Theatrical Theology

Theatrical Theology

Explorations in Performing the Faith

Edited by
WESLEY VANDER LUGT
and
TREVOR HART

CASCADE *Books* • Eugene, Oregon

THEATRICAL THEOLOGY
Explorations in Performing the Faith

Cascade Books
An Imprint of Wipf and Stock Publishers
199 W. 8th Ave., Suite 3
Eugene, OR 97401

www.wipfandstock.com

ISBN 13: 978-1-55635-072-6

Cataloguing-in-Publication data:

Theatrical theology : explorations in performing the faith / edited by Wesley Vander Lugt and Trevor Hart.

xx + 278 pp. ; 23 cm. Includes bibliographical references.

ISBN 13: 978-1-55635-072-6

1. Theater—Religious aspects—Christianity. 2. Performing arts—Religious aspects—Christianity. 3. Religion and drama—Christianity. 4. Arts and religion—Christianity. I. Vander Lugt, Wesley. II. Hart, Trevor A. III. Title.

PN2049 H24 2014

Manufactured in the U.S.A.

To friends and colleagues at the Institute for Theology,
Imagination, and the Arts,
who model and inspire constructive dialogue
between theology and the arts

Contents

Contributors

MARILYN MCCORD ADAMS is Distinguished Research Professor of Philosophy at the University of North Carolina, Chapel Hill. Her publications include *Horrendous Evils and the Goodness of God* (1999), *What Sort of Human Nature? The Metaphysics and Systematics of Christology* (1999), *Christ and Horrors: The Coherence of Christology* (2006), and *Some Later Medieval Theories of the Eucharist: Thomas Aquinas, Giles of Rome, Duns Scotus, and William Ockham* (2010).

DAVID BROWN is Professor of Theology, Aesthetics and Culture and Wardlaw Professor at St. Mary's College, University of St. Andrews. He has written extensively in the area of theology and the arts, including a five-volume series with Oxford University Press: *Tradition and Imagination: Revelation and Change* (1999), *Discipleship and Imagination: Christian Tradition and Truth* (2000), *God and Enchantment of Place: Reclaiming Human Experience* (2004), *God and Grace of Body: Sacrament in Ordinary* (2007), and *God and Mystery in Words: Experience through Metaphor and Drama* (2008).

RICHARD CARTER has been priest at St. Martin-in-the-Fields in London since 2006, and previously was chaplain to the Melanesian Brotherhood in the Solomon Islands, Vanautau, and Papua New Guinea. He is the author of *In Search of the Lost: The Death and Life of Seven Peacemakers of the Melanesian Brotherhood* (2012).

SHANNON CRAIGO-SNELL is Professor of Theology at Louisville Theological Seminary. She is the author of *Silence, Love, and Death: Saying Yes to God in the Theology of Karl Rahner* (2008) and *The Empty Church: Theatre, Theology, and Bodily Hope* (2014) and coauthor of *Living Christianity: A Pastoral Theology for Today* (2009).

DAVID CUNNINGHAM is Professor of Religion and Director of the Cross-Roads Project at Hope College. His books include *These Three Are One: The Practice of Trinitarian Theology* (1998), *Reading Is Believing: The Christian Faith through Literature and Film* (2002), *Christian Ethics: The End of the Law* (2008), and the forthcoming *Theatre to the World: Toward a Dramatic Doctrine of Revelation*.

JIM FODOR is Professor of Theology at St. Bonaventure University. He is the author of *Christian Hermeneutics: Paul Ricoeur and the Refiguring of Theology* (1995), coauthor with Stanley Hauerwas of "Performing the Faith: The Peaceable Rhetoric of God's Church," in *Performing the Faith* (2004), coeditor of *Theological Aesthetics after von Balthasar* (2008), and coeditor of *The Routledge Companion to the Practice of Christian Theology* (forthcoming 2015).

TIMOTHY GORRINGE is St. Luke's Professor of Theological Studies at the University of Exeter. His books in the area of theology and the arts include *God's Theatre: A Theology of Providence* (1992), *The Education of Desire: Toward a Theology of the Senses* (2001), *A Theology of the Built Environment: Justice, Empowerment, Redemption* (2002), and *Earthly Visions: Theology and the Challenges of Art* (2011).

TREVOR HART is Rector of Saint Andrew's Episcopal Church and Honorary Professor at the University of St. Andrews. He has lectured and published widely on theology, imagination, and the arts, including his most recent works, *Between the Image and the Word: Theological Engagements with Imagination, Literature, and Language* (2013) and *Making Good: Creation, Creativity, and Artistry* (forthcoming 2014).

PETER HELTZEL is Associate Professor of Systematic Theology and Director of the Micah Institute at New York Theological Seminary. His publications include *Chalice Introduction to Disciples Theology* (2008), *Jesus and Justice: Evangelicals, Race, and American Politics* (2009), and *Resurrection City: A Theology of Improvisation* (2012), and coauthor of *Faith-Rooted Organizing: Mobilizing the Church in Service to the World*.

TODD E. JOHNSON is William K. and Delores S. Brehm Associate Professor of Worship, Theology, and the Arts at Fuller Theological Seminary. He is coeditor of *Conviction of Things Not Seen: Worship and Ministry in the 21st Century* (2002), coeditor of *Common Worship in Theological*

Education (2005), coauthor of *Performing the Sacred: Theology and Theatre in Dialogue* (2009), and coauthor of *Living Worship: A Multimedia Resources for Students and Leaders* (2010).

IVAN KHOVACS is Senior Lecturer in Theology at Canterbury Christ Church University. He received his PhD in Theology, Imagination, and the Arts with the thesis "Divine Reckonings in Profane Spaces: Towards a Theological Dramaturgy for Theatre" (University of St. Andrews, 2007) and is the coeditor of *Tree of Tales: Tolkien, Literature, and Theology* (2007).

GEORGE PATTISON is Professor of Divinity at the University of Glasgow. In addition to numerous books on Kierkegaard, such as *Kierkegaard: The Aesthetic and Religious* (2nd edition, 2012), he has published widely in the area of theology and the arts, including *Crucifixions and Resurrections of the Image: Christian Reflections on Art and Modernity* (2009) and *Art, Modernity, and Faith: Restoring the Image* (2nd edition, 2010).

WESLEY VANDER LUGT is Lead Pastor of Warehouse 242 in Charlotte, North Carolina. His publications include *Living Theodrama: Reimagining Theological Ethics* (2014), and the coauthored *Pocket Dictionary of the Reformed Tradition* (2013).

KEVIN J. VANHOOZER is Research Professor of Systematic Theology at Trinity Evangelical Divinity School. His books include *Is There a Meaning in This Text? The Bible, the Reader, and the Morality of Literary Knowledge* (1998), *First Theology: God, Scripture, and Hermeneutics* (2002), *The Drama of Doctrine: A Canonical-Linguistic Approach to Christian Theology* (2005), *Remythologizing Theology: Divine Action, Passion, and Authorship* (2010), and *Faith Speaking Understanding: Performing the Drama of Doctrine* (forthcoming 2014).

SAMUEL WELLS is Vicar of St. Martin-in-the-Fields in London. He is the author of numerous books, including *Improvisation: The Drama of Christian Ethics* (2004), *God's Companions: Reimagining Christian Ethics* (2006), and *Be Not Afraid: Facing Fear with Faith* (2011).

Introduction

THEOLOGY IS INHERENTLY THEATRICAL, and it is so by virtue of its object, mode, and goal. First, theology is theatrical because its object is the triune God who says and does things in the theatre of the world. God created this cosmic theatre, but he also performs the lead role. He does this not merely by speaking from offstage, but by entering into the action, preeminently by becoming flesh and dwelling among us as Jesus of Nazareth. Theology is a response to and reflection on God's incarnate performance and his continual involvement in the world theatre as Spirit. In other words, theatrical theology deals not just with our human drama, but with the theodrama: the drama of God's being and action. Although theologians have long recognized the dramatic nature of God's revelation and redemption, Swiss theologian Hans Urs von Balthasar was the first to claim that theology should take a similar shape, a claim he explored extensively in his five-volume *Theo-Drama*.[1]

Second, theology is theatrical because it occurs within the theodrama it seeks to comprehend. Because of this, Balthasar borrows Hegelian categories to argue that both lyric and epic modes are inadequate for Christian theology. Whereas theology in lyric mode merely explores subjective experience and theology in epic mode seeks an objective viewpoint, Balthasar indicates how theology in dramatic mode transcends this dichotomy, since it describes a reality in which we are profoundly involved as participants.[2] Consequently, theology involves an attempt to articulate the theodrama in which we are inextricably intertwined, and so theology is by definition a provisional and contextual endeavor. However, by drawing on the testimony of past participants—whether canonical or

---

1. Balthasar, *Theodramatik*, 5 vols. (1973–83); translated into English as *Theo-Drama*, 5 vols. (1988–98).
2. Balthasar, *Theo-Drama*, 2:57.

otherwise—and by relying on the guidance of God himself, theatrical theology can gain enough perspective to avoid the tyranny of the present.

3.   Third, theology is theatrical because its goal is faith seeking performative understanding. Theatrical theology overlaps significantly with narrative theology, but it seeks to be more intentional about moving theology beyond understanding toward practical performance. The theodrama is not merely a reality to comprehend, but the real drama in which every human being has a role to play. The goal of theatrical theology, therefore, is to resource fitting participation in the theodrama in dynamic interplay with accurate perception of the theodrama. In this way, theatrical theology is the fruition of narrative theology, since, as George Lindbeck claims, the intelligibility and credibility of the biblical story arises out of faithful performance.[3]

Since Christian theology is inherently theatrical, it should come as no surprise that a growing number of contemporary scholars in various theological disciplines are discovering the potential for interdisciplinary dialogue between theology and theatre. Theologians have advanced, deepened, and at times challenged the seminal work of Balthasar, to the extent that there is now a large and growing body of scholarship that reflects a "theatrical turn" in theology. Nevertheless, suspicions still persist in some circles regarding the value of interdisciplinary approaches to theology in general and with theatre in particular, especially given the history of the church's "anti-theatrical prejudice" throughout the centuries.[4] The purpose of this collection of essays, therefore, is to pursue the conversation between theology and theatre further, gathering together contributions from theologians who believe theatre has something important to offer the theological task.

Given that theology and theatre have not always been amiable conversation partners, and because the words "theatrical," "drama," and "performance" sometimes carry negative connotations within non-theatrical usage, it is important to clarify how this language will be utilized in this volume. In contrast to associating "theatrical" with something that is pretentious or showy, this volume uses "theatrical" to indicate how theology arises out of the historical performance of God and resources the ongoing performance of the church. Likewise, "performance" has nothing to do with hypocrisy, insincerity, or the prideful attempt to achieve

---

3. Lindbeck, *Nature of Doctrine*, 131.

4. Barish, *The Antitheatrical Prejudice.*

salvation by works, and everything to do with active participation in the
theodrama. The "drama" in "theodrama," moreover, refers to the real and   3.
historical action of God in interaction with humanity on the world stage,
and "drama" on its own carries connotations of plot, interaction of characters, conflict, and resolution.

In determining the relationship between these various terms, the
distinction between drama and theatre is perhaps the most important.
Within the performing arts, drama is the script intended for public performance, whereas theatre is the live performance of that script. To speak
of "dramatic theology," therefore, would orient theology toward the script
out of which performance arises, which in Christian theology is normally
associated with Scripture and tradition. By contrast, to speak of "theatrical theology" is to orient theology toward its performance, particularly
its realization through various forms of life and liturgy. The title *Theatrical Theology*, therefore, indicates the bent of these essays in exploring the
performance of faith. Finally, it is important to note that we are using
"theatre" to refer to theatrical performance and "theater" to refer to the
place where performance happens. "Theatre" also happens to be the international spelling, which is gaining more widespread use within the
United States.

The present volume had its provenance in an international conference hosted by the Institute for Theology, Imagination, and the Arts at
the University of St. Andrews in August 2012. The purpose of this conference was to demonstrate the fruitfulness for constructive conversation between Christian theology and theatre by pursuing this dialogue
further, tracing some of the advances that have already been made, and
identifying new challenges and opportunities still to be reckoned with as
the interaction continues and develops further. Despite von Balthasar's
magisterial work, attempts to develop this particular interdisciplinary
conversation in a serious manner have been relatively few and far between, though the past decade has witnessed burgeoning interest in doing
so along a range of different theological fronts. The conference organiz-
ers hoped that by bringing some of the interested parties together for a
few days, a sustained engagement might result that would be identifiably
more than the sum of its various and already scripted parts. This hope
was duly realized, and much of the most valuable exchange occurred during the question and answer sessions and in personal conversations held
during coffee breaks. All the plenary speakers had opportunity to rework
their papers for publication, so at least some of that surplus of intellectual

foment is reflected here. Not all those invited to speak at the conference were able to attend, but some of them generously committed themselves to submit essays for publication. Finally, the editors solicited a handful of further contributions in light of the conference, which served to fill some of the gaps that had become apparent as the conversation unfolded and new possibilities were glimpsed. The result can hardly claim to be an exhaustive or even a comprehensive treatment of the subject, but the hope is to show the potential for bringing theology and theatre into conversation with thirteen essays from scholars who have been at the forefront of this exploration.

Kevin Vanhoozer's opening essay sets the concerns of the volume as a whole in the fitting context of a cosmic drama. The story of God's acts in history, he suggests, represents the perfections of God's own eternal nature and the outworking of the divine decree. The economic Trinity is the dramatic presentation of the immanent Trinity, and the characterization of God as King is identical with the substance of the gospel, the good news of the Trinity's establishment of a kingdom in which we are called to participate. Trevor Hart builds on the insights of Max Harris's work *Theater and Incarnation*, especially the notion of a "theatrical hermeneutics," by pursuing further the claim that meaning is always more than a matter of words alone, because our creaturely being straddles the spheres of material and immaterial reality. This theological-anthropological claim, Hart argues, must be worked out carefully in relation to the central Christian conviction that God's own Logos is inexorably bound up with the unique dynamics of the "enfleshment" of the eternal Son, a conviction with potentially dramatic implications for the way Scripture is engaged with in the church. Ivan Khovacs considers Christ's prayer in the garden through the lens of Aristotelian tragedy and the work of Susan Taubes in order to press Karl Barth and Hans Urs von Balthasar's readings of Gethsemane towards a specifically theological-dramatic account of the tragic.

Some of Peter Brook's writing on theatre in the late twentieth century invites the possibility of exploring theatre direction as a metaphor for providence. Like any metaphor, it has limitations, but it also has rich possibilities in pairing creaturely freedom with the overall vision and even overall control of the director. Timothy Gorringe shows how providence is a major feature in Shakespeare's *The Tempest*, reflecting on the practice of theatre, contemporary events, and the theme of providence in general. Shannon Craigo-Snell suggests that church is a disciplined performance of relationship with Jesus Christ, mediated by Scripture. Her exploration of this theme produces a nuanced picture of Peter Brook's ideal of Holy/ Rough theatre, a novel diagnosis of Karl Barth's not-quite-incarnational ecclesiology, and an appreciation of the value both men place on emptiness. As both gift and discipline, emptiness is a form of hope and response to grace and inspiration that ultimately comes from beyond the realm of human striving. George Pattison's essay sheds fresh light on Søren Kierkegaard as someone thoroughly immersed in the world of theatre, frequently attending performances, writing extensive reviews of contemporary productions, and peppering his writings with theatrical allusions. In *Repetition*, through the mouthpiece of his pseudonym Constantin Constantius, Kierkegaard gives an account of why theatre is an important element in human development and illustrates it with an anecdotal account of a visit to the Königstädter farce theatre in Berlin. Kierkegaard wrote no dramas, but his writing, Pattison suggests, was decisively shaped by his experience of theater-going. Furthermore, in terms of his own aesthetic theories, he is seeking, like the dramatist, to show us what the various possible positions vis-à-vis the decision of faith look like when taken out of the pages of theology textbooks and "staged" in life.

Jim Fodor brings theatrical theorists into conversation with philosophy and theology in pursuit of a theological-hermeneutical dramatics. Specifically, he deploys Hans-Georg Gadamer's influential account of "play" and David Ford's appeal to the biblical category of wisdom to propose a series of fruitful engagements between theology and theatre, focusing on the areas of play or re-playing, the performative dimensions of reading, the open structure of play in light of the audience, and the centrality of play in human flourishing and God's redemption. Todd Johnson draws both on sociologist Erving Goffman's suggestion that human life is a succession of accepting and performing roles and on philosopher Paul Woodruff's insistence that the phenomenon of theatre itself is vital to human social formation in order to explore what it means to be human and perform the life of faith. He insists that faith is not a static thing, but a process of participating in God's story in liturgy and in everyday life. David Cunningham, by engaging with *Hamlet*, *Angels in America*, and *Cat on a Hot Tin Roof*, argues that Christian ethical claims should look less like those produced by the study of law or logic and more like those evoked by the experience of theatrical performance. The essay concludes with a meditation on Gloucester's final line in *King Lear*, a line that encapsulates theatre's ability to present multiple voices simultaneously, and thereby to complicate any excessively immodest pronouncements about Christianity's moral truth. Marilyn McCord Adams looks to theatre theory, especially to Augusto Boal's *Theatre of the Oppressed*, for help in understanding how cultic drama, by symbolically enacting cosmic problems, may successfully produce cosmic effects. Boal's analysis of Aristotelian poetics and his own revolutionary replacements shed light on how eucharistic drama co-opts worshippers into "acting out" truths about what is at stake between God and human beings, and provokes participants into rehearsing for a revolution.

Richard Carter and Sam Wells consider theatre's power to communicate the gospel through action, by showing rather than telling. Reflecting upon Carter's experience as a performer and priest with the Melanesian Brotherhood in the Solomon Islands, their essay explores theatre as a vivid and appropriate form of ecclesial witness in the public square, enquires whether it might be especially significant in the light of its power to encourage a form of ecclesial democracy, and investigates how drama is a kind of evangelistic liturgy and exegesis, a place of potential revelation and transformation. In the spirit of Augusto Boal, Peter Heltzel argues that theologians today need to reimagine the church as a Theatre of the Oppressed, a Spirit-led community that improvises for love and justice. Drawing on the example of Youth Ministries for Peace and Justice, a youth-led, faith-rooted environmental justice ministry in South Bronx, New York, he considers ways in which, as Boal's productions sought to break the "fourth wall" between actors and audiences, prophetic Christian communities today need to break the "fourth wall" between Word and world. Finally, David Brown examines the factors that led to a renewed interest in relations between theatre and religion in the twentieth century and grapples with questions about the nature of religious experience, its significance, and its relationship to aesthetic experience. He does so not just theoretically, but through concrete examples—including instances as varied as Sophocles *Oedipus at Colonus*, Ibsen's *A Doll's House*, and Robert Lepage's 2012 direction of Wagner's *Ring*—in order to explore the possibility of religious experience being mediated through drama.

It is important to acknowledge the numerous players that made the publication of these essays possible. First, we are grateful for the Institute for Theology, Imagination, and the Arts (ITIA) at the University of St. Andrews, which is a community of scholars who model and inspire the kind of constructive, interdisciplinary dialogue demonstrated in this volume. We are also indebted to everyone who participated in the Theatrical

Theology conference hosted by ITIA in August 2012. It was because of the widespread interest in this topic, as well as the quality and depth of the presentations and conversations, that we were motivated to put together these contributions and offer them to a wider audience. We were honored to have such high caliber plenary speakers at the conference, and we are doubly honored to add contributions written by distinguished scholars from both sides of the Atlantic. Particular words of thanks are due to Robin Parry, who initially encouraged us to publish these essays and then edited them with skill, as well as to Christian Amondson and the incredibly capable team at Cascade Books. In addition, Natan Mladin was willing to read through each essay and provide detailed and invaluable editorial suggestions, which were worth their weight in gold. We would also like to thank Cole Matson and Wilson Ricketts for their careful perusal of the manuscript. Overall, it takes a village to create and sustain dialogue of this nature, and we are equally thankful for the numerous voices that we hope will take up the conversation from here and continue to pursue a theatrical theology.

1

At Play in the Theodrama of the Lord

The Triune God of the Gospel

KEVIN J. VANHOOZER

The Dramatic Essence of Christianity:
Gospel Theatre as Trinitarian Work

JOHN CALVIN COULD WELL lay claim to the title "patron saint of theatrical theology" inasmuch as he makes frequent reference to the world (i.e., the heavens and the earth) as the *theatrum gloriae*: a theater in which to behold God's glory.[1] The focus of Calvin's theater is consistently on nature, or what we might call the history of creation, rather than on grace and the history of redemption. A further problem is that sinners "wickedly defraud God of his glory" and "cannot by contemplating the universe infer that he is Father."[2] Stated differently, and more provocatively: at least in Calvin, theatrical theology has little to do with the gospel, or the triune God.

The situation is quite different in the Fourth Gospel, where what is being played out in the theater of the world is precisely God's love for the world, which the "world" rejects. John's Gospel is a courtroom drama where, on one level, Jesus' identity is on trial, more specifically,

1. Calvin, *Institutes* I.v.8; I.vi.2; I.xiv.20; II.vi.1.
2. *Inst.* II.vi.1 (order slightly changed).

1

his theologically revolutionary claim to be "one" with the Father (John 10:30). (On another level, however, it is the reader's ability to read the signs and make correct judgments that is on trial.) The whole of John's narrative structure alternates between accounts of Jesus' deeds and discourses, two types of signs—evidence!—that he is who he says he is. What Jesus says and does in the Fourth Gospel is, on his own account, the climax and fulfillment of a longstanding divine project that defines both his life and his ministry: "Jesus came into Galilee, proclaiming the gospel of God" (Mark 1:14).[3] In the Fourth Gospel, the drama arises from seeing how people respond to Jesus' words (John 3:34; 6:63) and to Jesus himself as the Word of God made flesh (John 1:14). It is precisely as the incarnate Word that Jesus not only proclaims but also enacts the "gospel of God." Indeed, Jesus *is* the gospel of God—God's great saving word/deed on the stage of world history—and hence the reason why the essence of Christianity is inherently dramatic: "in Christ God was reconciling the world to himself" (2 Cor 5:19).

If a theology oriented to the theater of redemptive operations (rather than creation alone) needed a proof text, John 5:19–20 could well fit the bill insofar as it is all about "seeing" and "showing" the wonderful works of God the Father and the Son: "Jesus said to them, 'Truly, truly, I say to you, the Son can do nothing of his own accord, but only what he sees the Father doing; for whatever the Father does, the Son does likewise. For the Father loves the Son, and shows him all that he himself is doing; and greater works than these will he show him, that you may marvel.'" The context of the passage is itself dramatic, occurring at a key moment in the millennia-long evangelical *oikonomia* of divine mercy that, according to Augustine, begins with the mark God puts on Cain (Gen 4:15). The immediate context concerns Jesus' healing an invalid on the Sabbath (John 5:9), a miracle that prompted Jewish opposition (John 5:16) and Jesus' retort "My Father is working until now, and I am working" (John 5:17). Jesus' answer made the Jews all the more determined to kill him "because not only was he breaking the Sabbath, but he was even calling God his own Father, making himself equal with God" (John 5:18): high drama indeed!

It is against this backdrop that Jesus makes the comments that serve as a lens through which the present essay seeks to discern how "deep" the theatrical qualifier goes. My question concerns the triune theodrama of

3. All Scripture quotations in this chapter are from the English Standard Version (ESV) unless otherwise indicated.

redemption, and whether it pertains to history only or stems from a plot conceived in eternity. On the surface, Jesus is defending his actions by claiming that, in healing on the Sabbath, he is simply doing what God is always doing (i.e., giving life). The repeated emphasis on *doing* and *showing* speaks directly to the theatrical nature of Christian theology, as does the emphasis on *seeing*.

Jesus' comments in John 5 comprise a brief summary of the drama of redemption, at the bottom of which (so to speak) we find the doctrine of the Trinity. Jesus' works are ingredients in a single overarching work that comes to a climax on the cross.[4] The Johannine Christ conceives of his life in terms of a single project, as evidenced in his prayer to the Father, "I glorified you on earth having accomplished the work that you gave me to do" (John 17:4) and by his last words, "It is finished" (John 19:30). Redemption is a theatrical work, something Jesus does in the theater of the world for the world's salvation and the glory of God.

In doing theatrical theology it is important to remember that "theatrical" is a qualifier, not the main subject. Theologians ought not elevate theatre studies to the rank of queen of the sciences; my appeal to the language of theatre and drama is strictly ministerial and heuristic. The substance of redemption is indeed dramatic inasmuch as it concerns what the triune God has done on the stage of world history: theodrama. It is important, however, to recognize the limits of the theatrical analogy. For example, a critic might ask what the Christian theodrama represents, assuming that drama always represents something "more real" than the actors and actions themselves. However, if Jesus is God made flesh, whom or what does he represent?[5] It is just here that our passage may shed unexpected light. I shall argue that the work the Son "represents" in time is God's own eternal life. More specifically: *God's mighty work in the history of redemption enacts the perfections of God's inner life.* To restate my thesis by adapting Rahner's Rule: the economic Trinity—God's

---

4. Leon Morris notes that *ergon*, the Greek word for "work," occurs twenty-seven times in the Fourth Gospel, eighteen times with Jesus as the subject, in both the singular and the plural. Significantly, it is the term the Johannine Jesus himself prefers when speaking of his sign-deeds/miracles: "John sees miracles from one point of view as *semeia*, activities pointing men to God, from another point of view he sees them as *erga*, activities which take their origin in God" (*Gospel according to John*, 690).

5. "But if God is the actor, whom is He going to represent? Who or what is the greater Reality which His actions might imitate and strive to be like?" (Pakaluk, "Play's Not the Thing," 29).

self-communication in history via the acts of Father, Son, and Spirit—
dramatically represents the immanent Trinity, God's own inner life.[6]

The argument proceeds in three steps. We begin by considering
Jesus' claim that "the Son can do nothing of his own accord, but only what
he sees the Father doing" (John 5:19) in light of the work of two theologians who represent, in different ways, the tendency of modern theology
either to overlook or misconstrue the immanent Trinity: Robert Jenson
and Hans Urs von Balthasar. Both theologians employ the category of
drama to explicate the Father-Son relationship, but they do so in radically
different ways. Neither theologian adequately accounts for the proper
relationship between God's triune being and the events of the gospel. The
one (Balthasar) imports dramatic conflict into God's own life; the other
(Jenson) exports God's own life into the history of Jesus. This dichotomy
sets the stage for the second step: a fresh proposal for retrieving traditional formulations of the relationship between the so-called "immanent
Trinity" and "economic Trinity," and for understanding how and why an
account of the former is necessary to maintain the integrity of the gospel.
The third step returns to earth and explores how what was determined
in eternity is demonstrated in redemptive history. Creation here appears
as a theater for God's righteousness (i.e., covenant faithfulness), for the
drama of redemption is fundamentally covenantal in its plot, climax, and
conclusion. The essay concludes by offering brief reflections on the role
of human actors in the theodrama today.

Theodramatic Coherence or Incoherence?
Understanding the Triune God of the Gospel

Seeing and Showing

Jesus' words in John 5:19 figured prominently in debates between the
Arians and the Pro-Nicene over the Son's divine nature. Augustine

---

6. "Rahner's Rule" refers to Karl Rahner's axiom that "The 'economic' Trinity is the
'immanent' Trinity, and the 'immanent' Trinity is the 'economic' Trinity" (Rahner, *The
Trinity*, 22). It is an attempt to spell out the relationship between God in himself (*in se*)
and God acting in history (*ad extra*) for us. The underlying issue concerns the worry
that, if there is not an identity between God's historical appearance and eternal reality,
then there is a "God behind God," and we have no assurance that the way God appears
to us in the history of Jesus Christ is the way God truly is in himself. See further Sanders, *The Image of the Immanent Trinity*.

observes in his *Tractates on the Gospel of John* that heresies arise "when good Scriptures are not well understood."[7] Heretics use this text in particular to argue that the Son is "lesser" than the Father. If the Son can do only what he sees the Father doing, Augustine asks, does it follow that he can walk on the sea only if he sees his Father doing so? Augustine wants no part in such absurdities. Instead, he proposes that Jesus' walking on water is the work of his flesh, but that this walking is an inseparable work of Father and Son: "I see both working there . . . whatever the Son does, he does not without the Father; because whatever the Father does, he does not do without the Son."[8] Stated differently: when Jesus walks across the stage, so too (in some sense) does the Father. Theatrical theology indeed!

That the Son can do only what he *sees* the Father *showing* him has proven to be a challenging proposition through the centuries, even to committed Trinitarian commentators. Many find it difficult to interpret this passage without implying that the Son is subordinate in power, or that he acts subsequently to the Father. The challenge is to understand the God of John's Gospel, and ultimately the God of the gospel. In particular: does the Son who "sees the Father doing" (John 5:19) refer to the pre-existent or incarnate Son? More broadly: what is the relationship between God as he is in himself (*in se*; immanent Trinity), and God as he shows himself to be in his works (*ad extra*; economic Trinity)?

A few recent biblical scholars follow C. H. Dodd's lead in viewing Jesus' words as a "hidden parable" about how sons learn from their fathers.[9] The passage is a "perfectly realistic description of a son apprenticed to his father's trade."[10] This is a reasonable attempt to describe the kind of dependence Jesus has in view, not least because John also tells us that the Son does not speak on his own (John 12:49) or come on his own (John 7:28; 8:42). And yet, must it follow that the Son *imitates* what he sees the Father doing, such that "the determinate sources and pattern of his actions are the deeds of his Father he sees and then repeats"?[11]

Augustine anticipated this line of interpretation and tried to nip it in the bud, especially in his reading of John 5:19 in *Tractate* 20.[12] It is too

---

7. Augustine, *Tractate* 18.2.

8. *Tractate* 20.6.

9. Dodd, "A Hidden Parable in the Fourth Gospel."

10. Dodd, *Historical Tradition in the Fourth Gospel*, 386 n. 2.

11. Van der Watt, "Father Shows the Son Everything," 264.

12. On Augustine's interpretation of this passage, see especially Johnson, "Augustine's 'Trinitarian' Reading of John 5" and Ayres, *Augustine and the Trinity*, chapter 9,

"carnal" an interpretation to think that "the Father sits and does a work, and shows it to the Son; and the Son . . . does another work in another place, or out of other materials."[13] This cannot be, Augustine never tires of reminding us, because "All things were made by him [i.e., the *Logos*; the Son]; and without him nothing was made" (John 1:3). Moreover, if the Son only copies what he sees the Father doing, then Augustine wants to know the location of the other light and the other firmament the Son must have made in imitation of the Father. If the Son indeed works *like* the Father, then there should be two worlds, not one (i.e., the world the Father made and the world the Son made after him). The futility of this line of interpretation, in addition to the positive teaching of John's Prologue, leads Augustine to his counter-proposal: "The works of the Father and the Son are inseparable."[14]

The Son, then, not only does the same work as the Father, he also does it *likewise*. Far from indicating subordination, then, Augustine believes that verse 19 affirms the equality of the Father and Son. Hence the Son does what he sees the Father doing "not in imitation, but in virtue of His sameness of nature."[15] To claim to be doing "only what he sees the Father doing" turns out to be simultaneously the humblest and the loftiest of claims, for it implies both the complete dependence of the Son on the Father and the complete unity of their respective activity. Augustine resolves the apparent contradiction by suggesting that the Son's "seeing" and the Father's "showing" are indirect expressions that ultimately pertain to the generation of the Son by the Father: "Hence, he sees the Father doing whatever he does, because he sees that he has the power of doing it from him whom he sees that he has the nature by which he exists."[16] That the Father begets the Son does not mean, however, that the Father precedes the Son in time, as if the Father were older. On the contrary, Augustine affirms the *eternal* generation of the Son: "Show me flame without light, and I show you God the Father without the Son."[17] Who the Son is and what the Son does is "all of the Father."[18] Augustine

---

"Showing and Seeing." Johnson comments that *Tractate* 20 contains Augustine's "most mature theological reflection on Trinitarian agency" (800), yet another reason to focus on John 5.

13. *Tractate* 21.4.

14. *Tractate* 20.3.

15. Westcott, *The Gospel according to St. John*, 189.

16. Augustine, *Contra sermonem Arrianorum* 9.14.

17. *Tractate* 20.8.

18. Ibid.

concludes by paraphrasing what he takes Jesus to be teaching: "I am equal [to God] in such a way that he begot me; I am equal in such a way that he is not from me, but I am from him."[19]

At this point, one can easily imagine a critic complaining that Augustine has effectively de-dramatized both the Son's "seeing" and the Father's "showing" by interpreting them in terms of eternal generation. This is precisely Robert Jenson's critique: the whole idea of an immanent Trinity wrongly partakes of the Greek philosophical notion that divinity must be immune to time. Jenson's counter-proposal, however, is to collapse the immanent into the economic Trinity, taking every metaphysical thought about God captive to Jesus' narrative history. Hans Urs von Balthasar represents an alternative approach that discovers drama (i.e., a "primal kenosis") in the immanent Trinity, yet in his case the cost of doing so is to inscribe conflict—suffering and loss—into the divine life itself, thus raising a question about whether the gospel, which promises life in and with God, truly overcomes distance, alienation, and forsakenness. Each theologian makes it difficult to understand what we mean by the "triune God of the gospel" and, in so doing, renders the very notion of a theatrical theology problematic. Jenson locates all the drama in history, so that it is not "representing" anything (i.e., it does not dramatize what is happening in the immanent Trinity). Balthasar, by way of contrast, thinks the economic Trinity represents the inner life of God, but only because he locates the primal drama not in history but in the immanent Trinity itself. Hence the challenge of the present essay: to consider an alternative way to think about the relationship of the triune God to the dramatic history of redemption.

Robert Jenson: Triune God as Gospel Theatre

On Jenson's telling, the traditional Western doctrine of the Trinity posits an "immanent" Trinity (the way God is in himself) behind or at a different metaphysical level than the "economic" Trinity known by the historical action between Jesus and his Father in their Spirit. As to what the immanent Trinity is, Western theology knows only "that" it is eternal, and that there is no "possibility" or temporality in God himself, "no actual participation in time's stories and chances."[20] The immanent

---

19. *Tractate* 20.4.
20. Jenson, *America's Theologian*, 92.

Trinity has no beginning, middle, or end and, as such, is "untouched by the triune gospel narrative."[21] The God of traditional theism is immune to time—metaphysically indifferent to temporal events, including those that comprise the story of Jesus.[22]

Jenson's counter-proposal is to rethink the triune God strictly on the basis of the narrative history of Jesus, the "second identity" of God.[23] Jenson admits that the whole argument of his *Systematic Theology* depends on the conceptual move that he makes "from the biblical God's self-identification *by* events in time to his identification *with those events*."[24] If God were not identified *with* Jesus' history, that history would not reveal God himself: "The revealing events would be our clues *to* God, but would not *be* God."[25] On Jenson's view, then, God's being *is* the history that happens in Jesus.[26] Accordingly, the "metaphysical center of gravity" shifts from an allegedly pre-existent beginning to an eschatological consummation, for it is only the end of a story that ultimately reveals a person's identity.[27] The one God is an event, a triune theater of the historically observed: "God is what happens between Jesus and his Father in their Spirit."[28]

On Jenson's view, the triune God is inseparable from the drama that culminates in the events of Jesus' death and resurrection. Jenson thus feels led to reject the *Logos asarkos*, that is, the notion of a pre-existent Son before and apart from the history of the man Jesus. What the Son sees the Father doing, therefore, cannot refer to some sort of pre-temporal interpersonal communion, but only to what happens between the man Jesus and his Father. Jenson suggests that divine sonship begins with the

21. Ibid., 93.

22. Jenson's whole project may be understood to be a "revisionary metaphysics" whose task is to "reinterpret being to accommodate the gospel" (*Systematic Theology* 1:212). As such, it is but one of several post-metaphysical Trinitarian theologies (e.g., Jürgen Moltmann; Catherine Mowry LaCugna) that have followed in the wake of Karl Barth.

23. Jenson, *Systematic Theology*, 1:127. "Identity" is Jenson's replacement term for *hypostasis*: "A divine identity is a *persona dramatis dei* who can be repeatedly picked out by a name or identifying description or by pronouns, always by relation to the other two" (106).

24. Ibid., 1:59 (Jenson's italics).

25. Ibid.

26. Sanders positions Jenson amongst the "radicalizers" of Rahner's Rule (*Image of the Immanent Trinity*, 107–12).

27. Swain, *God of the Gospel*, 64.

28. Jenson, *Systematic Theology*, 1:221.

historical mission (incarnation) rather than an alleged eternal procession (begetting). Strictly speaking, a pre-existent Son would, for Jenson, have no identity, for identity is a function of narrative, and a being that is immune to time has no history to be narrated. Jenson radicalizes Rahner's Rule, claiming that the drama of the Christ does not simply represent but *constitutes* the immanent Trinity: "Since the biblical God can truly be identified by narrative, his hypostatic being, his self-identity, is constituted in *dramatic coherence*."[29]

For Jenson, then, the gospel story and the event of God's triune being are one and the same: "God is one with himself just by the dramatic coherence of his eventful actuality."[30] The drama of the Christ determines both the identity of the triune God and the relationship of this God to human creatures: "It is a central contention, indeed motivation of the doctrine of the Trinity, that the story God lives with *us* and the story that is his *own* life, are not other than one another."[31] Whatever the distinction may be between an immanent and an economic Trinity, Jenson is sure that it does not involve two different dramas: rescuing Israel from Egypt and raising Jesus from the dead are determining events not only of salvation history but also of the triune life itself.[32] The triune God of the gospel is literally *of* the gospel—comprised of the events that together make up the drama that is Jesus the Christ of Israel. God proves himself to be God not by transcending history but by demonstrating self-constancy (faithfulness) through time: "The dramatic coherence of YHWH's identity is determined by the *outcome* of the biblical events and not at the beginning."[33] Until the end, that is, God's being is only a being-in-anticipation.

In insisting that the gospel events—in particular, Jesus' death and resurrection—are what constitute the dramatic coherence that is triune identity, Jenson clearly succeeds in making theology theatrical. The only question is whether he has located the drama in the right place (i.e., God's

---

29. Ibid., 64 (Jenson's italics).

30. Ibid.

31. Jenson, "Christ as Culture 3: Christ as Drama," 197.

32. Pannenberg comments that in Jenson's theology the difference between the immanent and economic Trinity "almost vanishes," with dire consequences: "Without that distinction, the reality of the one God tends to be dissolved into the process of the world" ("Books in Review: Robert W. Jenson," 51).

33. Swain, *God of the Gospel*, 89.

being).[34] Is it truly the case that the Trinity "happens" in the events that make up the drama of Christ? Is the triune identity constituted for the first time by the history of the man Jesus? What if God had not created, or had created but not sent his Son into the world? Would he still have been the God that he is? Jenson answers his own contrary-to-fact questions in the affirmative, but insists that we can say nothing more, because such a state of affairs is beyond narratability.[35] However, something more robust—something with positive content—needs to be said about the immanent Trinity, for the pre-existence of Christ is arguably "the basis for the incarnation as the free, gracious action of the Son."[36] Without the pre-existence of Christ, and hence an immanent Trinity, it becomes difficult in the extreme to understand the Son's free choice to "empty" himself, take on the form of a slave, and die on a cross (Phil 2:5–8).

Jenson's gospel is the good news that God has raised Jesus (the "son" that Israel should have been, and is in Israel's place) from the dead. This event is what constitutes God not simply as "our Father" but as "the Father." It is also the event that constitutes Jesus as the Son: "Jesus is constituted the Son, not because he is timelessly begotten of the Father, but because he is eschatologically raised by the God who sent him . . . ."[37] The death of Jesus is atoning because it is the event whereby God constitutes himself as Redeemer by defeating the principalities and powers, including death itself. The Holy Spirit's role in the drama, as the bond of love that settled on Jesus at his birth, is to ensure that the Father and Son remain one even as the Father abandons the Son on the cross.[38] The good news of the gospel is thus that the Spirit brings the church into this same resurrection future, saving humanity not *from* but *through* time by bringing them to time's *telos*, the end that provides closure and dramatic coherence. God, then, is the savior because he proves himself faithful through time, inviting humanity into his story—the conversational event that is the Father, Son, and Spirit—a storied event of love that has a narrative ending but no temporal end.

Must theatrical theology follow Jenson in identifying God not only *by* but also *with* these gospel events? There are three problems: first,

34. According to Gathercole, "drama *is* the metaphysics which provides the framework for his system" ("Pre-existence," 48).

35. Jenson, *Systematic Theology*, 1:141.

36. Gathercole, "Pre-existence," 41.

37. Swain, *God of the Gospel*, 137.

38. Jenson, *Systematic Theology*, 1:191.

Jenson's view makes God in some sense dependent on the world, for he would not be the triune God he is without it. Second, because God in Jenson's view is not complete in himself (i.e., transcendent and independent), it is not clear either how he can freely and graciously determine to create us or what he has (in himself) to give us.[39] Third, because God's identity is constituted by what happens in Jesus' history, Jenson's critics wonder whether evil thus belongs eternally to his identity as well, since the history of Jesus includes unjust suffering, thus raising the question, "Is the gospel of Jenson's triune God still good news?"[40]

Hans Urs von Balthasar: An Immanent Drama?

Whereas Jenson dramatizes the Trinity by identifying God's being precisely with what happens in the history between the man Jesus and the one he called "Father," Balthasar dramatizes theology by discovering a primal history within the immanent Trinity itself. Whereas Jenson attempts to derive the doctrine of the Trinity from the events of the gospel, Balthasar views the Trinity as the deep source and "inner presupposition of the doctrine of the Cross."[41] Yet Balthasar, too, has recourse to a theatrical model: "the play in his account offers a framework, and a set of resources, for thinking, not only of the whole of history, but of the whole of history in relation to God, and God in relation to history."[42]

We can include Balthasar, unlike Jenson, among those who in one way or another qualify Rahner's Rule (the "Restricters").[43] On the one hand, Balthasar affirms the independence, as it were, of the immanent Trinity. He sees the cross as "the privileged . . . locus of the Trinity's self-revelation" but not, contra Jenson, as the locus of the Trinity's authentic actualization.[44] The triune God has a rich inner life, and does not need the cross to become who he is. On the other hand, Balthasar finds drama not only in the history of redemption but, first and foremost, in the Godhead

---

39. "God's decision to be our God cannot be a decision to give God, for there is no antecedently existent God to be given" (Swain, *God of the Gospel*, 156).

40. See especially Hart, *Beauty of the Infinite*, 164–65 and McCall, *Which Trinity? Whose Monotheism?*, 139–40, 146–47.

41. Balthasar, *Theo-Drama*, 4:319.

42. Kilby, *Balthasar*, 58.

43. Sanders, *Image of the Immanent Trinity*, 133–45.

44. Balthasar, *Theo-Drama*, 4:321.

itself. In particular, there is a certain "liveliness" that characterizes God's being as love.

"God is love" (1 John 4:8); yes, but why should there be *drama* in the immanent Trinity, especially when other theologians have character-ized it in terms of eternal bliss? Balthasar is not interested in speculation, but he does want to discover what there is in the immanent Trinity that corresponds and gives rise to the love poured out on Christ's cross. He therefore reasons backwards, as it were, from the crucifixion to God's inner life: "The immanent Trinity must be understood to be that eter-nal, absolute self-surrender where God is seen to be, in himself, absolute love."[45] In other words, the eternal relations of Father, Son, and Spirit are fundamentally dramatic. Balthasar strays into speculative territory, however, in positing a supra-temporal proto-kenosis in God's immanent being. To be precise, he construes the Father's loving generation of the Son as a kenotic "event" in God's own life, an eternal self-emptying proper to the Father rather than the Son, where the apostle Paul and traditional Christology had located it (cf. Phil 2:5–11). Balthasar makes a striking theological innovation when he construes the eternal generation of the Son as a supra-temporal kenotic "event" of costly inner-Trinitarian love.

Balthasar therefore discovers "drama" in the immanent Trinity it-self. The triune life is full, and eventful, with a proto-kenosis at its heart: the Father takes a "risk" in giving himself (i.e., his divine essence) up to the Son. In Balthasar's words: "the Father strips himself, without re-mainder, of his Godhead and hands it over to the Son."[46] It follows that the historical event of the cross, and thus the whole drama of redemp-tion, is a kind of play within a play. To be precise: the economic Trinity plays out, in history, the eternal drama that is the life of the immanent Trinity. Balthasar rejects the notion that actions only become dramatic when they are historically realized in time and space. On the contrary, the immanent Trinity is itself a "primal drama": "the drama of the 'empty-ing' of the Father's heart, in the generation of the Son, that contains and surpasses all possible drama between God and a world."[47]

---

45. Ibid., 323.

46. Balthasar, *Theo-Drama*, 4:323. Kilby questions whether the Father's abandon-ment of the Son on the cross is possible "*only if* the eternal Trinitarian relations are characterized by infinite, absolute distance, radical otherness, separation" (*Balthasar*, 108).

47. Balthasar, *Theo-Drama*, 4:327.

Though both Jenson and Balthasar seek to do justice to the drama of the gospel in their Trinitarian theology, it will be my suggestion that neither theologian adequately accounts for the proper relationship between God's triune being and the events of the gospel. Where Jenson *historicizes* the drama, collapsing the immanent into the economic Trinity, Balthasar *eternalizes* it, importing the economic drama into the life of the immanent Trinity. As we have seen, Jenson is unable to account for the sheer gratuity of the divine self-determination to be who he is for us. Balthasar, for his part, speaks of the Father's self-giving as a giving *away*. However, Karen Kilby worries that this suggests loss (i.e., kenosis) and imports something "dark" into God's own life, thus eternalizing suffering by incorporating it into God's triune life: "And then, it seems to me, it becomes hard to understand how Christianity can possibly be 'good news.'"[48]

Fortunately, there is another way for theatrical theology to think about the triune God of the gospel. Contrary to expectations, the old Trinitarian theism provides a better framework than new versions of Trinitarian theism for understanding the drama of redemption. At least, this will be my working hypothesis, namely, that the transcendental conditions for theatrical Trinitarian theology are found not in Jenson or Balthasar but rather in Augustine, Aquinas, Calvin, and especially Jonathan Edwards. The rest of the present essay explores this perhaps counter-intuitive suggestion.

Immanent Perfection (Triune Communication *Ad Intra*): Procession, Glorification, and Covenantal Self-determination

"For the Father loves the Son and shows him all that he himself is doing." (John 5:20)

When does the Father love the Son and show him all that he is doing? There is no need to speculate, for Jesus tells us in no uncertain terms in his high-priestly prayer: "you loved me before the foundation of the world" (John 17:24). The love the Father shows the Son during his sojourn on earth is the historical realization of an eternal relationship. God does not, therefore, *become* love in the events that make up Jesus'

---

48. Kilby, *Balthasar*, 120.

history; rather, these events show us what God always/already *is*. And that, after all, is the task of the doctrine of the Trinity: "to describe the connection between God and the economy of salvation."[49]

Only the perfect life of the immanent Trinity preserves the integrity of the gospel and the gratuity of grace. The triune God of the gospel presupposes the freedom of an immanent Trinity that is already fully actualized (contra Jenson) and whose actuality is marked by a love characterized not by self-emptying/*kenosis* (contra Balthasar) but rather by fullness/*pleroma* (Eph 3:19; Col 1:19). It is out of the fullness of love that the Father shows everything he is and is doing to the Son, who eternally sees him. This showing and seeing are coordinated, two aspects in an ongoing activity of communication by which the Father and Son "make common" their very being.[50] The Spirit is involved as well, as bond and witness of this Father-Son love. My thesis in what follows is that the God who communicates himself to us in history is also eternally self-communicative in himself. What the triune God consequently communicates to the world—his light, life, and love—corresponds to what God antecedently is. "God is a communicative being" (Jonathan Edwards).[51]

Perfect Communion: Persons, Relations, and Processions

The doctrine of the immanent Trinity identifies the divine *dramatis personae*, the personal agents of our salvation. God in himself is the sheer positive plenitude of his own perfections. The perfect life of God is made up of various personal relations: the Father's *begetting* the Son, the Son's *begottenness*, and the Spirit *proceeding* from the Father and the Son. These relations of origin—paternity, filiation, spiration—*are* God's perfect life.[52] These are the "movements" or "doings" in the immanent Trinity that, as we shall see, ultimately form the template for the work of the Father and Son in the history of salvation. The technical term is "procession," a divine self-communication *ad intra*, in contrast to the "missions" of Son and Spirit, which are self-communications *ad extra*.

49. Sanders, "Trinity," 35.

50. The Son is the radiance of God's light, the word/act of the Father's self-communication, the "exact imprint of God's very being" (Heb 1:3). See Webster, "One Who is Son," 85–88.

51. Edwards, "Miscellany" 332, in *Works of Jonathan Edwards*, 13:410. Cf. Schweitzer, *God Is a Communicative Being*.

52. See Webster, "God's Perfect Life," 143–52.

Can we extrapolate from the history of Jesus to the conclusion that there is an equivalent "drama" in the processions that constitute the life of the immanent Trinity? I think we can, but not because there is conflict, or even risk in the Godhead, but rather because there is communicative activity. Scripture depicts the life of the Father, Son, and Spirit as a *doing* than which nothing greater can be conceived: a ceaseless activity of free and loving communicating whose beginning and end is triune communion.[53] This, I submit, is the immanent, eternal triune doing that gets dramatically represented in the economic triune doing as the history of redemption.

As we have seen, Augustine interpreted the seeing and showing of John 5:19 as shorthand for the eternal generation of the Son. The Father shows all that he does to the Son in the sense that he gives the Son an immediate knowledge of his works, and he does this by "begetting" the Son (i.e., communicating his own being and nature). Thomas Aquinas says that the Father shows him everything "insofar as he generates him as the brightness and concept of his own wisdom, and as the Word."[54] In brief, the Son understands that he is and receives his ability to do things "from" the Father.[55]

What Jesus is in his history on earth he is antecedently, in himself, as the eternal Son. Jesus' being born of Mary somehow corresponds to his derivation from his Father in heaven. "According to John, Jesus holds the unique divine identity in common *with* the Father *as* the Son *of* the Father."[56] It is important here to note that not every relation between the divine persons has to do with origins.[57] While "begetting" and "breathing"

53. This claim, as with all others about the immanent Trinity, is based on what we learn about the Father and Son by observing their interaction in the economy and by listening closely to what Jesus says about his filial relationship to the Father before the foundation of the world (John 17:24).

54. Aquinas, *Commentary on the Gospel of John*, 276. Like Augustine, Thomas Aquinas links the Son's seeing what the Father is doing to eternal generation as a procession, and eternal generation to wisdom, the "begetting" of knowledge through seeing: "for the Son to see the Father doing something is nothing other than to proceed by an intellectual procession from the acting Father" (273).

55. Cf. Augustine: "he [the Son] sees that he has the power of doing it from him [the Father] whom he sees that he has the nature by which he [the Son] exists" (*Contra sermonem Arrianorum* 9:14).

56. Köstenberger and Swain, *Father, Son and Spirit*, 112.

57. See Sanders, "Trinity," 43–45. Pannenberg argues that, although their mutual relations constitute the divine persons, not all relations should be construed as relations of origin (*Systematic Theology*, 1:143).

do account for the derivation of Son and Spirit from the Father, not every thing that pertains to the missions of Son and Spirit can be translated back into processions, at least not if processions pertain uniquely to relations of origin.

Is eternal generation a matter of origin only, or is there also some hint of eternal (filial) *obedience* in the Father-Son relationship? Whereas Balthasar's answer to the question, "What in the immanent Trinity corresponds to the Son's obedience unto death on the cross?" is a primal kenosis, I want to speak of a primal responsiveness. To do so is not to import lack or risk into the Godhead, but rather to recognize a positive quality and divine perfection. Let us call this filial responsiveness, together with other personal relations derived from the economy, *communicative relations*.[58] Is it possible that the "seeing" and "showing" that is the object of Jesus' discourse in John 5 pertains not to the Son's eternal generation (contra Augustine) but to one of these other communicative relations?

"Light from Light": Glorification as Radiant Communication

The few but significant communicative interactions of Father and Son, particularly as presented in the Fourth Gospel, yield further insight into God's inner life. The three persons are distinct communicative agents that nevertheless share a common communicative agency. There are three main topics of conversation: mutual glorification, the giving of life, and the sharing of love. Significantly, the dialogues "come at crucial moments in the narrative of the unfolding drama of the Trinity, and they mark the nodal points of the inner relations of the Trinity, worked out in time and space."[59] Given our present focus on John 5 about the Father's showing and the Son's seeing, I want to focus on the theme of glorification.

When Jesus realizes that his hour has come he prays, "Father, glorify your name" (John 12:28), only to be answered by a voice from heaven: "I have glorified it, and I will glorify it again." The Spirit, too, plays a communicative role. Jesus says: "He [the Spirit] will glorify me, for he will take all that is mine and declare it to you" (John 16:14). As with all God's

---

58. "As the Son's proper mode of being God consists in the pure relation wherein he receives his being from the Father, so the Son's proper mode of acting as God consists in the pure relation wherein he receives his action from the Father," a relation that Allen and Swain term "receptive filiation" (Allen and Swain, "Obedience of the Eternal Son," 123–24, 129).

59. Davies, *Theology of Compassion*, 199–200.

communicative action, glorification too is triune: a unified action with three aspects.

Glorification is the communication of God's majesty, the publication of God's excellence. It is also the main topic of Jesus' longest prayer, the high-priestly prayer of John 17, spoken on the eve of the drama's climax. What is striking is how Father and Son glorify—make known the glory of—one another: "Father, the hour has come; glorify your Son that the Son may glorify you" (John 17:1). Tellingly, however, Jesus indicates that his historical glorification (being "lifted up" on the cross—John 3:14; 8:28; 12:32–33) only makes known something he had already enjoyed in eternity: "and now, Father, glorify me in your own presence with the glory *that I had with you before the world existed*" (John 17:5; my emphasis). In the words of the seventeenth-century Scottish minister Robert Leighton: "It is most true of the Blessed Trinity, *Satis amplum alter alteri theatrum sumus* [each is to another a theater large enough]."[60]

There is good reason to think that the perfect life of the immanent Trinity involves, among other things, a mutual glorification between the three persons. The particular way in which the Son glorifies the Father corresponds to the way in which he has his being and activity "from" the Father—what I have termed "filial responsiveness." Aquinas, following Augustine, interprets Jesus' words in John 5:19 ("The Son can do nothing of himself") as meaning "I am equal to the Father, but in such a way as to be from him, and not he from me."[61] As the Image and Word of God, the Son is both radiant and "respondent"—the latter being a particularly apt term (from "to pledge [*spondere*] in return [*re-*]") for the Son's role in the immanent life of God. This captures something of the way in which the Son does what he sees the Father doing. This eternal filial responsiveness—the Son's ability to see and do his Father's works "from" the Father—is eventually played out in history as the obedience that leads to the Son glorifying the Father on the cross. "God" is the name for this common communicative (e.g., glorifying) activity of the three persons. And, according to Jonathan Edwards (see below), the whole point of the history of redemption is to play out in the theater of space and time the dynamic triune glorification that is God's perfect eternal life. The Son

---

60. Leighton, *The Whole Works of Archbishop Leighton*, 1:154 (comment on 1 Pet 1:23).

61. Aquinas, *Commentary on the Gospel of John*, 747.

glorifies the Father by communicating the perfect light, life, and love that God is in himself.[62]

Pactum Salutis: *Triune Covenantal Self-Determination*

In his high-priestly prayer, Jesus speaks of having accomplished the work the Father gave him to do, relates it to the project of glorifying God, and asks the Father to glorify him (the Son) with the glory he had with the Father "before the world existed" (John 17:4–5). The ultimate work of glorification, of course, takes place in the Son's being "lifted up" by his death on the cross (John 3:14; 8:28; 12:32, 34), the definitive instance of filial responsiveness to the Father's will. When did the Father assign the Son his task, and when did the Son accept it?

To construe this question of timing literally is to miss the point. We are not in the realm of chronology, but divine self-determination. We are in the realm of the Father's eternal love for the Son and his eternal show-ing the Son the work he was to do. It is this "showing" and "seeing," before the foundation of the world, that is played out in the history of salvation. The idea that the triune God freely determines *in se* ("in himself") to be *pro nobis* ("for us") is the deep background of the theodrama. Stated provocatively: the *drama* of redemption presupposes the *covenant* of re-demption, the (Reformed) idea that the gospel is an ordered execution in time of a pre-temporal divine plan, the *pactum salutis*. In the words of Jonathan Edwards: "The whole Trinity is concerned in the affair of our redemption. It is a work designed for the glory of each of the persons."[63]

What the Father and Son decide to do together is to give life (John 5:21), or rather, to share their own life, a project in which the Spirit par-ticipates too (Rom 5:8–11).[64] As we shall see, the Spirit shares in the love of Father and Son not only by witnessing it but also by pouring it into

---

62. For more on the way in which the economic Trinity communicates the light, life, and love that characterizes the immanent Trinity, see my *Remythologizing Theology*, chapter 5.

63. *Works of Jonathan Edwards*, 25:144.

64. In the important "Miscellany 1062," on the "Economy of the Trinity and the Covenant of Redemption," Edwards notes that the divine determination to redeem was "determined by the perfect consent of all, and . . . consultation among the three persons about it . . . there was a joint agreement of all, but not properly a covenant between 'em [sic] all" (*Works of Jonathan Edwards*, 20:442). McClymond and McDermott explain: "The covenant of redemption was a joint agreement among all three persons but a cov-enant only between the Father and the Son" (*Theology of Jonathan Edwards*, 204).

human hearts (Rom 5:5). What is most prominent, however, is the Son's perfect filial responsiveness, his mode of glorifying the Father in eternity, which is historically enacted when the Son humbles himself and takes on the role of Israel, the "son" God called out of Egypt to glorify him by their obedience and worship (Hos 11:1).[65] It is precisely because Jesus is the second person of the Trinity that he can execute, freely and perfectly, his role as royal son and suffering servant, namely, the mediator of the covenant by which God creates a new kinship unit, thereby enlarging, as it were, the scope of his familial relations.

The Son's appearance in history was neither a surprise nor contingency measure, but rather the result of a joyful collaboration conceived in eternity between the Father and the Son. To be sent is to be given a mission. As Augustine points out, the Son's sending precedes the historical event of the incarnation; hence the mission, like the Son, is preexistent.[66] The Son consents to being sent *before* the economy proper gets underway, *before* he takes on "the form of a servant" (Phil 2:7). The role the Son plays in the economy is thus the same one he plays in eternity, though we should probably speak of "identity" rather than role, for the Son is just the one whose proper work is joyfully to consent to being sent. Hence it should come as no surprise that the Son's mission on earth is "to do the will of him who sent me and to accomplish his work" (John 4:34; cf. John 5:30; 6:38). The Son's eternal obedience does not mean that there are separate wills in the Godhead. On the contrary, says Aquinas, the Father and Son have the same will, but "the Father does not have his will from another, whereas the Son does have his will from another, i.e., the Father."[67]

Economic Redemption (Triune Communication *Ad Extra*): Mission, Admission, and Communion

"And greater works than these will he show him." (John 5:20)

The works that the Father shows and the Son sees are the result of what the Father and Son determined to do to communicate their perfect life in

---

65. Swain rightly points out that the incarnation is a movement of "self-giving descent, not of self-realization or self-constitution" (*God of the Gospel*, 169), contra Jenson.

66. *The Trinity*, 4.27.

67. Aquinas, *Commentary on the Gospel of John*, 294.

and to the created sphere. Jesus had already worked miracles (e.g., healing the sick), but the "greater works" pertain to what he would do later in the story, namely, raise the dead and bestow life (John 5:21–29; cf. John 11:1–45).[68] These are the works that contribute to "the work" the Son came to finish (John 4:34; 17:4): the work of redemption. It is this work—communicating the light, life, and love of God—that makes for dramatic coherence, not only in the life of Jesus, but in the relationship between God *in se* (immanent Trinity) and God *ad extra* (economic Trinity).[69]

The History of the Work of Redemption: Salvation History as Covenant Plot

The missions of the Son and Spirit repeat *ad extra* the communicative relations *ad intra*. Webster summarizes much of what I was saying in the previous section when he comments that the works of God "repeat" the immanent being of God. *God's mighty acts in history theatrically represent the perfections of God's nature and the outworking of God's decree.* Revelation is essentially "theatrical" representation: a triune operation in space and time that enacts the drama of redemption conceived and covenanted in eternity. The historical missions of Son (e.g., incarnation) and Spirit repeat—represent in time—eternal processions (e.g., begetting). The work of redemption is part and parcel of the mutual glorification of Father, Son, and Spirit.

The gospel is the execution and exhibition in time and space of what was freely decided in eternity. The covenant of redemption is a kind of script to which the Son is a willing conscript. The missions of the Son and Spirit are the acting out, in the history of Jesus, of what has been going on in God's triune life eternally, namely, the communication of God's light, life, and love: "God *enacts* his perfection."[70] Stated axiomatically: the economic Trinity *communicates* the immanent Trinity. The economic Trinity—the actions of God in the history of redemption—is

---

68. Rae characterizes the "greater works than these" that Jesus does as the work of creation and new creation ("The Testimony of Works in the Christology of John's Gospel," 295–310).

69. Cf. Webster: "Soteriology . . . has its place within the theology of the *mysterium trinitatis*, that is, God's inherent and communicated richness of life as Father, Son, and Holy Spirit" ("Soteriology and the Doctrine of God," 20).

70. Webster, "God's Perfect Life," 147. Cf. Bavinck: "The pact of salvation makes known to us the relationships and life of the three persons in the Divine Being as a covenantal life" (*Reformed Dogmatics*, 3:214).

itself a space-time representation of the way God always/already is in eternity. Father, Son, and Spirit play out in time the triune perfections. In a nutshell: the missions of the Son and Spirit are *dramatic representations* of the eternal processions in the theater of created space and time.[71] And, most importantly: the drama of redemption is not the place where God first becomes the God of steadfast love, but the place where the perfection of God's steadfast love—God's very being—is rendered historically present.

According to Jonathan Edwards, the end for which God created the world was to *communicate* himself, to share with creatures his own life: his knowledge, love, and joy. In this perspective, creation is a theater not for general revelation or natural theology but for grace and soteriology. Though Edwards was never able to complete his plan for *A History of the Work of Redemption*, he did leave some hints, including an extended sermon series with the same name.

The first sermon is programmatic, affording an overview of the whole project. It presents the history of redemption as a dramatic display of God's righteousness, which for Edwards means God's faithfulness to his covenant promises.[72] The actual work of redemption begins with the fall of Adam and continues to the end of the world. The history of redemption is one work, and thus has dramatic coherence: "'Tis but one design that is done to which all of the offices of Christ do directly tend, and in which all the persons of the Trinity do conspire and all the various dispensations that belong to it are united, as the several wheels in one machine, to answer one end and produce one effect."[73] What was agreed in eternity is thus enacted in time: Edwards refers to the "lower world" as "the stage of this wonderful Work [of Redemption]."[74] And though the Son declares, "It is finished," in one sense the work continues, for Edwards acknowledges that the effect of this work (e.g., calling, justifying, glorifying—Rom 8:30) is ongoing.

Clearly, Edwards is thinking in terms of one drama of redemption with many acts. Edwards lists several things the great work of redemption is designed to accomplish, but the overarching aim is the

71. Cf. Dodd: "The human career of Jesus is, as it were, a projection of this eternal relation (which is the divine *agape*) upon the field of time" (*Interpretation of the Fourth Gospel*, 262).

72. *Works of Jonathan Edwards*, 9:114.

73. Ibid., 118.

74. Ibid., 118–19.

self-communication of the triune God, the sharing of God's own life, and in particular the sharing in Jesus' sonship, together with all the rights, privileges, and honors that accompany it.

The High Point of the Work of Redemption: The Gospel as Covenant Climax

We are now in a better position to appreciate the intrinsic and necessary connection between the triune God and the gospel. According to Edwards, the Son's principal role in the dramatic history of redemption was to purchase redemption in the narrow sense of the term, that is, the deliverance from sin and death. We could speak here of the covenant's climax in terms of "conveyance" (i.e., a transfer of title to goods, property, and kingdom from one person to another): "He has rescued us from the power of darkness and transferred us into the kingdom of his beloved Son" (Col 1:13). The Son accomplishes this work by his death and resurrection, themselves communications of what God is: faithfulness and steadfast love. In other words, through the events of the gospel, God is communicating himself. Indeed, for Edwards, God's self-communication is the "end" for which the world was created.

The gospel is the announcement that the resurrection of Jesus *is* the end of creation, and the beginning of the new creation in which "God may be all in all" (1 Cor 15:28). It is the announcement that God's covenant purpose—to redeem the world in Christ; to extend the scope of his "familial" relations and invite human creatures into the fellowship that is the triune life—has been realized.[75] For the work of the Son enables what was his by nature (i.e., sonship) to be the believer's by grace. Indeed, one way to view the work of redemption is as a communication of Christ's filial responsiveness—the disposition that constitutes the Son the image of God—to men and women. In short: what God communicates is ultimately himself, and he does so by uniting them to Christ through the Spirit.[76] Such union with Christ is the result of what we might call

---

75. "The gospel . . . concerns the history of fellowship—covenant—between God and creatures" (Webster, "Soteriology and the Doctrine of God," 15).

76. The prime task of the Spirit is to communicate Christ. The Spirit comes into his own in the play only after Jesus' resurrection and ascension, the twin conditions for Pentecost ("as yet the Spirit had not been given because Jesus was not yet glorified" John 7:49). The sending of the Spirit is the condition for believers to join in the work the triune God is doing (e.g., knowing and loving God and others; glorifying God).

a drama of adoption, and is thus "theological shorthand for the gospel itself."[77]

The Trinity is the sum of the gospel because the good news concerns how the Father invites us to share in the divine life in the Son through the Spirit: "the good news of salvation is that God, who in himself is eternally the Father, the Son, and the Holy Spirit, has become for us the adoptive Father, the incarnate Son, and the outpoured Holy Spirit."[78] The gospel thus has a Trinitarian shape. Indeed, the gospel is the theatrical (i.e., economic) realization of the triune *pactum salutis*. It is the fulfillment, in the history of Jesus Christ, of the Father's promise and the Son's compliance to pour out eternal life on the elect. George MacDonald eloquently captures the way in which the Son's economic work theatrically represents his filial relation to the Father in God's immanent perfection: "When he died on the cross, He did that, in the wild weather of His outlying provinces, in the torture of the body of His revelation, which he had done at home in glory and gladness."[79]

In defeating sin, death, and the devil, the Son is recognized as the king he always has been, hence the bending of every knee and confessing of every tongue (Phil 2:10–11). The Son's glorification is thus a coronation. Yet the drama is redemptive only because of who the Son is: "Apart from Jesus' metaphysically prevenient identity as God's beloved Son, we are unable to appreciate that which distinguishes his embassy from the embassy of the Father's other servants."[80] The logic of the gospel—becoming reconciled to God—depends upon Jesus' being the incarnation of the Word that was God in the beginning: "For those [in the early church] engaged in these debates [about the Trinity], if Jesus was not truly and fully God, then we are not saved."[81]

Finally, and most significantly in light of the present essay, Edwards thinks the work of redemption was "designed to accomplish the glory of the blessed Trinity."[82] As the Father forms an idea of himself in the Son, the brightness of his glory, and delights in himself by flowing forth in love towards himself in the Spirit, so "God glorifies himself towards the

---

77. Billings, *Union with Christ,* 1. Calvin rightly saw that "union with Christ" is the font from which all the other blessings of redemption spring (*Institutes* III.xi.10).

78. Sanders, *Deep Things of God,* 165.

79. MacDonald, *Unspoken Sermons,* third series, *The Creation in Christ,* #173, 88.

80. Swain, *God of the Gospel,* 169.

81. Keating, "Trinity and Salvation," 444.

82. Edwards, *Works,* 9:125.

creatures also two ways," namely by communicating both his knowledge (i.e., the Son) and love (i.e., the Spirit).[83] United in Christ by the Spirit, the elect are not only brought into union with one another, but also glorified, to the extent that the image of God in Christ is communicated to them as well. The high point of the work of redemption, then, is triune glorification through triune communication. What is ultimately at play in the theodrama of the Lord is the communication of the glory of the Lord.

By now it should be clear why it is both proper and important for theatrical theology to treat the immanent Trinity. First, contra Jenson, the drama of the Christ is a drama of redemption only because of who Christ already is—the eternal Son of God. If Jesus were not the eternally begotten Son, his death would be simply one more human tragedy. As Aquinas says, the primary reason why knowledge of the divine persons is necessary "is to give us a true notion of the salvation of mankind, a salvation accomplished by the Son who became flesh and by the gift of the Holy Spirit."[84]

It is not enough, however, simply to posit an immanent Trinity whose communicative actions and relations the economic Trinity re-enacts dramatically; one must make the right ontological inferences from the historical events of the gospel. So second, contra Balthasar, the cross of Christ does not mean that one should import the idea of suffering loss into the self-giving that is the triune God's own life.[85] The cross does indeed dramatize something always true of the immanent Trinity, namely, the extent to which the Son joyfully consents to the will of the Father. Jesus' death was his obedient response to the mission for which he was sent, which is why, despite its horror, the cross has become part and parcel of the good news: as one of the means by which the triune God communicates eternal life. It is only because the Spirit unites us to the Son's bloody history, signified in baptism by our being buried and raised with him (Rom 6), that we, as adopted children, are able to share in his eternal Sonship: "the Son's economic obedience is the means whereby

83. Edwards, "Miscellany" 448, in *Works*, 13:495.

84. *Summa Theologiae* I, q. 32, a.1, ad 3.

85. Kilby worries that Balthasar, in construing God's self-giving as a giving *away*, blurs the distinction between love and loss. If these are linked eternally in God, then suffering is given a positive valuation and takes on "an ultimate ontological status" (*Balthasar*, 120).

other sons and daughters come to share as creatures in his filial relationship to the Father."[86]

The Effect of the Work of Redemption: Communion as Covenant Blessing

"And you shall be my people, and I will be your God." (Jer 30:22; cf. Exod 6:7; Lev 26:12)

Edwards says: "The great thing purchased by Jesus Christ for us is communion with God, which is only in having the Spirit."[87] What gets played out in the drama of redemption is not a primal kenosis but a primal *covenance*[88] for the end of conveyance: namely, an eternal divine covenantal self-determination to execute in time the transfer of humans who were not God's people into the kingdom of his Son (Col 1:13). It is only in the Son, through the Spirit, that fellowship with the Father—eternal life—is possible. It is only in the Son that men and women attain the end for which they were created, namely, "to glorify God and enjoy him forever."[89]

The greatest blessing communicated to those in Christ is, therefore, the *end* of communication: interpersonal communion, the kind of union Jesus had in mind when he petitioned his Father "that they [the disciples] may be one, even as we are one" (John 17:11). To speak of the triune God of the gospel (or the gospel of the Trinity) is ultimately to describe *divine communicative action oriented to the end of covenantal communion*. John Owen describes this blessing as follows: "Our communion, then, with God consists in his communication of himself to us, with our return unto him of that which he requires and accepts, flowing from that union which in Jesus Christ we have with him."[90] In brief: the triune God of the gospel is the Father, Son, and Spirit working—communicating!—in perfect communion to extend this communion even further, "from one degree of glory to another" (2 Cor 3:18).

---

86. Allen and Swain, "Obedience of the Eternal Son," 133.

87. Edwards, "Miscellany" 402, in *Works* 13:466.

88. I owe this term to Daniel Block.

89. *Westminster Shorter Catechism*, Q. 1.

90. Owen, *Communion with the Triune God*, 94.

Conclusion: Participating in the Triune Play

"... that you may marvel." (John 5:20)

Christian theology is inherently theatrical insofar as what lies at the heart of its gospel core is the work of redemption that the Father shows, the Son sees, and both do. Although many today associate drama and theo-drama with the theologies of twentieth-century theologians like Jenson and Balthasar, I have argued that more traditional forms of Trinitarian theism are, in fact, better suited to take up the mantle of theatrical theology, inasmuch as they better account for (1) the identities, economic *and* immanent, of the divine *dramatis personae* and (2) the intelligibility of the action, that is, the way in which the gospel communicates in time the eternal perfection and purposes of the triune God. The Trinity is the sum and substance of the gospel, I concluded, because the good news concerns how the one whose own life is perfect communion invites us to share in that life through the missions of the Son and Spirit.

The history of Jesus Christ is a "doing than which nothing greater can be conceived," not least because it is the realization in time of an eternal triune self-determination—to be pro-covenant, and hence *pro nobis*. The gospel is God playing out in time the eternal loving faithfulness and responsiveness that characterizes his own triune life. Jesus healed the sick, cast out demons, and did "greater works than these" (i.e., raising the dead; being raised from the dead as head of a new creation), which rightly lead the disciples, and us, to marvel (John 5:20). Theatrical theology is short-circuited, however, if we remain spectators only. The disciples were right to ask Jesus, "What must *we* do to perform the works of God?" (John 6:28, NRSV). Jesus' answer, "This is the work of God, that you believe in him whom he has sent" (John 6:29), indicates that there is indeed something for his followers to do. Disciples too have a role to play in the theodrama.

As John Owen rightly noted, communion is not simply a static condition but a "fellowship in *action*," a joint participation in a project. It is the way in which those who have rightly received God's communication (i.e., Christ) make "return unto him."[91] Interestingly, the term "participation" is used sixteen times in the Vatican II document on the liturgy, *Sacrosanctum Concilium*, twelve times with the qualifier "active," the point being that the laity make "return" to God by engaging more fully

91. Owen, *Communion*, 94.

in worship "by using their voices and bodies to experience the action of nothing less than the Trinity at work among us through the rites and prayers of the sacred liturgy."[92] When saints participate in both formal liturgy, and the informal liturgy that is life, they participate in the theater of the gospel: the communication of God's own triune life.

To be a "communicant" in the theodrama of the Lord is to participate, not least by acting, in a fellowship of actions and relations that are the effects and consequences of the triune work of redemption, and which ultimately derive from those actions and relations that comprise the perfect life of God *in se*. The work of redemption, the theme of the theodramatic play, is the good news that the Father's and Son's common work of seeing and showing has enlarged the circle of loving communion, making room for human communicants—"spect-actors" enlivened by the Spirit to *see* and *show* the glory of the Christ (John 17:24).[93]

Bibliography

Allen, Michael, and Scott Swain. "The Obedience of the Eternal Son." *International Journal of Systematic Theology* 15 (2013) 114–34.

Aquinas, Thomas. *Commentary on the Gospel of John, Chapters 1–5*. Translated by Fabian Larcher and James A. Weisheipf. Washington, DC: Catholic University of America Press, 2010.

Augustine. *Tractates on the Gospel of John, 11–27*. Washington, DC: Catholic University of America Press, 1988.

Ayres, Lewis. *Augustine and the Trinity*. Cambridge: Cambridge University Press, 2010.

Balthasar, Hans Urs von. *Theo-Drama*. Vol. 1, *Prolegomena*. San Francisco: Ignatius, 1988.

———. *Theo-Drama*. Vol. 4, *The Action*. San Francisco: Ignatius, 1994.

Bavinck, Herman. *Reformed Dogmatics*. Vol. 3, *Sin and Salvation in Christ*. Grand Rapids: Baker, 2006.

Billings, J. Todd. *Union with Christ: Reframing Theology and Ministry for the Church*. Grand Rapids: Baker, 2011.

Davies, Oliver. *A Theology of Compassion*. London: SCM, 2001.

Dodd, C. H. *The Interpretation of the Fourth Gospel*. Cambridge: Cambridge University Press, 1953.

———. *Historical Tradition in the Fourth Gospel*. Cambridge: Cambridge University Press, 1963.

———. "A Hidden Parable in the Fourth Gospel." In *More New Testament Studies*, 30–40. Manchester: Manchester University Press, 1968.

92. Irwin, "Foreword," ix.

93. My thanks to James Gordon, Jon Hoglund, Ike Miller, and David Moser for their comments on an earlier draft.

Edwards, Jonathan. *Works of Jonathan Edwards*. Vol. 9, *A History of the Work of Redemption*. New Haven: Yale University Press, 1989.

———. *Works of Jonathan Edwards*. Vol. 13, *The "Miscellanies," entry nos. a-z, aa-zz, 1–500*. New Haven: Yale University Press, 1994.

———. *Works of Jonathan Edwards*. Vol. 25, *Sermons and Discourses: 1743–1758*. New Haven: Yale University Press, 2006.

Frei, Hans. *Eclipse of the Biblical Narrative*. New Haven: Yale University Press, 1974.

Gathercole, Simon. "Pre-existence, and the Freedom of the Son in Creation and Redemption: An Exposition in Dialogue with Robert Jenson." *International Journal of Systematic Theology* 7 (2005) 38–51.

Hart, David Bentley. *The Beauty of the Infinite: The Aesthetics of Christian Truth*. Grand Rapids: Eerdmans, 2003.

Irwin, Kevin. "Foreword." In *Toward a Trinitarian Theology of Liturgical Participation*, by R. Gabriel Pivarnik, ix–xi. Collegeville, MN: Liturgical, 2013.

Jenson, Robert W. *America's Theologian: A Recommendation of Jonathan Edwards*. Oxford: Oxford University Press, 1988.

———. "Christ as Culture 3: Christ as Drama." *International Journal of Systematic Theology* 6 (2004) 194–201.

———. *Systematic Theology*. Vol. 1, *The Triune God*. Oxford: Oxford University Press, 1997.

Johnson, Keith E. "Augustine's 'Trinitarian' Reading of John 5: A Model for the Theological Interpretation of Scripture?" *Journal of the Evangelical Theological Society* 52.4 (2009) 799–810.

Keating, Daniel A. "Trinity and Salvation: Christian Life as an Existence in the Trinity." In *The Oxford Handbook of the Trinity*, edited by Gilles Emery and Matthew Levering, 442–55. Oxford: Oxford University Press, 2011.

Kilby, Karen. *Balthasar: A (Very) Critical Introduction*. Grand Rapids: Eerdmans, 2012.

Köstenberger, Andreas, and Scott Swain. *Father, Son and Spirit: The Trinity and John's Gospel*. Downers Grove, IL: InterVarsity, 2005.

Leighton, Robert. *The Whole Works of Archbishop Leighton*. Vol. 1, *A Practical Commentary Upon the First Epistle of Peter*. London: Ogle, Duncan, 1820.

McClymond, Michael J., and Gerald R. McDermott. *The Theology of Jonathan Edwards*. Oxford: Oxford University Press, 2012.

Morris, Leon. *The Gospel according to John*. Grand Rapids: Eerdmans, 1971.

Owen, John. *Communion with the Triune God*. Wheaton, IL: Crossway, 2007.

Pakaluk, Michael. "The Play's Not the Thing." *Edification: The Transdisciplinary Journal of Christian Psychology* 4 (2010) 28–30.

Pannenberg, Wolfhart. "Books in Review: Robert W. Jenson, *Systematic Theology* vols. 1 and 2." *First Things* 103 (2000) 49–53.

———. *Systematic Theology*. Vol. 1. Grand Rapids: Eerdmans, 1991.

Rae, Murray. "The Testimony of Works in the Christology of John's Gospel." In *The Gospel of John and Christian Theology*, edited by Richard Bauckham and Carl Mosser, 295–310. Grand Rapids: Eerdmans, 2008.

Rahner, Karl. *The Trinity*. New York: Crossroad, 2003.

Sanders, Fred. *The Deep Things of God: How the Trinity Changes Everything*. Wheaton, IL: Crossway, 2010.

———. *The Image of the Immanent Trinity: Rahner's Rule and the Theological Interpretation of Scripture*. New York: Lang, 2005.

————. "The Trinity." In *The Oxford Handbook of Systematic Theology*, edited by John Webster et al., 35–53. Oxford: Oxford University Press, 2007.

Schweitzer, William M. *God Is a Communicative Being: Divine Communicativeness and Harmony in the Theology of Jonathan Edwards*. London: T. & T. Clark, 2012.

Swain, Scott R. *The God of the Gospel: Robert Jenson's Trinitarian Theology*. Downers Grove, IL: InterVarsity, 2013.

Van der Watt, J. G. "The Father Shows the Son Everything. The Imagery of Education in John 5:19–23." *Acts Patristica et Byzantia* 18 (2007) 263–76.

Vanhoozer, Kevin J. *Faith Speaking Understanding: Performing the Drama of Doctrine*. Louisville: Westminster John Knox, 2014.

————. *Remythologizing Theology: Divine Action, Passion, and Authorship*. Cambridge: Cambridge University Press, 2010.

Webster, John. "God's Perfect Life." In *God's Life in Trinity*, edited by Miroslav Volf and Michael Welker, 143–52. Minneapolis: Fortress, 2006.

————. "'It Was the Will of the Lord to Bruise Him': Soteriology and the Doctrine of God." In *God of Salvation: Soteriology in Theological Perspective*, edited by Ivor J. Davidson and Murray Rae, 15–34. Farnham, UK: Ashgate, 2011.

————. "One Who Is Son: Theological Reflections on the Exordium to the Epistle to the Hebrews." In *The Epistle to the Hebrews and Christian Theology*, edited by Richard Bauckham et al., 69–94. Grand Rapids: Eerdmans, 2009.

Westcott, Brooke Foss. *The Gospel according to St. John*. Vol. 1. London: Murray, 1908.

2

Beyond Theatre and Incarnation

Trevor Hart

The Incarnation and the Fleshiness of Theatre

THE CENTRAL AND MOST striking claim of the Christian faith is that God's own eternal Word or Son became flesh and dwelled among us, playing out his distinctive part on the stage of human history. Whatever else it means, this claim compels Christians to reckon much more seriously with the nature and significance of the "flesh" in question than has sometimes been the case. According to the mainstream of christological understanding in Scripture and creeds alike, the enfleshing in question was permanent rather than temporary. Our own creaturely nature, having once been assumed into union with the person or *hypostasis* of the Son, and having fully shared in the drama of human birth, life, action, suffering, and death, was not now set aside in the way that an actor may legitimately step out of character upon leaving the stage at the end of a performance. On the contrary, this creaturely nature remains forever bound up with the Son's own identity as such, more substantial now than it ever was by virtue of its resurrection and ascension (taken back "into heaven" to the Father's right hand to use the inevitably mythological categories of kerygma and liturgy), modifying the very being of God himself in the process.[1]

1. Despite the qualifications that need to hedge such a claim, and despite the proper insights and concerns attaching to theological notions of divine "immutability," that

30

Such a radical conjunction between Word (*Logos*) and flesh (*sarx*), in which the uncreated Lord of heaven and earth himself now so penetrates our humanity with the fullness of his own being as henceforth to be identified with it and identifiable as one of us, prohibits any attempt on our part to ascribe to the flesh any merely fleeting or illustrative significance, as though it were a stepping stone to be left behind in the bid for a meaning or reality with which, finally, it has nothing to do. That the Word himself has become flesh means that, for creatures like us—ones possessed of both body and "soul"—no such discarnate reality is either available or even desirable. Whatever encounters and intercourse we take ourselves to have with "spiritual" or non-material entities are in any case earthed securely and without loss, in one way or another, in our amphibious entanglement in the realm of space-time materiality.[2] Hitherto this observation might have been merely empirical, perhaps even (as in various forms of dualism and idealism) resented and resisted, fuelling eschatological hope for an eventual escape from the unseemly limits of our inconvenient situation in the body. But God himself has appeared among us, clothed with his own "fleshy" mode of being and showing no sign of sloughing it off again at the earliest opportunity. As a result, both the craving for engagement with a pure *Logos asarkos* and any aspiration on our part towards eventual personal disembodiment (a phrase arguably now rendered oxymoronic in the context of a theological anthropology at least) are seriously flawed. To be human is to be wedded inexorably to and part of a material creation, even if our humanity will not submit to any accounting conducted in material terms alone. The assumption of Jesus' resurrection body as a permanent feature in the triune life of God compels such an acknowledgment and forces a re-evaluation of the significance of the flesh: for God and for us.

With the incarnation, we might say, a decisive new significance is bestowed upon the flesh, for us and for its primordial maker and newest inhabitant; and we are bound to attend to it henceforth with a new curiosity and expectation. Not any or all "flesh"—in the first instance at least—but the very particular instantiation of it has no being except as

---

notion, when philosophically rather than biblically derived, and in the form in which it is sometimes presented and understood, seems to me finally to be incompatible with the radical implications of christological orthodoxy for our thinking about God.

2. "Humans are amphibians—half spirit and half animal. . . . As spirits they belong to the eternal world, but as animals they inhabit time." Screwtape in Lewis, *The Screwtape Letters*, 44.

the form of God's own unique dwelling among us, now as one of his own creatures. Language falters here, and so it should. How could it be otherwise? The humanity of Jesus, which is God's *own* humanity, the presence among us humanly of the one through whom all things were made in the beginning, resists our attempts to capture and to speak meaningfully of it in the terms of everyday discourse, subverting and renewing those terms even as we use them. And thereafter, *all* flesh must appear differently to us, inasmuch as it falls now within the penumbra of the claim that here God has made our "flesh" his own in a radically new manner and with universal redemptive intent and accomplishment.

Taking seriously the economy of the flesh, then, is *de rigueur* for Christians in their approach to the world in all its complex reality, visible and invisible. That which God has made his own through a supremely costly and risky venture,[3] and drawn bodily into the celebration of his own eternity, clearly has a premium and price surpassing human understanding. Nevertheless, we must strive to grasp it and to respect it in our own ascriptions of value and worth to the phenomena of creaturely experience. And, although the "flesh" (Heb. *bāśār*, Gk. *sarx*) of biblical and patristic testimony refers to our creatureliness as a whole, and thus in human terms to our material form in its integral union with the "invisible" realm of persons, meanings, and values etc.,[4] it certainly *includes* our embeddedness as "ensouled bodies" in the material cosmos, together with all its glorious messiness and unavoidable earthiness. "Flesh" in the more familiar and precise sense, therefore, is something Christians can neither neglect nor decry, but must grapple with and take seriously as a reality laden with value and significance deeper and more considerable than that with which we may, from time to time, choose to invest it.

It may seem needless to say that the arts are bound up with the economy of flesh, despite the persistent idealism that has occasionally plagued Western aesthetics. It is clear enough that a work of art is always more than its physical manifestation in clay, egg tempera smeared on wooden substrate, vibrating strings or air forced through tubes, soaring stonework, or whatever the chosen medium might be. Unless there is indeed

---

3. On the sense in which God may properly said to have put himself at "risk" in the incarnation and atonement, see helpfully Lewis, "Kenosis and Kerygma."

4. See Bratsiotis, "bāśār;" Schweizer and Meyer, "sarx." For a careful analysis of the uses of *sarx* and *sōma* (body) in fourth and fifth century christological discussion see "A Neglected Aspect of Athanasius's Christology" in Dragas, *Athanasiana*. Cf. Dragas, *St Athanasius Contra Apollinarem*.

something more than sensory presentation alone allows (some value or meaning or pattern apprehended by imagination), we should hardly be inclined to identify any object as "art" at all. But to identify this non-material imaginative surplus as the true "work," something contained complete in "the mind of the maker," seems problematic on empirical grounds alone, let alone in light of the sort of theological considerations we have just addressed.[5] The true work of art, as the product of a fully human engagement with the world, is necessarily implicated in the world of the flesh. Rather than seeking to resituate us in a world of pure "spirit" or "idea" by capturing our attention, art at its best draws us more fully and profoundly into a material cosmos already fully charged with spirit and meaning.[6] Among the arts, theatre and drama—more fully even than the dance or opera—has a peculiarly close and incorrigible relation to the stuff of human flesh and blood. As a form centered on the presence and action of actual bodies performing in the presence of an audience in real time and space, theatre is more than usually resistant to the bid for complete abstraction which has sometimes seized artistry of other sorts. As Max Harris notes, though "the human body may generate arbitrary sign systems of gesture, movement and expression, the body on stage is not, like the word 'corpus' or a particular configuration of paint, an arbitrary signifier of human being."[7] Here, the relationship between signifier and signified is much more complex and ambiguous, a fact that has a good deal to do with theatre's peculiar power as art. Taking "flesh" in both its broader and more narrow senses, therefore, "(w)hatever may be true of other art forms, . . . the theatre is irredeemably fleshy."[8]

A Proper Dwelling Place for God

First published more than twenty years ago now, Harris's work *Theater and Incarnation* remains one of a small handful of books to engage with the phenomenon of theatre in a sustained and serious manner from a

5. Perhaps the most familiar version of aesthetic idealism is that of R. G. Collingwood in *The Principles of Art*. For a discussion of Collingwood's influence on the attempt by Dorothy L. Sayers to sketch a distinctly Christian aesthetic grounded in the dogma of the incarnation, see Hart, *Making Good*, chapter 12. Cf. Sayers, *The Mind of the Maker*, 26–34; Sayers, "Towards a Christian Aesthetic."

6. See Hart, "Through the Arts."

7. Harris, *Theater and Incarnation*, 38.

8. Ibid., 39.

theological standpoint and, so far as I am aware, the only one to do so with the incarnation as its central doctrinal motif. Given the suggestive resonances between theatre's irredeemable "fleshiness" and faith's most distinctive claim that the meaning of our humanity and of the wider creation itself is to be found finally in the dramatic "enfleshment" of God's own Word in the *theatron* of human history,[9] one might perhaps have expected more in the intervening decades by way of an effort to pursue some of Harris's core insights and observations further.[10] Also surprising is the paucity of allusions to, let alone actual engagements with, his work or the issues at the heart of it in other contributions to this volume. Whatever the reason for this relative neglect, it is a pity, because despite some interesting and important work published in the field in the last decade or so, *Theater and Incarnation* remains by far the best example to date of a genuine conversation between theatre and theology. Of course there are, as with any book, no matter how well conceived and written, points at which one might have hoped for something more or different in the precise execution, and there are certainly lines of further enquiry to be picked up and pursued. What I propose to do in this essay, therefore, is to give the reader some sense of the burden of concern that drives and informs Harris's book and to attend to a few points at which it might prove fruitful to press beyond the range of his own consideration.

The starting point for Harris's reflections lies in his recognition of resonances, to which I have already alluded, between the logic of the incarnation (a concept compressing the dynamics of what is already a highly "dramatic" and "theatrical" event) and the peculiar challenges and opportunities afforded by the attempt to stage meaningful theatrical performance. In addition, one might mention the long and uncomfortable history of Christian suspicion, hostility, and indifference shown variously to theatre arts in general.[11] This persistent "antitheatrical prejudice" had

9. The familiar image of the world stage is appropriated by metonymy in 1 Cor 4:9: "(W)e have become a spectacle (*theatron*) to the world, to angels and to mortals."

10. Harris appears in the bibliography but not the name index, for example, of Kevin Vanhoozer's major 500-page contribution to the area. See Vanhoozer, *The Drama of Doctrine*. Vanhoozer's focal concern is, to be sure, the nature of doctrine and the uses of Scripture, but Harris's work already directs us wisely to the inseparability of a "theatrical hermeneutic" from considerations of Christology as such, and encourages treatment of the incarnation not simply as a central plotline within a drama cast in other terms, but as a way of framing the drama as a whole. A brief critical engagement with Harris (and Vanhoozer) is to be found in Joshua Edelman, "Can an Act be True?"

11. See Harris, *Theater and Incarnation*, 68–72. For a thorough account see Barish, *The The Antitheatrical Prejudice.*

its provenance early in patristic reactions to the vulgar "spectacle" of ancient Rome's equivalent to reality TV (in which, quite apart from the moral and spiritual dubiety of many of the carefully staged "happenings," it should be remembered that Christians often fared rather badly), conveniently theorized in terms of Plato's (perfectly reasonable, but lop-sided) worries about the negative impact of certain sorts of theatre on its audiences and actors. Puritan heirs to this cheerless tradition of nay-saying had conveniently in their sights some of the more earthy and bawdy excesses of the form, such as the Comedy of Manners, which exploded onto the stage in 1660 with the Restoration of Charles II to the English throne after eighteen years of enforced prohibition by Cromwell's republican regime. But they, too, sought a broader theoretical ground for urging Christian avoidance of theatre, appealing to the lexicon, for example, to establish that "play-acting" was an accepted definition of the New Testament's *hypokrinomai/hypokrisis* (feigning or "hypocrisy"), one of the very things Jesus himself had been at pains to condemn. The silliness and partiality of such arguments mounted as a case against theatre as a whole is easy enough to see, but we should not underestimate the impact they have had on Christian sensibility over the last 450 years.

In direct response to such sweeping views (and to less clearly articulated impressions and attitudes derived from them), Harris proposes that the incarnation and theatre may actually be shown to function as paradigms of one another, inasmuch as "the idea of the Incarnation is through and through theatrical, and . . . the theatre, at its most joyous, occupies common ground with the Incarnation in its advocacy of . . . 'the good gift of [our] humanity.'"[12] His angle of approach to this interlacing of the theological and the theatrical is first to consider the doctrine of revelation, both in its guise as a virtual *alter ego* of the doctrine of the incarnation itself (the enfleshed Word himself *is* the fullness of God's self-disclosure to us) and in its more familiar linkage to the written script—the Bible—that "bears witness to God's acts of grace" in "the theatre of [His] covenant."[13] Then, in the latter chapters, Harris suggests that theatre endorses the value of the "flesh" of our creaturely space-time existence and thus resonates with the incarnation's witness to the same as "a proper dwelling place for God and therefore for humankind."[14] In what

12. Harris, *Theater and Incarnation*, viii. The cited phrase is from Karl Barth whom Harris adopts as an occasional theological interlocutor and unexpected witness for the defence throughout the book.

13. Ibid., 7. Again, as it happens, the brief citation is from Barth.

14. Ibid., ix.

follows, I will attend chiefly to the first of these parts, leaving numerous important and worthwhile themes for a more sustained response to the book on another occasion.

Revealing Script, Transforming Performance

Harris traces a likeness between the modes of God's self-revealing action and the ways that theatrical texts typically become the bearers of meaning in performance. Texts, he reminds us, do not impress determinate meanings upon pliant and passive readers. Instead, as so-called reception theories of reading associated with Wolfgang Iser, Hans Robert Jauss, Stanley Fish, and others are at pains to point out, texts anticipate and solicit responses of one sort or another from those who pick them up and read them, and the meanings that arise in the process are always in part the product of what readers bring with them to texts, as well as what they find there.[15] Literary texts such as novels and poems are prone to higher levels of "incompleteness" in this regard than texts of some other sorts—telephone directories, tenancy agreements. They deliberately engage the reader's imagination to make a constructive contribution to the fictional worlds they generate,[16] suggesting rather than specifying meaning in a prescriptive way, and thus leaving themselves open to a variety of possible interpretations and imaginative elaborations. Texts, we might say, remain inert physical artefacts until, in the act of reading, they become the generative source of meanings courtesy of the dynamic process we call interpreting or, in a telling phrase, "making sense" of what is to be found on their pages.

If Harris rather underestimates the extent to which this is true of other literary works, he is nonetheless surely correct to insist that dramatic texts in particular are manifestly incomplete as works of art, providing only the verbal cues and clues for a radical transformation, which performance alone is able to provide.[17] Thus the playwright typically solicits rather less immediately from the imagination of the audience than a novelist does from his or her reader, calling precisely upon the mediation of the actors to "flesh out" further the world of the work and to draw

15. For a useful and relative brief overview see Eagleton, *Literary Theory*, 74–90.

16. On the imaginative construction of fictional worlds and the imaginative projection of "worlds" attendant upon works of art see helpfully Walton, *Mimesis as Make-Believe*, 57–69; Wolterstorff, *Art in Action*, 122–50.

17. Harris, *Theater and Incarnation*, 1.

upon more than words alone in exploring, constructing, and showing possible meanings. The resulting circumstance is complex, though, and certainly does not make meaning in the theatre straightforward or easy to grasp. On the one hand, a snatch of dialogue which on the page remains potentially ambiguous is bound to have a particular construction placed upon it by its utterance now with a particular vocal inflection, and taken up into a larger, multi-layered "language" of bodily deportment, action, and movement all occurring within a carefully "staged" set of spatial and temporal relationships. Of course, all this compels us to hear and to feel the significance of the words in one particular way rather than a host of other possible ways. Of necessity, with enfleshment of the word comes particularity rather than abstraction.

And yet while a particular reader is quite likely to read the same novel as essentially "the same novel" even upon repeated revisiting, picturing characters, places, and events in substantially the same way, an individual theatergoer is far more likely to be confronted by a rich variety of different performances of the same drama by attending different productions, to the point that he or she may feel almost as though a quite different play is being staged, despite the underlying continuity represented by the script. Performance transforms text. Furthermore, while words may "come alive" for us when clothed in the flesh of an actor's particular rendition of them, words are not the only sort of language available or at work in the theatre, and where languages of other sorts are concerned, the movement is not always identifiably in the direction of hermeneutic determinacy. In his proposal for a "theatre of cruelty," Antonin Artaud sought to exploit to the full the power of theatre's physicality to communicate depths of meaning that were, he held, independent of words. Western theatre as a whole was, he believed, too much in the thrall of words and those aspects of our humanity bound up identifiably with words, and had shown far too little concern for the significance of "everything . . . specifically theatrical in theatre"—the unique communicative force of music, dance, gesture, voice inflexion, architecture, lighting, décor, plastic art, and so on.[18] One need not subscribe to the metaphysic undergirding Artaud's insistence on all this,[19] nor share his

18. Artaud, *Theatre and Its Double*, 28.

19. For an account of Artaud's convictions concerning the primal cosmic forces (some of them very dark) to which the "body-language" or physical poetry of theatre was, he believed, naturally rather than merely conventionally wedded, see Harris, *Theater and Incarnation*, 42–44, 123–28. Cf. Artaud, *Theatre and Its Double*, 64–67.

confidence in the pre-linguistic purity (i.e., undefiled by language and its constructs) of an experiential-expressive substrate composed of such theatrical elements, in order to grant the basic point that theatre "speaks" with a voice made up of more than words alone. Indeed, some of its most dense and hermeneutically resistant utterance is to be found not in dramatic texts but precisely in what is "specifically theatrical in theatre." It is this that can leave an audience gasping for breath and wondering at the power and the mysterious surplus of meaning that remains to be accessed, even when the most detailed critical dissection of all the available words has been carried out.

How, then, does all this bear upon an understanding of the modes and means of God's revealing of himself? In several ways, all centered on the claim that in the incarnation of the eternal Son of the Father we have, in effect, the "performance" through enfleshing of a previously discarnate Logos or Word, and thus its transformation into something possessed of new force and depth for humankind. Let's begin, though, with the putative analogy between theatrical script and the Scripture which the church in some sense identifies as Word of God in textual form. We can perhaps already sense the difficulties and complexities with this analogy given the above. The incarnate Word does not, after all, *perform* this script, which is instead an attempt to capture the gist of his performance after the event.[20] Indeed, if Scripture is to be a script for performance, then it can only be so for the church rather than Christ himself, but even this is less than satisfactory as a model once one pursues the suggestion very far.[21] It is of the essence of a metaphor, though, that it should not offer wholesale correspondences so much as suggestive links between two terms, being characterized precisely by high levels of difference. And here we can limit ourselves with impunity to the following suggestion ventured by Harris: if God's own Word, in communicating himself to us most fully, does so not by a download into our inner lives of digitized ideas or purely "spiritual" data, but by taking flesh and making truth concrete and particular and "earthy," addressed as much to our senses as to any other part of our

---

Artaud's eventual descent into insanity counsels caution, perhaps, to those who would dismiss his claims as speculative and wholly unfounded.

20. Harris rather sidesteps the awkwardness at this point by stepping back from the issues of temporal sequence: "As a play script bears testimony to a past or future performance, so, Barth would suggest, the Bible bears witness to God's acts of grace in 'the theatre of his covenant.'" Harris, *Theater and Incarnation*, 7.

21. Wesley Vander Lugt pursues this further in *Living Theodrama*.

humanity, might it not be the case that the written form of God's Word (i.e., the Bible) is naturally prone to interpretation in ways which take this same "irredeemable fleshiness" seriously? That is to say, might its meanings be accessed most fully and powerfully when we read it in a manner that seeks ever to clothe it again with flesh, rather than abstracting from it principles, facts, ideas, and other more intellectually "hard-edged" bits and pieces readily systematized into bodies of doctrine, moral teaching, and the like? Our concern is for more meaning and truth to be broken out of God's Word rather than less, and perhaps also for greater intellectual humility and a willingness to acknowledge and to live with mystery where it presents itself and lies infuriatingly beyond our intellectual and imaginative reach, as that which presents itself bound up with the inherent contingencies and ambiguities of the flesh so often does.

Narrative theology insists on attending to the storied dimensions of particular biblical texts and to Scripture as a whole, considered as a single overarching narration of the character of God in his dealings with Israel and, through Israel, the whole of creation. Furthermore, narrative theology draws attention to the action and drama shot through the pages of the Bible, and by doing so has gone some way, perhaps, to rekindling an imaginative disposition towards it, reinvesting the biblical story with the "flesh" of imagined particularities rather than transmuting it instead into a series of bloodless abstractions. Ignatian spirituality, of course, has a long history of this sort of thing, encouraging the reader consciously to embellish the biblical text which is, as Auerbach reminded us long since, like most theatrical scripts, mostly "replete with background"; in other words, it is devoid of precisely the sort of detail that imagination craves and needs in order to appropriate and make sense of what is offered to it.[22] This is nowhere more fully the case than in the Gospels. What did Jesus look like? In what tone of voice should we imagine him having delivered a particular bit of dialogue? What was going on with body language as he spoke? And so on. Lest anyone complain that to ask and answer such questions is to go beyond the reach of what Scripture permits and to incline in the direction of a particular "construction" of the text, it suffices merely to observe that we cannot help doing so, having in our mind's eye and ear *some* version of what we read or hear read. The only question is whether we do so consciously—and thus with a self-critical awareness of other possible ways of imagining things—or permit

---

22. See Auerbach, "Odysseus' Scar," in *Mimesis*, 3–23.

some long since sedimented and habituated way of seeing, hearing, and feeling the text to reign unchallenged as the "authorized version."

It is this sort of thing that Harris advocates when he suggests the need for a "theatrical imagination" and a "theatrical hermeneutics." A good piece of literary criticism carried out on a dramatic text will, he suggests, seek precisely to make good "the weakness and helplessness of the written word," animating the text in the act of interpreting it. Likewise, the sensitive reader of Christian Scripture, as one committed to the conviction that God revealed and reveals himself most fully by taking flesh, must seek to do no less.[23] So, dealing with the Johannine account of Jesus' first "sign" at Cana in Galilee and his curt "reproach" of Mary, as most commentators have tended to view it (and to seek to justify it), Harris invites us to make some adjustments to our habituated ways of reading and imagining the encounter.

> Envisage Jesus turning to his mother with a grin on his face, a twinkle in his eye and a full cup of wine in his hand, and saying with good humour, "My good lady, what's that to us? I'm not on call right now!" (This is a colloquial but fair paraphrase of the Greek). If Mary were then to laugh, looking at her son with love and full confidence in his ebullient generosity, the exchange would have an entirely different flavor and would lead more naturally into the miracle that follows.[24]

My point here is not to concur with Harris's particular reading, but simply to endorse the principle on which he arrives at it. Biblical texts will often "come to life" in a wholly new way if we attend to them with the expectation born of faithfulness to a Word who is himself known only as he "takes flesh," and an imagination primed and open to receive new meanings rather than resting content with the imagined *textus receptus*.

Replete with background, biblical texts so often cry out for the *poetic* work of imaginative construction and reconstruction, lending themselves, in an "incompleteness" directly analogous to that of the theatrical script, to a variety of different possible "performances," more than one of which may well be wholly fitting and appropriate for particular readers on particular occasions. The idea that a biblical text has a single authoritative meaning that must trump all others seems to me to be born of a reductionist mindset, which fails to celebrate the richness and depth

23. Harris, *Theater and Incarnation*, 12. The citation is appropriated from R. E. Palmer.

24. Ibid., 25.

of meaning invested by God through the imaginative labors of authors and readers alike. If more than one interpretation can be shown to be a legitimate possibility when a text is situated in its canonical context, and when other relevant critical considerations have been taken on board, it seems more faithful to the text's presumed authority to hold each of them in tension with the others rather than presuming to elevate one of them. After all, the acknowledgment that several different ways of "playing" *King Lear* or *Measure for Measure* are possible and equally rich in their exploration of the territories of human meaning does not lead inexorably into the quagmire of critical relativism. It is still perfectly possible to prefer one "reading" of these plays to others (and to articulate persuasive grounds for doing so) and, more to the point, to make the judgment (if relevant) that a particular rendition is not just "different," but badly done or unfaithful to the relevant traditions of performance.

Gesturing towards the Stage

Where Harris leaves us, on this particular issue at least, is facing the persuasive suggestion that an approach to biblical texts armed with a "theatrical imagination" sensitive to and able to summon into the mind's "eye" the sensory richness of action staged in real time and space, is likely to do fuller justice to these texts as a means of God's continual address to us than the more purely "literary" approach to which we are accustomed. But why stop here? Might one not go further and suggest that, whereas in the Temple and the synagogue it may have sufficed perfectly well for the divine Word to be read aloud and made concrete within the mind's eye of its more imaginative hearers, in the congregation of those whose faith is in *the Word made flesh*, a different liturgical possibility presents itself for consideration? If, as Harris insists throughout his book, the divine Word presents itself most fully not as text or utterance but in the flesh and blood realities of an embodied existence, surely we ought to consider whether a natural and proper mode of the rehearsal and interpretation of this same Word in its form as Scripture might lie in actual embodied performances of those portions of the biblical text that lend themselves naturally to it. In other words, instead of just reading portions of text aloud and letting them hang in the air, why not act them out in the midst of our worship, granting them (albeit temporarily) a particular lodging within the dynamics of time and space, specific "body language" and inflection of voice. What I have in mind would be rather different from the way Christian drama "sketches" are occasionally deployed in church merely to "illustrate" a text already read (and probably soon to be interpreted in a torrent of words from the pulpit). Instead, it would itself be a primary mode of the Word's careful reiteration and re-presentation in the congregation gathered around it, with all the semantic force of that "flesh" that Christian faith holds to be the Word's most natural and fulsome abode. We ought not to expect any sermon subsequently to be able to distil the meaning of such performance satisfactorily into words for us. To expect or desire this would be indeed to miss the point, that the meaning would be cast in the "language" of a particular embodied performance itself, existing at many levels to which words alone cannot aspire to take us. Something along these lines seems to be the natural conclusion of the case Harris begins to build with regard to a distinctly Christian hermeneutic, though he does not himself drive it home.

Of course, such a suggestion raises all manner of challenging hermeneutical considerations, but most if not all of them seem simply to be sharper versions of issues arising already in the treatment of the biblical text as "text" to be read and heard. That the issues of meaning and interpretation present themselves more forcefully and vividly in relation to embodied performance seems to be an argument *for* rather than *against* the idea, potentially driving us further and deeper into the semantic surplus of the texts as we grapple with them together. More theorizing and down-to-earth practical reflection would obviously be needed before moving to act on such a suggestion, and there is not scope for that here. But it seems worthwhile, in a volume of this sort, at least to air a thought that, while it goes identifiably beyond *Theater and Incarnation*, seems to be entirely consonant with its vision and to build on the basic theological and theatrical insights its author so helpfully brings into conversation.

Bibliography

Artaud, Antonin. *Theatre and Its Double.* Translated by Victor Corti. London: Calder, 1993.

Auerbach, Erich. *Mimesis: The Representation of Reality in Western Literature.* Translated by Willard R. Trask. Princeton: Princeton University Press, 1953.

Barish, Jones. *The Antitheatrical Prejudice.* Berkeley: University of California Press, 1981.

Bratsiotis, N. P. "bāśār." In *Theological Dictionary of the Old Testament*, edited by G. Johannes Botterweck and Helmer Ringgren, 2:317–32. Grand Rapids: Eerdmans, 1975.

Collingwood, R. G. *The Principles of Art*. London: Oxford University Press, 1958.

Dragas, George. *Athanasiana: Essays in the Theology of St. Athanasius*. London: n.p., 1980.

———. *St. Athanasius Contra Apollinarem*. Athens: Church and Theology, 1985.

Eagleton, Terry. *Literary Theory: An Introduction*. Oxford: Blackwell, 1983.

Edelman, Joshua. "Can an Act be True? The Possibilities of the Dramatic Metaphor for Theology within a Post-Stanislavskian Theatre." In *Faithful Performances: Enacting Christian Tradition*, edited by Trevor Hart and Steven R. Guthrie, 51–72. Aldershot, UK: Ashgate, 2007.

Harris, Max. *Theater and Incarnation*. 1990. Reprint. Eerdmans, 2005.

Hart, Trevor. *Making Good: Creation, Creativity and Artistry*. Waco, TX: Baylor University Press, 2014.

———. "Through the Arts: Hearing, Seeing and Touching the Truth." In *Beholding the Glory*, edited by Jeremy S. Begbie, 1–26. London: Darton, Longman and Todd, 2000.

Lewis, Alan E. "Kenosis and Kerygma: The Realism and the Risk of Preaching." In *Christ in Our Place: The Humanity of God in Christ for the Reconciliation of the World*, edited by Trevor Hart and Daniel Thimell, 70–91. Exeter, UK: Paternoster, 1989.

Lewis, C. S. *The Screwtape Letters*. London: Bles, 1941.

Sayers, Dorothy L. *The Mind of the Maker*. London: Methuen, 1941.

———. "Towards a Christian Aesthetic." In *Our Culture: Its Christian Roots and Present Crisis*, edited by V. A. Demant, 50–69. London: SPCK, 1947.

Schweizer, E., and R. Meyer. "sarx." In *Theological Dictionary of the New Testament*, edited by Gerhard Kittel, 7:98–151. Grand Rapids: Eerdmans, 1971.

Vander Lugt, Wesley. *Living Theodrama: Reimagining Theological Ethics*. Aldershot, UK: Ashgate, 2014.

Vanhoozer, Kevin J. *The Drama of Doctrine: A Canonical-Linguistic Approach to Christian Theology*. Louisville: Westminster John Knox, 2005.

Walton, Kendall. *Mimesis as Make-Believe: On the Foundations of the Representational Arts*. Cambridge: Harvard University Press, 1990.

Wolterstorff, Nicholas. *Art in Action: Toward a Christian Aesthetic*. Reprint. Carlisle, UK: Solway, 1997.

3

The Intractable Sense of an Ending

Gethsemane's Prayer on the Tragic Stage

IVAN PATRICIO KHOVACS

"Life has passed me by . . . Loser."[1]

"My Father, if it is possible let this cup pass me by.
Still, not how I want it, but how you do."[2]

The Sound of a Breaking String

TRAGEDY DELIVERS A HARD grace. The sound of a breaking string, the signature ending to Anton Chekhov's *The Cherry Orchard*, ushers in the passing of an old order dispossessed by time, exhausted of its future tense. It also signals, if in a nerve-shattering key, possibilities better left for an audience to consider. The play begins with someone on an armchair waking from sleep and ends with someone else, in the same chair,

---

1. Here and elsewhere, my translation of the closing scene in "The Cherry Orchard," Chekhov, *Вишневый Сад*, 522.

2. Matt 26:39. "Πάτερ μου, εἰ δυνατόν ἐστιν, παρελθάτω ἀπ᾽ ἐμοῦ τὸ ποτήριον τοῦτο. Πλὴν οὐχ ὡς ἐγὼ θέλω ἀλλ᾽ ὡς σύ." This translation occurs along with those of parallel passages in the other gospels in Ruprecht, "Gethsemane," 1–25.

44

his dimming eyelids betraying no ordinary exhaustion. The lone figure left behind by his companions simply drops into an armchair mumbling something to the effect that "life has passed me by," to which he enjoins the self-extinguishing epithet, "Loser," before falling asleep, never to wake again. Tragedy does not get better than this. Signaling the twilight of gods and heroes, the final frame in Chekhov's final play plunges an audience into the existential fear of impersonal orbits colliding in the human sphere: "After a long silence, the sound of a breaking string is heard in the distance, as if coming from the sky, fading away mournfully. The sound of an axe striking against a tree in the orchard is heard. Then, *Curtain*."[3]

The following discussion brings us to another orchard, to the Garden of Gethsemane, as tragedy breaks over the Christ, isolated on the world stage and about to face his final curtain. I am centrally concerned with the intractable sense of the tragic, its depths sounded in prayer as Christ kneels in anticipation of the end. I propose bringing the performative insight of the tragic stage into a reading of Christ's prayer in the Gospel narratives of Gethsemane. For if the anguish Jesus faces in Gethsemane turns on the opposition between the human will not to die and the divine will that offers itself to death,[4] then the whole drama of redemption anticipated in everything assumed by the incarnation reaches a climax there in the garden. At stake is nothing less than God's action in history and its purchase on the human condition. To paraphrase the patristic axiom, that which was not assumed is not redeemed.[5] In Gethsemane, I propose, Christ's taking up human suffering in the shape of the tragic both affirms its terminal force and anticipates its redemptive end.

Even as Jesus drops to his knees, his prayer to "let this cup pass from me" appears to give in to a gravitational pull away from the will of the Father. Inconceivably, we are left to reckon with the possibility that Jesus in his humanity dissents from divine prerogative. The force is seemingly reversed, however, in the subsequent "not my will but yours be done." I wish to explore this dual movement in close interaction with Karl Barth's "Excursus on Gethsemane," and Hans Urs von Balthasar's equally discerning reading of Christ's suffering in the garden. Reading the Gethsemane narratives against the backdrop of tragic theatre will excavate

---

3. Chekhov, *Вишневый Сад*, 522.

4. This phrasing is borrowed from Ratzinger, "On St. Maximus the Confessor," para. 11.

5. Gregory of Nazianzus, Epistle 101.

the drama at the heart of Jesus' agonizing prayer. This is not to say that Christ's prayer and subsequent act of submission attract divine punishment as if in conclusion to a Greek tragedy. However, Christ's prayerful struggle, as evidence of a faith pressed to its limits, does invite *divine action performed in the manner of his human action*. This confirms not only that the Father's will is immanently done in the Son of God, but in terms of the doctrine of incarnation, that in Jesus this action is predicated on a dramatic economy of divine will performed vicariously in the manner of human willing.

The problem hangs essentially on the doctrine of hypostatic union, which I understand concisely in terms of how divine being in Christ relates to his being human. However, since this is a straightforwardly theological proposition, taking Christ's prayer—"My Father, if it is possible, take this cup from me"—and bringing it into focus through the lens of the theatre requires some justification. On my definition, theatre is an essentially vicarious event; it is the performance of an action by way of some other action: "Theater is the one art form that imitates human action in the medium of human action."[6] From the point of view of both actor and audience, vicarious action drives the dramatic performance. "The actor is that unique creature who passes through a whole life in a few hours and in so doing carries the spectator vicariously with him."[7] In terms of the theological drama wrought in the crucible of Gethsemane, if God's performance in the manner of the Son's human willing is essentially vicarious—"not my will but yours be done"—there is some logic in using theatre as theological analogue, and crucially for my argument, in thinking of Christ's being as the theatre of divine life made flesh. This dynamic underpins my hypothesis that a theological-dramatic interpretation positions the human audience accountably before Gethsemane's tragedy.

In saying "accountably" I am focusing prominently on the fact that the narrative form of the Gospels presumes a human audience. Jesus lives his story for God and for the sake of humanity. And if this anticipates an active response on our part, it is simply that all theology demands audience participation in some sense. The Gethsemane prayer narratives are no exception. This insight coheres with and is most readily appreciated from a theatrical perspective. In fact, reading Christ's prayer against

6. States, *Great Reckonings in Little Rooms*, 45. The original quotation is abridged for style.

7. Ibid.

the backdrop of the stage will beg questions about an element of *grace* inherent in the performance of tragedy classically conceived. In that regard, Gethsemane claims a note of *hope* piercing through the intransigent "fourth wall" separating audience from the tragic performance. Theologically, this enables me to reconsider the role of the human audience in Gethsemane represented by the figures of the sleeping disciples, hence, to reappropriate Christ's command to "watch and pray" as a stage direction that both anticipates and transcends the intractability of the tragic end.

The Sorrow and the Pity

Central to this discussion is an understanding of the tragic stage inevitably directed by Aristotle's farsighted suggestion that "Tragedy is the imitation of an action of serious and ultimate consequences in the form of action effecting through pity and fear the *katharsis* of such suffering."[8] As this abridged translation of Aristotle's contested passage would have it, tragedy stages suffering in terms of its limits and consequences. The tragic stage, in other words, denotes an experimental space in which life's suffering is pressed to its logical extremes, thereby confronting and being confronted by the surdity and cecity of otherwise incomprehensible endings.

Aristotle's insight that *katharsis* is the aim of the tragedy could, nevertheless, pose an obstacle at this point, at least if we were to insist on interpreting *katharsis* strictly as the "purgation" of emotion in the sense of an uninhibited, empathetic response to suffering on the stage. Aristotle's phenomenology of the tragic, however, anticipates a sobering horizon coming into view at the limits of affect and emotion. For Aristotle, a measure of the suffering portrayed on stage obtains in the self-disclosure demanded of the theatrical audience. To state the obvious, Aristotle's canons of the tragic focus entirely on the stage performance, its composition and ultimate reception.[9] Consequently, taking the performance as our point of reference, Aristotelian *katharsis* is comprehensively understood in terms of *self-dispossession*, a displacement of self (*autos*) in favor of taking in, and so apprehending vicariously the suffering of the other (*al-*

8. Aristotle, *Ars Poetica*, §1449b; my translation from the classical Greek.

9. In the *Poetics*, Aristotle is conscious that tragedy may be "judged both by itself, in the abstract, and in relationship to our theatre audiences," and, therefore, carefully notes that his analysis relates primarily to tragedy in theatrical performance. Cf. Aristotle, *Poetics*, 38.49a (G. Else, trans.).

los). On one hand, therefore, the vicarious nature of the stage frees the witnessing audience from delusions of limitless autonomy; on the other hand, it places suffering in the perspective of contingency, limits, and terminal consequences. Olympians subject their body to pain if they are to achieve their prize, and comedians set aside pride for a laugh, but the promise of the tragedy is some clarifying understanding in the face of suffering. This demands nothing less than total abandonment to the theatrical experience. Insight gained from the tragic stage comes from losing something of oneself to the performance, intellectually and emotionally. Tragedy, therefore, already dissenting from comedy's self-healing ends, abhors the escapist devices of the cheaply comedic.[10] So, unlike the kind of comedy played just for laughs, tragedy cannot be the object of mere entertainment precisely because it works on the premise that suffering is ultimately and by definition exhausting.

This is where Aristotle's anatomy of performance affords perspective on Gethsemane's tragedy. The *Poetics* plots a three-fold structure around the encompassing nature of the tragic, namely:

1. *agon*, the central struggle;

2. *anagnorisis*, the recognition of one's part in the ensuing calamity, resulting in, and itself being the requisite condition for

3. *pathos*, which relates the experience of suffering to tragedy in a universal sense.[11]

On the classical stage, this narrative structure leads ultimately to the tragic hero being eliminated from the scene. Critical to the tragic vehicle, however, are the spectator's vicarious sensibilities, hence the "pity and fear" through which audiences confirm in themselves something of the hero's sense of suffering and damning recognition of "the end." The very structure of the tragedy, "the particular shape and emphases of a tragic plot,"[12] mapped around high points of conflict and incommensurable consequences, conspires against detached, objectifying perspectives on

---

10. Aristotle opposes the tragic portrayal of suffering to comedy, which he understands essentially as entertainment, a "painless" imitation of the ludic, or even an exaggeration of the base and grotesque, though without malice, hence causing "no pain or destruction." Ibid., lines 23–24.

11. Greek tragedies, however, do not follow a single order of events, but rather plot patterns and trajectories characteristic of a tragic fate. See Peter Burian on the tragic plot and its exposition of conflict from the perspective of overarching myths. Cf. Burian, "Tragic Plot," 178–208.

12. Ibid., 179.

the performance of suffering. We might say, in fact, that the virtue of the Aristotelian tragedy, as an aesthetics of contingency, is the exercise of *self-dispossessed identification with the suffering other*. This, at least, is how I understand Aristotle's otherwise ambiguous use of "katharsis."

Suffering, of course, operates on a cosmic economy. The stage tragedy therefore invites self-dispossessing catharsis in favor of the global perspective. The intractable endings anticipated by the tragedy solicit and confirm suffering arising from one's sense of finitude in the face of tectonic forces opposing existence itself. Seen in their ultimate scale, such losses converge on oppositions between human conceit and divine prerogative, which precipitate conditions of a terminal order. Vicarious suffering and insight into humanity's fate under such threatening conditions are both the result and essential pattern of the tragic stage. For in the tragedy

> a structure comes into being that depends upon a kind of complicity of the audience in order to be fully realized. Seen in this light, a tragic plot inheres not simply in a poetic text, but also in the dialectic between that text in performance and the response of an informed audience to the performance.[13]

In staging the tragic fate, that is, audiences court something of the intractability portrayed in such endings, and thereby enact in theatrical "play" a clarifying perspective on the awful nature of things otherwise unfathomable. The devastation of the hero on the tragic stage signals the unmasking of an audience's fears of facing diminishing returns on a cosmic scale. Here, then, lies the significance of staging the tragic condition, of scripting and rendering on stage "an action of ultimate consequences . . . mediating between pity and fear the sense of such suffering."[14]

---

13. Ibid.

14. I am translating in paraphrase this critically contested passage of the *Poetics* (1449b.1), placing emphasis on the total and terminal nature of tragic endings. Aristotle's emphasis on the performative nature of the tragic stage might be more fully rendered as "*the imitation of an action of serious and terminal consequences in the form of an action mediating between feeling and understanding the sense of such suffering.*" I propose these as working correlates on which to build the ensuing discussion, and not as definitive of Aristotle's text. Aristotle, *Ars Poetica*, 1449b.1:24–25, 28; my translation.

Tragedy, Theology, and the Tragic Stage

Bringing tragedy into theological discourse, however, remains problematic and cannot be taken for granted. The argument that Christianity
undermines on principle the totalizing aesthetics of the tragic has long
been recognized. George Steiner, for example, ventures that Gethsemane
signals the end of the questioning privileged on the tragic stage, including questioning of the gods and their divine order. For Steiner, at this
point in the Christian narrative, "the morality play of history alters from
tragedy to *commedia*" because Gethsemane, even from the depths of
Christ's agony, points to the possibility of a *peripeteia*, a "fortunate reversal" redirecting the tragic towards a "celestial epilogue."[15] From the critic's
standpoint, Gethsemane is the beginning of a tradition whose promise of
a heaven tidies things up far too neatly to be compatible with suffering
and loss conceived on the widest possible scale.

Steiner's suspicion, moreover, points to the problem of collapsing
"tragedy" (in its theatrical sense) into "the tragic," understood as the
sense of life's dreadful events. However, if Aristotle's observations about
tragedy are insightful, then the problem is not categorical but constructively built into the nature and purpose of the tragic stage: tragedy in
the aesthetic arena reckons with the nature and sources of life's suffering.
Consequently, reading Christ's prayer in Gethsemane through the lens
of the tragic stage does not require resolving tensions between theatre
and life as such. On the contrary, relating Christ's agonizing prayer in
Gethsemane to the tragic performance presumes the inclusivity of questions about suffering and its ultimate consequences in the drama of life.
At this point, however, these theological aims and their underpinning
presuppositions call for some qualifying remarks.

First, none of this signals commitment to a view that Gethsemane
is tragedy in the classical sense, let alone that Christ is a tragic hero in
Aristotelian terms.[16] Nevertheless, I take seriously the tenor of Christ's

---

15. Steiner, *Death of Tragedy*, 13.

16. Presenting Jesus as a "tragic hero" problematically requires some account of
hamartia, the fault of "overweening pride" and cause of his downfall. In classical drama,
hamartia leads to the tragic fate, but not as a consequence of divine decree, predestina-
tion, or some other *force majeure*: it is the result of a course of *action*, of choices made
that over time show the deeply grained patterns of the tragic. Theologically, however,
Christ's action of assuming humanity's capital offence through the instrument of the
cross resists the classical tragic pattern (cf. Burian, "Tragic Plot," 181, esp. Easterling's
note, 349). Biblical drama on the stage is often thought problematic in this regard. So,
for example, although *Jesus Christ Superstar* (Andrew Lloyd Webber/Tim Rice, 1971)

suffering in Gethsemane. The divine/human tension presumed to be central to Christ's prayer in Gethsemane remains the subject of transaction models, in which, for example, Jesus exchanges the autonomy of "my will" for the infinitely undivided good of the Father's will. However, to see the *commercium* with the Father's will simply in terms of Christ's divinity colluding with the Father to trump his human nature is no satisfying solution. From the point of view of the hypostatic union, we may speak in an orthodox sense of two wills, but must nevertheless accept that they speak in one voice, in the one person Jesus Christ. Furthermore, to subordinate Christ's human will to his divine nature compromises what we might say about humanity's share, if any, in Gethsemane. Hans Urs von Balthasar, for one, recognized that appealing to Christ's singular resolve in favor of his divine nature reduces his humanity to a kind of *Deus ex machina*, a vehicle for the god waiting in the wings, whose primary business is to clear the stage of vain mortality. Such a move would bring into question the anticipated turn apparent even from the perspective of Gethsemane of the *Deus vivus ex mortuis*.[17] In stark contrast, Karl Barth's "Excursus on Gethsemane"[18] outlines a drama taking place almost entirely above the human plane, so much so that divine providence coordinates the workings of evil itself. In Barth's model, Christ's prayer "If it be your will . . ." is evidence of divine will taking this and every such thought captive, as it were, that Christ might bear evil on his journey to the cross. The present discussion, however, follows my intuition that reading the prayer of Gethsemane against the pattern of the tragic stage can yield some observations about hope in the midst of life's intractable endings.

Second, I assume a narrative continuity in the synoptic presentations of Gethsemane in the Gospels, the fine points in the witness of each author being of negligible consequence to my aims. This is not to say that differences in the Gethsemane narratives are negligible in themselves. Indeed, there is much to be said for Louis Ruprecht's reading of textual variants, near-cognate phrasings, and possible intertextualities between Christ's prayer and texts emerging from antiquity. Such a reading finds in the Gospel of Mark a tragic bias in the irresolvably unstable three-part phrasing:

---

exploits the "man of sorrows" motif without suggestion of resurrection, play productions nevertheless have used the final bows to prompt something of the Gospel's redemptive ending.

17. Balthasar, *Explorations*, 3:411.

18. Barth, "Judge Judged," 259–73.

> Abba, the Father, all things are possible for you.
>
> Take this cup away from me.
>
> Still, not what I want, but what you do.[19]

Ruprecht's literary-exegetical approach to each of the Gospels queries the non-interrogatory voice attributed to Christ in what the author understands as Mark's "performance" of the prayer in Gethsemane. He concludes that, failing to set the prayer in question form, Mark's rendition sounds out the depths distancing Christ's humanity from God's presumptive will. The near-accusatory mood is said to betray the tragic profile of the Greek stage—hence, for Ruprecht, the gospel's implied sense of a suppliant knowingly and heroically attracting divine retribution. The performative approach I intend, however, presumes some virtue in reading Christ's prayer thematically and in its canonical whole. Theologically, this will enable me to learn from as well as query Barthian and Balthasarian readings on this point.

Third, and despite Barth's provocative reference to a momentous "pause" underscoring with cosmic intensity Christ's sense of estrangement in his prayer to the Father,[20] reading Gethsemane against the background of the tragic stage does not presume that Christ's prayer is reducible to a hermeneutics of doubt. In my reading, Christ's agony in Gethsemane is not defined by self-doubt, divine discontent, an existentially divided self, or the like. Philosophically, I do not question that suspicion and doubt are essential for critical reflection on the object held in question. Theologically, moreover, doubt can function as an apophatic form of verification. However, taking my intuition to its logical conclusion would suggest that even if Christ, who inhabits God in word and

19. I offer this translation per Ruprecht, "Gethsemane," 9, 11 et passim. See also Ruprecht, "Heart of Christian Compassion," 37–78.

20. Barth does not resort to tragedy as a category, but neither is he insensitive to the rendition of the prayer, not in question form, but in a statement suggesting divine inevitability. He speaks, therefore, of a "pause," a "stumbling," a "moment," a "trembling," even a "proviso," and implicitly, a questioning of divine necessity on this point (270). Jesus is "sorrowful unto death" (Matt 26:38) in view of "another possibility than that which will in fact be realised relentlessly and by divine necessity" (Barth, "Judge Judged," 264–65). Ruprecht, however, presses this moment of disruption to its literary extremes—i.e., Mark's "performance" of the prayer in a non-interrogatory form denotes "the *vertical* dimension of Jesus' tragedy" (10). God's non-response underscores the caesura between heaven and earth characteristic of the tragedy: "Jesus' last agonized prayer meets only with the awful loneliness of some dark recessed corner in a broken world, the dreadful silence of heaven. . . . *That* is the essence, the tragic in a tragedy." Ruprecht, "Gethsemane," 12, original emphasis.

flesh, asserts noetically what he has to do, there is nevertheless a sense in which, experientially, the full consequences of his decision to drain the cup to its bitter end remain opaque to his sight. Indeed, is there any point denying that, on some level, Christ's faith is tested by the absence of God's audible voice in Gethsemane and in the events that follow?

Fourth and finally, going beyond Balthasar's theological dramatics, and resisting Barth's speculation about a drama of supranatural proportions, my approach places the human audience directly before Christ's moment of struggle in its excruciating intensity. So, without diminishing the source of the divine/human conflict in Christ's person, but taking exception to the near-mythical clash of wills in the conquest of evil both Barth and Balthasar imagine, my tragic reading rescues an element of hope evident in Christ's prayer in Gethsemane. *That this act of hope implies a protest against the tragic condition itself is an insight emerging from and fundamental to the performance of the tragedy.* I will therefore conclude in my performative reading of Christ's prayer that the faith demonstrated in Gethsemane—which need not be "heroic" but simply consistent with the mustard seed of faith of which Jesus spoke in his teaching—entails a hope-filled perspective communicated to (because it is performed *for*) the human audience. For in facing his sense of the intractable ending awaiting him, Christ stages *pro nobis* something of humanity's remonstrance against suffering. In Gethsemane, the drama of salvation is realized in the drama of self-dispossessed divinity at once agonizing in the face of and offering itself to death.

Tragedy: The Medium Is the Message

Tragedy enacts on the theatrical stage binary lines extending from the cosmic plane into the sphere of human destiny; its primary concern is the terminal scope of such oppositions. The tragic plot unfolds when the distance separating divine order and finite existence is threatened by or can only be maintained at the expense of the weaker force. This emphasis on the chasm itself as an impersonal source of suffering was brought to light by Susan Taubes in her contemporary reading of Greek tragedy and the Shakespearean stage.[21] Taubes construed tragedy in terms of human protest threatening the balance between infinite will and man's ability to forge a destiny in the fated ordering of the universe. For it is one thing to

---

21. Taubes, "Nature of Tragedy," 193–206.

know that ordinary mortals cannot commune with the gods freely and on their terms, but it is another thing altogether to query the nature of the caesura, to arrogate to oneself knowledge that, properly speaking, could only reference the willing and doing of the divine. It is entirely human to recognize the distance between a universally presumptive precept such as justice and the failings of its demands, but to question why this must be so, as does the biblical Job, is to shake a fist at heaven.[22] Faced with injustice, the human figure is left standing on the edge of the abyss asking "Why?" only to have the question echo back hollow and unheard, *but not unopposed.*

In Taubes' account, in fact, the destructive scope of the tragic depends on some point of reference, whether heaven's recoil or some overriding principle relating the tragic character to "the larger context of a universe where domains that equally claim man's loyalty come into opposition, and where the good attainable to man is an always precarious balance of contrary forces."[23] So, for example, Antigone disobeys a royal decree against mourning a traitor. Her brother's treason has brought calamity on Thebes so that in giving him a burial, Antigone is subject to royal condemnation. She is damned as a direct consequence of her all-too-human but nevertheless imposing desire to honor family. Conflicts between allegiance to kin and country converge on the tragic hero whose questioning will signals an inevitable demise.

Similarly, in Euripides's tragedy, Medea rages against her husband's betrayal with another woman and takes revenge by killing their offspring. Violation of the sanctity of the marriage bed triggers a violation of the divine prohibition against infanticide. But the fact that Medea's wrath is unleashed in protest of injustice makes her crime the worse for it, and she pays the price for both. Another example is Oedipus, Sophocles's tragic protagonist, who openly questions and attempts to escape cosmic fate, only to fall into the hands of ignominious destiny. So, as a general principle, and as George Steiner has noted, "Tragedies end badly. The tragic personage is broken by forces which can neither be fully understood

22. This was both the tenor and critique behind Elia Kazan's Broadway production of Archibald McLeish's *J.B.* (1958), a modern re-contextualization of the biblical drama of Job championing man's "pseudo-Promethean" prevailing over "an absurd universe." Wheeler, "Theology and the Theatre," 342.

23. Taubes, "The Nature of Tragedy," 195.

nor overcome by rational prudence. . . . Tragedy is irreparable. . . . It mocks and destroys us."[24]

The stage tragedy plots a geography of suffering in which the universal passes through the crucible of the particular in inverse proportions: loss on a human scale is inversely proportional to divine or impersonal universals. On this reading, divine will need not be coercive to extract loss in the human sphere: its mere presence is the costly content of a speech like "Not my will, but thine be done."

> The tragic stage is a balance where human action is weighed, where man's will is measured against the working of the gods, meaning against futility, order against chaos. . . . For tragedy means that the relation between man and the noumenal sphere, upon which his survival and happiness depends, has become uncertain, conflictual, strained to the limit, and can be expressed only in terms of contradiction and paradox. Man does not enjoy certainty and assurance either in divine authority or in his own autonomy; he is dependent on the gods but he can no longer count on them.[25]

More importantly, however, Taubes perceived a kind of *grace*, a cathartic self-abandonment emerging from the performance of tragic, intractable endings. For even as "[t]he tragic play balances perilously between the extreme poles of hope and nihilism,"[26] in some sense, its performance confirms *faith* as constitutive of human struggle, and not simply as some illusory promise dangled before the suffering hero. Consequently, the pleasure in performing and watching the tragedy

> is not in man's suffering, but in the entire chain of events set off by the hero's transgression, and culminating in his downfall, *which assures us that there is a final limit to destruction.* . . . The paradoxality and thus the fascination of tragedy consists in sustaining the alternatives in a perilous balance that leaves the door open to nihilism *as well as to faith.*[27]

It would appear that rehearsing our worst fears on the stage bounds tragic nihilism, now logically suspected of being self-destructive in the extreme, within the forces of *faith and hope* for the "perpetual restoration

24. Steiner, *Death of Tragedy*, 8–9.
25. Taubes, "The Nature of Tragedy," 195.
26. Ibid.
27. Ibid., 204, added emphasis.

of the human order."[28] The tragic stage restrains the pull toward fatal-
ism, and implicates an audience existentially in its protest and claim
that this cannot be the way things are—there must be some other way.
Bad endings rehearse the kind of clarifying perspective possible in
Chekhov's sound of a breaking string: the intractable fortune visited
on the tragic hero sounds in an odd but compelling way a hopeful note
intended for the audience. Nor is such hope reducible to utopian reverie,
as Terry Eagleton points out in his critique of Steiner's insistence on "pure
tragedy" without Christian insight:

> Pure tragedy, Steiner claims, must be immune to hope; but hope
> is bound up with human possibility, which is in turn bound up
> with value. And without some sense of value there can be no
> tragedy. Nor, for that matter, can there even be pessimism. One
> could not be a pessimist about the human condition if one could
> not even conceive of its being other than it is. . . . If *Waiting for
> Godot* is pessimistic, it must be because the idea of Godot's com-
> ing must always have been conceivable. What makes for tragedy,
> often enough, is exactly the fact that we can indeed conceive
> of a more humane condition. . . . The red herring of utopian
> perfection is cynically intended, among other things, to distract
> us from this outrage.[29]

So, if life's tragedy extends invariably towards the universal, irre-
versible, and absolute, its performance on the stage telescopes into perspective things of ultimate value so that audiences leave the theatre with
questions that affirm rather than deny love and truth, the strong bonds
of family and community, the need for a body of law predicated on some
notion of justice and peace, the limits of power, and in the end, life itself.
In this sense, tragedy becomes an object of enjoyment. On my argument,
catharsis, as a clarifying perspective, is tragedy's purpose and promise.
Or, to follow Taubes, "The hopeful message of tragedy is that though evil
is irrepressible it is not endless, that human life has meaning and dignity,
though the odds are against man."[30] Tragedy, in other words, is a medium
through which creaturely resilience to crushing forces beyond human
control is given some sense of order and meaning.

Ironically, it would seem that a bad day for Oedipus or Hippolytus
or Lear, or for the protagonists in the Scottish play, betokens hope of a

---

28. Ibid., 206.
29. Eagleton, "Commentary," 157–58.
30. Taubes, "The Nature of Tragedy," 206.

better day for the human audience. The ordurous endings haunting the tragic figure, the *kakos* native to the play, pierces through the proscenium line and is received by an audience under protest. Underpinning such straightforwardly bad news is the cathartic realization that the destruction wrought by the tragedy has its limits, that the dying of the light does not go on interminably but is at some point eclipsed by shadow.

> Out, out, brief candle!
> Life's but a walking shadow, a poor player
> That struts and frets his hour upon the stage
> And then is heard no more.[31]

So much for life. But the same can also be said of death. Tragedy will get its man or woman, the tragic hero will die, but in the process, death's instrument, otherwise threatening on the ascendant, will unprise from our orbit, if only for a moment. Tragic theatre, as a vehicle of hope, likewise rehearses "that note of calm and sober grief that follows upon great natural calamities."[32] The sobering note on which the stage tragedy concludes is evidence enough that the forces consuming the tragic hero eventually consume themselves, for such is the self-destructive nature of life's negating other. "Death, be not proud" says the Christian on his death bed, prescient of an end to tragedy's own device, "And Death shall be no more: Death, thou shalt die!" *In tragedy, therefore, the medium is the message; to stage the tragedy is to stage proleptically something of its ending.*

But granting that Gethsemane's plaintive but recognizably human prayer echoes the dynamics of the tragic stage, is it possible to speak of Christ's action in the garden as protest against suffering "rehearsed" on behalf of and before a human audience? Is it a performance of the tragic and of hope costumed in a "will" uniquely human and divine? The conclusion I am driving toward is that the hermeneutics of hope inhering in the staging of the tragic is key to Christ's performance of self-dispossession in Gethsemane. I argue that the cathartic thrust of Christ's prayer, cathartic as I have so far defended, is evident in a dual movement: for Christ abandons anything that is "my will alone and undifferentiated" in favor of both (a) "my will" performed as "your will," and (b) "your will" performed in the manner of human willing and not apart from it. *For,*

---

31. Shakespeare, *Complete Works*, "Macbeth," V.5:23–26.
32. Taubes, "The Nature of Tragedy," 206.

in faith, Jesus relinquishes control of his life, but not of his destiny as Logos incarnate. In Christ, divine life is performed not at the expense of but in and through human action: God is made theatre in the flesh.

Barth and Balthasar on Tragedy

In my interaction with Barth and Balthasar and their readings of Gethsemane, I am conscious that the question of Christ's prayer to the Father comes under the grand scope of their respective theological ends. Unfortunately, this also means that their shared theological interest in the drama of Gethsemane falls prey to reductive arguments about nature and grace. A summary of how this conflict bears on our central question will furnish the rest of the discussion with the relevant doctrinal context.

Balthasar understands the tragic dimension of Christ's passion as taking up and thereby signaling the fulfillment of the very questions underpinning the *agon* in the Greek tragedy. His underlying hypothesis is that if truth was enacted in the pre-Christian tragedy, and to the extent that truth is always God's truth, then struggle on the tragic stage was both an account of suffering and evidence of protest demanding the verdict of the cross. In Gethsemane, Christ takes up the problem at the heart of the tragic stage and both judges and redeems it in the crucible of his suffering. The redemptive catholicity of his passion instantiates the reversal of the tragic order. We might say that for Balthasar God's *Logos* was suggested, if inauthentically and only in muted tones, in the words of the tragic poets. Christ, therefore, authenticates the tragic theatre's rendering of human struggle in the question "If it be possible . . ." central to his prayer. Divine grace, evident though frustrated in the natural order, is thereby taken up and redirected towards fulfillment in the salvific events of the cross and resurrection. For Balthasar, from the retroactive perspective of Gethsemane and the ensuing drama on Golgotha, Greek tragedy was, without knowing it, essentially Christian.

Barth, for his part, steering clear from the cultural dimensions of the tragedy, approaches Gethsemane with an unwavering emphasis on its uniqueness, thus leaving no room for doubt about Christ's redemptive suffering and any participatory accretion on the part of humanity. That said, Barth's reading of Christ's prayer as a *pro nobis* event affirms the tragic dimension of Christ's suffering, even as he denies the possibility that such sorrow inheres in humanity's struggle in an abstract, universal sense. For Barth, redemption is not the perfecting of an existing natural order but its complete denaturing, so to speak, and regeneration as nature animated for its Creator through the agency of the Redeemer. This pattern of divine will is concretely evident in Christ's bodily resurrection, and is continually rehearsed as the theatre of Christ's body, the church. In Gethsemane, however, Jesus heroically grinds out a victory by exhausting the opposition from within its own operative resources: Christ plays into the hands of all-consuming evil, letting it take hold of him that he might effectively take hold of it from the root and turn its negative force inside out.

In sum, and at the risk of oversimplification, Balthasar reads Gethsemane as the climactic installment on which is predicated the truthfulness of the tragic stage. By contrast, Barth, taking little interest in the cultural scene, sees tragedy in Gethsemane exclusively in terms of Christ's inner life being laid open and made consequent to sin. Both readings rightly question possible tensions that might otherwise suggest a conflict of wills, not to say persons, between Father and Son. However, in their self-conscious drive towards a climax in which Jesus, mustering supranatural resolve, sets aside impertinent questions in favor of doing the will of the Father, both theologians show a bias towards the other side of Golgotha. Their underlying logic is that all theology is always-already presumptive of the resurrection. The logic may be unimpeachable, but there is nevertheless reason to suspect that the bifocal perspective of Good Friday and Easter Sunday affords a sharper focus on Gethsemane than either Barth or Balthasar would allow. Therefore, setting aside the generalities of grace and nature arguments, a detailed look at Barthian and Balthasarian approaches should set the stage for my suggestion that Gethsemane courts a particular human sensitivity that Christ lives in himself, though not only for or by himself, but with his fellow human audience.

Balthasar's Passion of the Christ

Balthasar sees Gethsemane as the beginning of a process in which Christ absorbs in his person humanity's failure, including everything the history of the tragic stage intended to say but could not speak as God's word, let

alone perform in the sphere of the sacramental.[33] In this crucible of suffering, "[s]ince the sin of the world is 'laid' upon him," Christ is reduced
to obedience, to a heroic resolve to identify with humanity so that he
"no longer distinguishes himself and his fate from those of sinners."[34] For
Balthasar, the collapsed perspective shows that "Christ's anguish was a
co-suffering with sinners."[35] Christ assumes and thereby averts on behalf
of humanity ultimate suffering due in consequence of creaturely rebellion. His is a substitutionary act "of such a kind that the real loss of God
which threatened them . . . was assumed by the incarnate Love of God
in the form of a *timor gehennalis*."[36] Accordingly, Balthasar confidently
claims with reference to the Last Supper, "a universal sacrament in the
centre of the history of the world recapitulating all the quasi-sacramental
events of the Greek stage."[37] Greek tragedy, in other words, which could
only represent suffering as inner groans without the *Logos*, and though
truthful in its apprehension of the need for divine resolution, is fulfilled
and transcended in the godlessness of Christ's suffering.

Mythological in its proportions, this reading emerges in Balthasar's
distinctive but highly critiqued contribution to the doctrine of *kenosis*,
which sees the intensification of all tragedy in Christ's descent into hell.[38]
In essence, though, Balthasar allows constructively that, on some level,
Christ performs an act of faith. Jesus' prayer is not simply evidence of
an obedience-mechanism enabling divine will to instrument tragedy's
defeat: Jesus is not a Sophoclean figure bearing creaturely sin to the cross;
prayer is not the *deus ex machina* on Gethsemane's tragic stage. Christ's
prayer of obedience is the performance of faith (and not merely evidence

---

33. So, for example, it is not merely that the Son's *mission* takes place in history (cit-
ing Joseph Moignt, "[il a] reçu de Dieu une mission qui engage la totalité de l'histoire"),
but that Christ in his being *inhabits* and gestates redemptive history. Balthasar, *Theo-
Drama*, 4:273.

34. Balthasar, *Mysterium Paschale*, 104.

35. Ibid.

36. Ibid.

37. Balthasar, *Explorations*, 3:401–2.

38. Accordingly, sinning humanity's desire to exist for itself without God is met
with divine presence in the person of the Son, not triumphantly exercising authority
over the gates of hell, but *dead*, in ultimate solidarity with those damning themselves,
yet going beyond their "No" to God as the divine "Yes" is pronounced on his life. From
within those depths, Christ frustrates hell's hold with Life made new in his flesh. A critical treatment of Balthasar on this point is found in Quash, *Drama of History*, 193–95ff.
See also the critical overview of Balthasar's doctrine in Barbeau Gardiner, "Light in
Darkness."

of a resigned or rejected tragic hero, though he may be both).[39] In other words, Christ's prayer is the point at which humanity's otherwise ineffective faith seems articulate in the face of a God from whom, in the garden of Gethsemane, we do not hear. *The questioning faith of a human audience is thereby spoken into Christ's self-dispossession in faith to the will of the Father.*

Taubes understood tragedy as operating on the disturbing premise that the world is broken, but that this reality is evident only relative to an unbroken whole. Likewise for Balthasar, "The encounter of . . . 'tragedy' and 'faith' is deeply significant, for that which is broken to pieces in the tragic presupposes a faith in the unbroken *totality*."[40] In Balthasar's dramatics, an unbroken totality and healed brokenness presupposed by the cross, the very idea of a reconstituted whole perceived in faith, is a lived and not merely notional reality; it is a "fact of our experience, something we know [in faith]."[41] Consequently, the "totality" which, from the perspective of the tragic, is "shattering into fragments (or has already been shattered) can be only the object of a *faith*, perhaps a faith that flies in the face of all reason."[42] To speak of an inherently theological orientation in the theatre, therefore, is simply to recognize that the stage tragedy excites in an audience a longing for the restored whole.

Tragedy's "longing" begs questions of what Balthasar calls "the gift of reconciliation" made to humanity through Christ "because the love of God in Christ has undergirded all our contradictions in such a way that they have become the perfect expression of the eternal Yes of God to us."[43] Christ's faithful "Yes" to the Father performed for humanity even in the shedding of human tears on Gethsemane's receptive earth means that believers, not ones for "merely sitting in the space for the spectators of the tragedy, but taking [their] part in the action of the stage," are therein made public spectacle for the sake of Christ, "'*theatrizesthai* [being put on the stage],' as the Letter to the Hebrews says."[44] Therefore, from the

---

39. "[T]he one who suffers is genuinely the one rejected instead of all those chosen, so that all rejected sinners may be able to be chosen in his stead." Once again, there is a question of emphasis, as Balthasar is concerned principally with the consequence of the sin Christ draws onto himself, not with how this inheres positively in his act for humanity. Balthasar, *Explorations*, 3:402.

40. Ibid., 391.

41. Ibid.

42. Ibid.

43. Ibid., 402.

44. Ibid., 402–3. Is there, then, a place for tragic aesthetics in a post-resurrection

perspective of Gethsemane and the cross, the believer's performance appropriates God's primordial "Yes" to humanity articulated in the act of creation and reconstituted in Christ's "Yes" costumed in and spoken through the mask of creaturely life.

To sum up, Balthasar asserts that Christ's passion signals the beginning of the end of tragedy as such, but he does so under the pressure of a totalizing aim to baptize the tragic stage as Christian in its theological orientation. According to the logic, Greek tragedy recapitulates suffering in terms of a collision between divine and human spheres; equally, though unknowingly, it presumes the apotheosis anticipated by the *agon* of Gethsemane. Whatever the merit in this strategy, and if indeed the disciples in the Gethsemane narratives represent unfaithful humanity, it is clear that Balthasar understands the audience as actors on Gethsemane's stage, and not merely as passive receivers of images passing before their dozing eyes. The thrust of the theatrical analogy now comes into view: the stage tragedy is a performance laboratory for open-ended questioning; the theatre of suffering frees an audience to raise and reckon with questions of ultimate significance, to rehearse both an always-shattering reality and an existentially anticipated whole, and to do so, as Aristotle so succinctly put it, with "pity and fear." In Balthasar's performative reading of Gethsemane, humanity is included in the finite perspective of Christ's prayer insofar as God's will accommodates itself to the sobering sorrow and self-dispossessed compassion of one pleading that the cup might pass him by.

Karl Barth's Excursus on Gethsemane

Barth, on the other hand, sees Christ as the archetypical tragic hero, though he is destroyed *not* on account of an insidious *hamartia* (the fatal flaw of the tragic character)[45] but by *his* resolve to bear in his body the pestilence and thereby spare humanity the terminal consequences of the disease. Barth's reading does not so much avoid as transcend the language of the tragic with insight on the satanic stratagem particular to

---

stage? Is there room, Balthasar asks rhetorically, for a "post-Christian [i.e., post-resurrection] tragic element of our existence?" His answer is framed in terms rivalling Greek and Shakespearean tragedy, to the extent that the church "understands herself to be definitively redeemed [but] is always on the run, blindly, head over heels, from the cross that God intended for her." Ibid., 409.

45. On *hamartia* and the tragic portrayal of Christ, see footnote 16 above.

Christ's hour. Barth avoids mythical scenarios in which God is somehow hemmed in by the limits of human intention, or in which divine will is commandeered above the human plane by Promethean determination, thereby violating both divine freedom and creaturely finitude. Crucially, though, Barth's lengthy and meticulously plotted reading of Gethsemane commits Christ to a fate far more distantiating from his human audience than the tragic staging would allow. It is as if Christ performs his sacramental action in Gethsemane with his back to the audience. So singular is the action of the Actor on the Barthian stage that one commentator goes so far as to say that, "at the conclusion of his struggle, [Christ] 'stands upright with a supreme pride' . . . setting out to crucify himself, even as he is crucified by others."[46]

From that position, he commands the operations of evil under the guise of God's punishing love of the Son. For Barth, Gethsemane is nothing less than the orbit of *das Nichtige*, the staging of the *nihil*, and is therefore Christ's master solo in an active *decision* to submit to the will of God. There is no suggestion of a participatory role for the human audience, for in Gethsemane, Barth tells us, "the act of God in Jesus Christ had absolutely nothing to correspond to it in the existence of those who believe in Him. They could not watch with Him even one hour. *He alone watched and prayed in their place.*"[47]

For Barth, the intimacy of Gethsemane's prayer, spoken but a stone's throw from the sleeping disciples (Luke 22:41), isolates Christ well away from the human audience in a spiritual struggle that began in earnest with the temptations in the desert. Barth grounds the inner *motivation*, missional *objective,* and the satanic *obstacle*—a rather conventional dramatic triad—in the ἀγωνία (*agon*)[48] dramatized uniquely in Jesus during the forty days in the wilderness. In the desert, temptation "break[s] over Him—the temptation which . . . has never broken over man before or since, the temptation with which He alone could be assailed."[49] For Barth, Gethsemane's climax to Christ's determination born of fierce opposition is the reason why this scene, including the ambiguously nuanced prayer, is preserved in the Synoptic Gospels.

The intensity and cosmic implications are such that impersonal evil attaches itself to the Son's bodily existence with indescribable ferocity.

46. Jones, "Barth on Gethsemane," 49–50.
47. Barth, "The Judge Judged," 268, added italics.
48. Ibid., 261.
49. Ibid., 261; cf. 260–64, 267.

Barth resorts almost inconceivably to the rhetoric of the personal, asserting that perhaps on this and only this occasion could one speak of evil attaining an interiority bordering on being:[50]

> Satan now spoke with him as the prince of this aeon, triumphantly avenging His contradiction and opposition in the wilderness. *The will of God was done as the will of Satan was done.* The answer of God was identical with the action of Satan. . . . The coincidence of the divine and the satanic will and work and word was the problem of this hour, the darkness in which Jesus addressed God in Gethsemane.[51]

Barth clearly takes seriously the prayer "if you are willing" as something that actually resonates in Jesus' being, like the sound of an eternally breaking string. He therefore speaks with complete integrity relative to his broader argument of a dual direction in Christ's passion, both as *God's act for humanity* and as God's act for humanity *in the medium of human action.*[52] However, if the governing semiotic in Gethsemane is "the passion of Jesus Christ as the act of God *for us*," it is only in virtue of being "the act of God for us as the passion of *Jesus Christ*"; following Barth's rhetoric, "[i]n this, and this alone . . . there stands or falls the truth of Christian experience."[53] Consequently, Barth dismisses any suggestion that humanity (i.e., "nature") in some way witnesses and anticipates (let alone participates in) Christ's saving work.

In the end, Barth affirms the theologically disturbing direction suggested in the first part of Christ's prayer but, at the same time, sublimates its dramatic and potentially tragic dimensions under a hierarchy of divine primacy over human will. Barth grants that the prayer signals a previously unknown struggle in Christ's being, but he quickly shores up potentially embarrassing suggestions (not least, from the point of view of Christology) with a strategy designed to preserve Christ's prayer as *sine qua non* evidence of his human surrender to the superintendent will of God. The drift of Barth's argument goes as follows:

50. This is shared by Balthasar, whose theological dramatics also feature centrally the incorporation of evil into divine will. Accordingly, in Gethsemane "God ceases to dispose of [Christ], and his enemy does so instead." Balthasar, *Mysterium Paschale*, 108.

51. Barth, "The Judge Judged," 268.

52. Ibid., 249. Barth's excursus on Gethsemane is an auxiliary hypothesis to his thesis on reconciliation, but is related centrally to the question of dual agency in Christ's saving work.

53. Ibid. Emphasis added.

a. "If it had been the will of God that the cup should pass from him, then Christ would have wished and affirmed that to be the case."[54] However, it should be evident that:

b. "It is not God's will"[55] for anything other than the crushing way of the cross.

c. Moreover, Jesus would have pressed the point "if it had corresponded to the real will of God,"[56] and he "clearly wished [but did not will] that it might have been so."

d. In fact, however, Jesus was always "determined to surrender to ['the real will of God']."[57] And in any case, "He only prays. He does not demand." For Jesus did not "set his will in this direction."[58]

In short, the first part of the prayer confirms and is evidence of Christ's innermost being coming to terms with the necessity of his suffering. The second part of the prayer, though confirming the truth of the preceding moment, galvanizes willful obedience to God's supreme action for a humanity whose exclusion from the garden is iconographically associated with the abandonment and helplessness of the sleeping disciples.

Christ's performance on this stage is indisputably performed *for* humanity, *on* our behalf, and *in* our place. Jesus' determination to drink the cup is the script to which the prayer of Matthew 23:37 becomes a retroactive postscript, "Jerusalem, Jerusalem, you who kill the prophets and those sent to you, how often have I longed to gather your children under my wings . . . ." In the event, Barth's take on Christ's theatre of suffering leaves one wondering whether there is any indication of an act of faith performed, as it were, *with* the human audience. Barth's position in the excursus on Gethsemane could not be any clearer: from the perspective of Gethsemane's garden, the human audience lies numb to the workings of their disease, proverbially "like a patient etherized upon a table," under the skill of a surgeon whose operating theater, in any case, is *not* of this world.

---

54. Ibid., 269.
55. Ibid.
56. Ibid.
57. Ibid.
58. Ibid., 270.

Gethsemane on the Tragic Stage

To summarize the preceding discussion, both Balthasar and Barth take seriously the ambiguity in Christ's prayer in Gethsemane, but for reasons conforming to particular theological programs. Though they are as one on the heroics of suffering, which vindicate Jesus in his role as Savior, their respective readings of the supplication to the Father yield distinct notions of humanity's place on Gethsemane's stage. For the Catholic Balthasar, Christ's prayer is of a piece with his perfecting in himself humanity's sincere but inadequate attempts to make sense of suffering through the mythology of the stage. By answering his own question ("yet not my will but yours be done") and following its consequences to the end in the face of all possibilities to the contrary, Christ's suffering sheds the starkest possible light on the intractability of bad endings. There can be no destiny worse than his. The universal significance of Christ's suffering in Gethsemane unfolds a mythology not so much to forfeit suffering myths performed on the pre-Christian stage as to narrow their *agon* towards fulfillment in the tragedy of the cross. Balthasar shapes a Christian suffering *mythos* in which, in the place of Aristotelian sorrow and pity, fear and courage "divinized in the most adorable Heart of the Lord"[59] actualize the Son of God's resolve to embrace death in order to transcend it.[60] The excruciating resolve demanded of Christ as he faces humanity's deepest fears in himself ploughs into fallow creaturely soil so that a divine "Yes" may begin to germinate. A universe of inexhaustible perspectives thereby opens on the world stage, so that the faith of mere mortals might perceive in the light of resurrection an eternal "Yes" spoken both in God and man, that humanity might hear the shattering of nay-saying when God speaks from the whirlwind of Pentecost. By the same token, however, and to complete the myth, the plough drives human suffering deep into the heart of God.

Barth, for his part, zeros in on the historical significance of Gethsemane's suffering in virtue of the particular history it encompasses: Christ's alone for only Christ in his humanity can be tempted to depart from God's intention; only he can contemplate a will other than his

---

59. Balthasar, *Theo-Drama*, 1:399.

60. Balthasar poignantly recalls the George Bernanos character in *The Diary of a Country Priest* who, unbowed in the face of martyrdom, is sustained by a sense that "in the perspective of the Mount of Olives, . . . the distinction between fear and courage practically collapses." Ibid.

Father's because he alone embodies it in history.[61] Everything that takes place as "Jesus realizes that his life constitutes the exclusive point of conflict between what humankind intends for itself (sin and the propagation of evil) and what God intends for humanity (freedom in companionship with God)"[62] is uniquely Christ's. The human audience, as evidenced by the disciples who cannot stand watch and pray, remains unawed in its silence. The theatre of Christ's suffering plays before faithless eyes. Only in retrospect, and only then from the other side of the cross, will the force of the drama come fully into their view.

Methodologically, Barth's argument runs on two levels, one relating to divine rejection of evil, the other to Christ's embrace of this rejection. Christ appropriates in himself God's eternal rejection of evil, and does so by embodying the *néant* temporally and historically, as it were, giving "to airy nothing a local habitation and a name."[63] To do so in the freedom exposed between two wills in Gethsemane constitutes positively the beginning of the end of God's rejection of evil. However, following Paul Dafydd Jones's reading of Barth on this point,

> for this to occur, there must [be] the event of the cross, whereby the "true human" himself affirms *both* God's uncompromising disapproval of humanity's "previous" involvement with evil *and* assists in effecting the expulsion of evil from the created realm. . . . He must choose the history of rejection for himself: his "unsubstitutionable" identity must come to an "unsubstitutionable" end, as he constitutes himself as the one burdened with sin.[64]

To be clear, there is no question of a role for humanity in the outworking of this eternal, covenantal event historicized "unsubstitutionably" in the person of Jesus; anything relating to humanity can only be said in virtue of Christ's journey to the cross and the response it demands from the human audience. But even Barth's suggestion of an unsubstitutable opposition between human will and divine priority "[i]n the continuation of the prayer"[65] brings Gethsemane into the environment of the tragic drama: its implications are potentially terminal and of the highest order. At stake is nothing less than salvation, hence everything Christ

61. Barth, "The Judge Judged," 251.

62. This summary is found in Jones, "Barth on Gethsemane," 157.

63. Shakespeare, *Complete Works*, "Midsummer Night's Dream," V.1:16–17.

64. Jones, "Barth on Gethsemane," 167.

65. Barth, "The Judge Judged," 262.

may assume in himself and subject to the redemptive judgment of divine life become flesh. So, a more complex picture of "my will" comes into view than is at first evident in Barth's reading of Gethsemane, and not without some implications for a participatory audience.

Barth accepts that Christ's opposition of his undifferentiated human will to the actual will of God in an agonizing prayer would effectively rule out the authority of "your will." So, logically, the vocatively phrased, "Not my will but yours be done" signals for Barth the death of human will in Christ for the sake of his divine Other. In tragic terms, therefore, the hero fatefully submits mortal flesh to the workings of divine destiny. Nevertheless, there is a sense in Barth that Christ's dying to human will in Gethsemane, as was the case in the desert, is predicated on divine providence performed in the manner of human willing. Barth allows at least provisionally that "my will" in the latter part of the prayer is for Christ "the real will of God as His own will." [66]

The Sense of an Ending

Barth does not thematize the implications of such a rhetorical turn. This language, however, coheres rather unexpectedly with my thesis that the end of tragedy is catharsis, understood as self-dispossession. For Christ, as "fully God and fully man," self-dispossession is not the same as the suppression of his human nature. Chalcedonian Christology, in fact, compels an anti-heroic reading of Christ "who, though being in nature as God, emptied himself into the form of man," to paraphrase the canticle in Philippians 2. This is no less true of Jesus' prayer in Gethsemane, which on my reading is further evidence of divine appropriation of human nature in the downward movement of incarnation. As Balthasar would have it, this is the Son of God "vicariously taking on man's Godlessness."[67] The questioning prayer, in other words, invites the full consequences of the incarnation: it allows that God *qua* Son registers under protest the anticipation of his tragic end.

Though admittedly walking a knife-edge between orthodoxy and heresy,[68] I propose that Christ undertakes his pilgrimage to the cross

---

66. Ibid.

67. Balthasar, *Theo-Drama*, 4:324.

68. This is a risk of which Balthasar is keenly aware, as pointed out in Nichols, *No Bloodless Myth*, 166.

in trust that God the Father will perform his will, not supra-materially but—in effect of his self-squandering in the Son—precisely *in the manner of* Jesus' human action. This includes, necessarily, the action of his questioning prayer. In Gethsemane we hear Jesus raise divine protest against suffering and injustice, and at the same time pray in faith, that is to say, against evidence to the contrary, that his walk to Golgotha should indeed become God's story performed in the midst of human history; that his story would become God's story. Jesus' "knowing all that was to happen to him" (John 18:4) is therefore itself subject to his acting in faith. Not surprisingly, in Luke's narrative of Gethsemane, an angel offering Jesus comfort does not depict heroic resolve typical of epic drama, but rather strengthening of faith as self-dispossessing trust, faith as it were in terms of "the assurance of things hoped for, the conviction of things not seen" (Heb 11:1).

More insightfully, however, a participatory perspective for the human audience opens up when Barth's provocative suggestion that God's will is performed *as* Christ's human willing is held in tension with Balthasar's insistence that Christ *acts in faith*. Gethsemane is a performance of tragedy and hope costumed in Christ's trust that divine will conforms to the all-too-human shape of his action. Yet far from being isolated on some mythical, cosmic stage, the suffering Christ of Gethsemane rehearses protest on behalf of and before a human audience.

Theologically, whatever we might say about action above the human plane, Christ's prayer in Gethsemane is evidence of action taken in faith. Gethsemane points to Christ's sense that his actions are done *as if* and in the belief that they are coherent with and indeed *are* in themselves the actions of God in him. This will have some bearing on the Scripture's isolation of Christ's suffering as unrepeatably his. For it now implies that God's action is performed *in the manner of* a historically unique will, and not just abstractly in solidarity with humanity. In Gethsemane, the will of God is performed precisely *as*, and not apart from, Christ's particular humanity.

The tightrope stringing Docetism, Adoptionism, Semipelagianism and other possible heterodoxies tautens. Nevertheless, I propose reading the Gospel drama of Gethsemane as a performance of the tragic, which in the terms I have argued, implies reading it as a narrative plumbing the depths of human suffering with questions of divine justice and hope. In theatre, tragic performance necessarily implies the hope of a redemptive end. Tragedy enacts protest against brokenness in view of a possible whole, a perspective ultimately inhering in the participatory position of the audience. This theatrical dynamic allows me, therefore, to press a final point in regard to Christ's prayer in Gethsemane, namely, that although clearly unique to his person and mission, *Christ's agony in the garden includes and encompasses whatever distance keeps him from his human audience.*

The plea in the garden for some other way is Christ's alone, something that is amplified and voiced in full in the cry of dereliction from the cross. However, formulating his prayer in terms of a possibility other than one that would destroy the protagonist, Jesus echoes the way in which the tragic stage raises questions in the place of and in order that an audience might appropriate them as their own. Similarly, in my argument, the vocatively formulated "Father, if it is possible, let this cup pass from me" is integral to Christ's *faithfulness to humanity*, for which cause he chooses the way of the cross. In other words, Christ's question is not only his question, but is also a question intended for and asked on behalf of— and, indeed, *with*—the human audience. Here, I am merely amplifying a doctrine that Christ as the Son of God suffers, that this is a suffering fully assumed by the Word, and that this includes the questioning and even protesting orientation of a human audience. Or, as Katherine Tanner has put it, "Jesus does not overcome temptation until he is tempted, does not overcome fear of death until he feels it, at which time this temptation and fear are assumed by the Word. Jesus does not heal death until the Word assumes death when Jesus dies . . . ."[69]

I conclude from this that, on Gethsemane's stage, "my will" is always "my will aligned with and in agreement with your will." This implies, however, unity as well as distance. So, the hypostatically distinct "my will" is also differentiated from "your will," which is by definition differentiated from creaturely willing, hence, from nature as such. Jesus therefore brings before the Father "my will" in its economic whole, trusting in faith that God will redeem an all-too-human will that "this cup should pass from me." In this sense, "your will" becomes "my will" *only* insofar as it is performed in the manner of human willing, that is, in Christ's hypostatic act of faith.

In this economy of self-dispossessed divinity, Christ embodies the full consequences of his identification with humanity and breaks free from the shackles of the tragic, from the tyranny of distrust and unbelief.

---

69. Tanner, *Jesus, Humanity and the Trinity*, 28.

In Christ, the reversal of tragedy is birthed in an act of faith performed on a human scale. This prevenient grace bridging the distance between Christ and his disciples establishes that, from this point forward, the only possible tragedy of *ultimate* consequence is an unformulated, unrequited, or spectating rather than participatory faith. Positively, in regard to the human audience presumed by the drama of Gethsemane, it suggests that to address oneself in the vocative to the living reality that is God, hence, to "watch and pray"—even in the modality of some doubting or dozing disposition—already implies an act brought into the open and cathartically exposed to the light of redeeming Life, a prescient embodying of tragedy's "the end."

Bibliography

Aristotle. *Ars Poetica*. Edited by R. Kassel. Oxford: Clarendon, 1966. Online: http://www.perseus.tufts.edu/hopper/text?doc=Perseus:text:1999.01.0055.

———. *Poetics*. Translated by Gerald F. Else. Ann Arbor, MI: University of Michigan Press, 1970.

Balthasar, Hans Urs von. *Explorations in Theology*. Vol. 3, *Creator Spirit*. San Francisco: Ignatius, 1993.

———. *Mysterium Paschale: The Mystery of Easter*. Edinburgh: T. & T. Clark, 1990.

———. *Theo-Drama: Theological Dramatic Theory*. Vol. 1, *Prolegomena*. Translated by Graham Harrison. San Francisco: Ignatius, 1988.

———. *Theo-Drama*. Vol. 4, *The Action*. Translated by Graham Harrison. San Francisco, 1994.

Barbeau Gardiner, Anne. Review of *Light in Darkness: Hans Urs von Balthasar and the Catholic Doctrine of Christ's Descent into Hell*, by Alyssa Pitstick. *New Oxford Reviews* 54.7 (2007) 43.

Barth, Karl. "The Judge Judged in Our Place." In *Church Dogmatics*. Vol. 4.1, *The Doctrine of Reconciliation*, translated by G. W. Bromiley, 259–73. Edinburgh: T. & T. Clark, 1997.

Burian, Peter. "Myth into *Muthos*: The Shaping of the Tragic Plot." In *The Cambridge Companion to Greek Tragedy*, edited by P. E. Easterling, 178–208. Cambridge: Cambridge University Press, 2003.

Chekhov, Anton. *Вишневый сад: Полная Хрестоматия По Литературе*. Moscow: Olma, 2002.

Eagleton, Terry. "Commentary." *New Literary History* 35.1 (2004) 151–59.

Jones, Paul Dafydd. "Karl Barth on Gethsemane." *International Journal of Systematic Theology* 9.2 (2007) 148–71.

Nichols, Aidan. *No Bloodless Myth: A Guide through Balthasar's Dramatics*. Edinburgh: T. & T. Clark, 2000.

Quash, Ben. *Theology and the Drama of History*. Cambridge: Cambridge University Press, 2005.

Ratzinger, Joseph, as Pope Benedict XVI. "On St. Maximus the Confessor." *ZENIT* (25 June 2008). Online: http://www.zenit.org/article-23016?l=english.

Ruprecht, Louis A., Jr. "The Heart of Christian Compassion: The Prayer in Gethsemane." In *This Tragic Gospel: How John Corrupted the Heart of Christianity*, 37–78. San Francisco: Wiley, 2008.

———. "Mark's Tragic Vision: Gethsemane." *Religion & Literature* 24.3 (1992) 1–25.

Shakespeare, William. *Shakespeare: Complete Works*. Edited by W. J. Craig. Oxford: Oxford University Press, 1980.

States, Bert O. *Great Reckonings in Little Rooms: On the Phenomenology of Theatre*. Berkeley: University of California Press, 1985.

Steiner, George. *Death of Tragedy*. New Haven: Yale University Press, 1996.

Tanner, Kathryn. *Jesus, Humanity and the Trinity*. Minneapolis: Fortress, 2001.

Taubes, Susan. "The Nature of Tragedy." *The Review of Metaphysics* 7.2 (1953) 193–206.

Wheeler, Burton M. "Theology and the Theatre." *Journal of Bible and Religion* 28.3 (1960) 334–44.

4

Raising a Tempest

Brookian Theatre as an Analogy for Providence

TIMOTHY GORRINGE

"How came we ashore?" asks Miranda in *The Tempest*, as her father tells her the story of his banishment and their arrival at their island. Prospero responds, "By Providence divine" (I.ii.160). Later in the play, when Alonso, Ferdinand's father, finds him playing chess with Miranda, he asks:

> What is this maid with whom thou wast at play?
> Your eld'st acquaintance cannot be three hours:
> Is she the goddess that hath sever'd us,
> And brought us thus together?

Ferdinand replies:

> Sir, she is mortal;
> But by immortal Providence she's mine:
> I chose her when I could not ask my father
> For his advice, nor thought I had one. (V.i.185–94)

Several times Shakespeare reprises the "happy fault" theme of the Easter exultet. Miranda asks:

> What foul play had we, that we came from thence?
> Or blessed was't we did?

Prospero replies:

> Both, both, my girl:
> By foul play as thou say'st, were we heav'd hence,
> But blessedly holp hither. (I.ii.60–64)

Similarly, as Gonzalo watches Ferdinand and Miranda he says:

> Look down, you gods,
> And on this couple drop a blessed crown!
> For it is you that have chalk'd forth the way
> Which brought us hither. (V.i.201–4)

In what was probably his last great play, Shakespeare weaves together reflections on providence, the divine, and theatre. An act of 1606 had prohibited the mention of God on stage in any way that could be construed as profane, but Shakespeare manages triumphantly to explore these themes in *The Tempest* without contravening the statute.

As is well known, Shakespeare drew on the account of a real shipwreck that happened two years before he wrote the play in 1611, when a fleet of nine vessels carrying colonists to Virginia encountered a storm and one was beached on Bermuda and had to spend the winter carrying out repairs. The event was read in terms of providence. William Strachey, who recorded the events in a 1610 letter, describes the island as a place "feared and avoided [by] all sea travellers alive above any other place in the world." He continues, "Yet it pleased our merciful God to make even this hideous and hated place both the place of our safety and means of our deliverance" and concludes that "the ground of all those miseries was the permissive Providence of God."[1] Sylvester Jourdain's *A Discovery of the Bermudas*, also published in 1610, tells us "they were forced to runne their ship on shoare, which through God's providence fell betwixt two rockes, that caused her to stand firme, and not immediately be broken."[2] Shakespeare knew many of the people involved in the Virginia enterprise and it is generally accepted that he knew these documents. In *The Embarrassment of Riches*, Simon Schama has shown that seventeenth-century

---

1. Strachey, "True Reportory of the Wracke and Redemption of Sir Thomas Gates, Knight," 136.

2. Jourdain, "Discovery of the Bermudas," 141.

Holland was saturated in the idea of providence, and this correspondence suggests the same goes for Britain. It would be a surprise if Shakespeare did not pick that up.

Although we certainly cannot say that this play is "about" providence any more than it is "about" nature, art, colonialism, enchantment, or any other themes that scholars have proposed, it has always been acknowledged that providence is one of the prominent themes. When *The Tempest* was performed after the great storm of 1703, in which 15,000 people died, including the Bishop of Bath and Wells and his wife, the production was regarded as blasphemous. Many people viewed the storm as God's judgment on official failures in the War of Spanish Succession. The Bishop of Oxford, William Talbot, preaching in Westminster Abbey on the national day of repentance, said that the production represented an "unprecedented piece of Profaneness" that was an "affront to God, unparalleled by any civilized nation."[3] Jeremy Collier, theologian and scourge of the theatre, said that the players and playwrights had "attempted as it were to scale the sky, and attack the seat of omnipotence: they have blasphemed the attributes of God, ridiculed his providence."[4] To stage a play that began with a storm and celebrated a benign providence in which all mariners and ships were safe in this context obviously raised problems with which the church was not willing to deal.

There are at least two ways of understanding providence in *The Tempest*. First, though Prospero understands himself in the hands of providence, as we see from his answer to Miranda, in some respects his studies enable him to echo it:

> Ye elves of hills, brooks, standing lakes and groves,
> And ye that on the sands with printless foot
> Do chase the ebbing Neptune and do fly him
> When he comes back; you demi-puppets that
> By moonshine do the green sour ringlets make,
> Whereof the ewe not bites, and you whose pastime
> Is to make midnight mushrooms, that rejoice
> To hear the solemn curfew; by whose aid,
> Weak masters though ye be, I have bedimm'd
> The noontide sun, call'd forth the mutinous winds,

---

3. Talbot, *A Sermon*, 17.
4. Collier, *Mr. Collier's Dissuasive from the Play-house*, 16.

And 'twixt the green sea and the azured vault
Set roaring war: to the dread rattling thunder
Have I given fire and rifted Jove's stout oak
With his own bolt; the strong-based promontory
Have I made shake and by the spurs pluck'd up
The pine and cedar: graves at my command
Have waked their sleepers, oped, and let 'em forth
By my so potent art. (V.i.33–57)

Although Prospero is *under* providence he *is* providence in terms of the play. As the epilogue suggests, he also in some way stands for the playwright who, in crafting the story, enacts providence for all his or her characters. We learn from Prospero that providence lies in wisdom, which is not just knowledge, but knowledge exercised for loving purposes: selflessly and with self-control. As Prospero prepares to meet his brother and Alonso, he soliloquizes:

Though with their high wrongs I am struck to the quick,
Yet with my nobler reason 'gainst my fury
Do I take part: the rarer action is
In virtue than in vengeance: they being penitent,
The sole drift of my purpose doth extend
Not a frown further. (V.i.24–30)

Prospero, though recognizing evil and moved to anger by it, is virtuous and controls his anger for good and loving purposes. Precisely because Prospero is providence, it is significant that he has no interest in clinging to this power:

But this rough magic
I here abjure, and, when I have required
Some heavenly music, which even now I do,
To work mine end upon their senses that
This airy charm is for, I'll break my staff,
Bury it certain fathoms in the earth,
And deeper than did ever plummet sound
I'll drown my book. (V.i.33–57)

Here the theme of kenosis is introduced. Prospero renounces his pseudo-providential power, exchanges his magic robe for his ducal cloak, and goes back to Milan to prepare for death.

A second way providence is displayed in *The Tempest* is through the transformation of evil into good, as in the Joseph story or the crucifixion. Pardon and forgiveness sound insistently throughout the latter part of the play. In Prospero's opening narrative we are back in Genesis 4: brother seeks to kill brother. But now, as in other late plays of Shakespeare, "pardon's the word for all."

> Flesh and blood,
> You, brother mine, that entertain'd ambition,
> Expell'd remorse and nature; who, with Sebastian,
> Whose inward pinches therefore are most strong,
> Would here have kill'd your king; I do forgive thee,
> Unnatural though thou art. (V.i.74–79)

When Alonso finds Ferdinand, he says, "How oddly will it sound that I must ask my child forgiveness!" Prospero replies:

> There, sir, stop:
> Let us not burthen our remembrance with
> A heaviness that's gone. (V.i.197–99)

When Stephano, Trinculo, and Caliban finally appear, Prospero says to Caliban:

> Go, sirrah, to my cell;
> Take with you your companions; as you look
> To have my pardon, trim it handsomely.

Caliban replies:

> Ay, that I will; and I'll be wise hereafter
> And seek for grace. (V.i.291–95)

The possibility of forgiveness represents the possibility of a return to Eden, the "brave new world" that Miranda rapturously acclaims. Evil and suffering are providentially overcome. The happy ending is brought about by divine direction. So Shakespeare suggests the possibility of an *apokatastasis*, or universal forgiveness. All this is compared to the business of theatre in the epilogue.

Now my charms are all o'erthrown,
And what strength I have's mine own,
Which is most faint: now, 'tis true,
I must be here confined by you,
Or sent to Naples. Let me not,
Since I have my dukedom got
And pardon'd the deceiver, dwell
In this bare island by your spell;
But release me from my bands
With the help of your good hands:
Gentle breath of yours my sails
Must fill, or else my project fails,
Which was to please. Now I want
Spirits to enforce, art to enchant,
And my ending is despair,
Unless I be relieved by prayer,
Which pierces so that it assaults
Mercy itself and frees all faults.
As you from crimes would pardon'd be,
Let your indulgence set me free. (Epilogue, l 1–20)

Shakespeare tells the audience that the magic they have just witnessed rests with them. Shakespeare's art, an analogue of Prospero's, has created a vision of a world restored to peace, where forgiveness reigns. He hands this vision to the audience. The magic, it is clear, is imagination, as Wordsworth puts it at the end of *The Prelude*:

This spiritual Love acts not nor can exist
Without Imagination, which, in truth,
Is but another name for absolute power
And clearest insight, amplitude of mind,
And Reason in her most exalted mood. (XIV, 188–92)

But Shakespeare suggests that beyond the benign magic of theatre is prayer to the providence to which Prospero himself is subject, "Mercy itself," which "bound everyone over to disobedience so that he might have mercy on them all" (Rom 11:32). This reading might be called into question by the great revels speech after the wedding masque:

Our revels now are ended. These our actors,
As I foretold you, were all spirits and
Are melted into air, into thin air:
And, like the baseless fabric of this vision,
The cloud-capp'd towers, the gorgeous palaces,
The solemn temples, the great globe itself,
Yea, all which it inherit, shall dissolve
And, like this insubstantial pageant faded,
Leave not a rack behind. We are such stuff
As dreams are made on, and our little life
Is rounded with a sleep. (IV.i.146–63)

So is life itself illusion? Might Macbeth be right after all? I suggest that the midrash on this passage are the closing lines of Peter Brook's *The Empty Space*. In theatre, unlike in life, he says, it is always possible to start again. "In everyday life, 'if' is a fiction, in the theatre, 'if' is an experiment. In everyday life, 'if' is an evasion, in the theatre 'if' is the truth. When we are persuaded to believe in this truth, then the theatre and life are one."[5] I take it that the meaning of these gnomic lines is that theatre is part of life as interpretation, as imaginative reflection on the intractable reality of the everyday, and that, as such, it can function somewhat as Aristotle imagined it.

Theatre Direction and Divine Providence

Brook's book, which is a reflection on the process of direction, provides, as I suggested more than twenty years ago, an analogy through which we might understand providence.[6] "It is a strange role, that of the director," wrote Brook, for whom *The Tempest* was always a favorite play. "He does not ask to be God and yet his role implies it."[7] Brook probably has in mind a Being with all the answers, and yet his whole essay on theatre and direction, according to which the director succeeds only by sharing his or her fallibility (for which the theological correlate would be the divine "weakness"), is profoundly suggestive for the doctrine of providence. In

---

5. Brook, *The Empty Space*, 157.

6. Gorringe, *God's Theatre*.

7. Brook, *The Empty Space*, 43.

God's Theatre, I pulled out four themes, but in this chapter I extend this to seven.

Brook's artistic career has been a sustained attack on what he calls "deadly theatre," theatre in which there is no real event between players and audience but simply hollow spectacle: entertainment. According to Brook, the director who comes to the first rehearsal with all the moves and business noted down—rather like some accounts of the predestinating God—is "a real deadly theatre man." He describes how, on the evening of his first rehearsal with the Royal Shakespeare Company in 1946, he spent his entire time pushing around little cardboard models of the actors trying to get the shape of the first scenes in his mind. The next morning, with his prompt book in front of him and the appropriate sequence of moves outlined, he asked the actors to do what he had worked out for them. As soon as they began he realized it was no use, as everyone moved at different paces and the shape was all wrong. Then, Brook writes, "I stopped, and walked away from my book, went in amongst the actors, and I have never looked at a written plan since."[8]

This suggested to me a way of thinking about God's activity. If we do in fact learn about God in Christ, then it should be clear that God rejected the prompt book option from the very beginning, and has been from the start "in amongst the actors." God works without script and without plan but with, to continue the metaphor, a profound understanding of theatre and the profoundest understanding of the play. The theme of the play is love and the realization of love. In his unauthorized account of Brook's production, David Selbourne records how Brook demanded that the actors find the "inner impulse" of their part, the play, and the rhythm of their lines. Interestingly, Brook remarked early in the rehearsal process that there was a particular rhythm to be found and a particular actor to find it, and this demanded "an almost metaphysical explanation."[9] All the director can do is illuminate the play and demand that the actors find their own inner resources. Often Brook simply sat in front of the stage drumming out a rhythm. Something like this is what God demands of us. With his cardboard models, Brook was actually preparing prompts for a puppet theatre—exactly the mistake so many theologians have made in their understanding of the "theatre" of world history, encouraged by classical analogies of God's activity. "To love within the growth

8. Ibid., 138.

9. Selbourne, *The Making of Midsummer Night's Dream*, 21.

of a community," writes Paul Fiddes, arguing that God must be subject to change, "is to allow it to develop in its own way and to make its own impact and contribution; otherwise it is not a community of free persons but a puppet show."[10] Like Brook's cardboard models, the possibility of a community of persons in the creator's mind cannot be quite the same as the actuality, since the actors will move too fast or too slow, grouping themselves according to their own dynamics.

An objection against this analogy is that it conceives of God as simply one agent among many, just as Selbourne sometimes wondered whether Brook was just one actor among many. This would reduce God to the status of a finite being. The giveaway here is the emphasis on "simply." God is indeed one agent among many, but he is the only *unique* agent, just as there is only one "director." God is the Creator and Sustainer, interacting with, and reacting to, in free and sovereign grace.

In place of a plan, Brook says, a director must have "a formless hunch":

> that is to say, a certain powerful yet shadowy intuition that indicates the basic shape, the source from which the play is calling to him. What he needs most to develop in his work is a sense of listening. Day after day, as he intervenes, makes mistakes or watches what is happening on the surface, inside he must be listening, listening to the secret movements of the hidden process. It is in the name of this listening that he will be constantly dissatisfied, will continue to accept and reject until suddenly his ear hears the secret sound it is expecting and his eye sees the inner form that has been waiting to appear.... The work is the work of an artisan, there is no place for false mystification, for spurious magical methods. The theatre is a craft. A director works and listens. He helps the actors to work and listen.[11]

What we can take from this theologically, I think, are two things. The first is the idea of a listening God, who listens not simply to fulfill the petitions of prayer, but who listens to the creature, as Paul suggests in Romans 8, praying through us. The second is that God, like Brook's director, has no time for spurious, magical methods, which is precisely what we learn from the cross. So if the cross is the epitome of providence, we learn that God disowns all such methods: like Prospero, the staff is broken. This relates directly to the suffering and evil that always call

10. Fiddes, *The Creative Suffering of God*, 55.
11. Brook, *There Are No Secrets*, 119.

the understanding of providence into question. In the '60s critics complained about new plays that seemed to concentrate on the sordid, and they called them "dirty plays." In Shakespeare and in great classical art, the critics said, one eye is always on the stars. Brook agreed but argued that what the critics wanted was not a holy theatre, a theatre of miracles, but simply a nicer and more decent theatre. "Alas, happy endings and optimism can't be ordered like wine from cellars. They spring whether we wish it or not from a source and if we pretend there is such a source readily at hand we will go on cheating ourselves with rotten imitations."[12] Perhaps in railing against providence when things go wrong we are like the critics wanting decent and nicer theatre in place of a holy theatre and a theatre of miracles. In place of happy endings and miracles, Christian theology puts instead a theology of hope rooted in the cross, which both interprets and redeems evil and suffering. In place of spurious, magical methods there is real magic, which is what Brook gave us in the *Dream* and what Shakespeare gives us in *The Tempest*: falling in love, music, the natural world, art not intended to deceive, and forgiveness.

A third aspect of Brook's account of direction that is suggestive for theology is that it is not simply a matter of "letting be." "When a director speaks of 'letting the play speak for itself,' suspicions are aroused, because this is the hardest job of all. If you just let a play speak, it may not make a sound. If what you want is for the play to be heard, then you must conjure its sound from it. This demands many deliberate actions."[13] The worst director of all is the honorable, unassuming one, the one who cultivates non-intervention as a way of "respecting" the actor. The idea that a company or an actor can do without leadership he calls a "wretched fallacy." In theological terms, this resembles deism, according to which the autonomy of the universe is only respected by God's non-intervention. The God presented by Maurice Wiles, for instance, falls exactly into the category of the honorable and unassuming director. Against such a view, and pressing the Brookian analogy, Christians believe that without divine direction there would really be "no speech nor language." Like the good director, God must be capable of imposing God's will, as Court History suggests (the story of David in 2 Samuel 12–20). The question is: how can this be done without resorting to *force majeure* or manipulation? This is a question both for the theatre director and for God.

12. Brook, *The Empty Space*, 53.
13. Ibid., 41.

The answer, to draw a fourth lesson from Brook, is in terms of mutual exploration between director and actor:

> The director must look for where the actor is messing up his own right urges—and here he must help the actor to see and overcome his own obstacles. All this is a dialogue between director and player. A dance is an accurate metaphor, a waltz between director, player and text. Progression is circular, and deciding who's the leader depends on where you stand. The director will find that all the time new means are needed. . . . He will follow the natural principle of rotation of crops: he will see that explanation, logic, improvisation, inspiration are methods that rapidly run dry and he will move from one to the other.[14]

We may conceive God to work in a similar manner. The dialogue between director and player is prayer, which Baelz calls a "creative participation in divine activity," but which might also be understood as divine participation in human activity.[15] Thus Buber spoke of an "I-Thou" relationship between God and human beings, resulting in what he called "active history" through which God's purpose is fulfilled in and through human purpose.[16] Brook insists that a director cannot understand a play by himself but only with the actors, and as the production progresses the director understands everything differently.[17] In some such way, God's providence evolves and grows together with the human.

This leads to a fifth point. Genuine dialogue involves the possibility of surprise. Surprise, I take it, is an integral part of human life, history, theatre, and also providence. "The theatre must not be dull," Brook wrote in some later reflections. "It must not be conventional. It must be unexpected. Theatre leads us to truth through surprise, through excitement, through games, through joy."[18] Barth at one point saw fit to praise the bourgeois virtues, and one can see the point. The unexpected only makes sense in the context of the expected, and a world of constant excitement and surprise would be unsustainable. Nevertheless, it is the dialectic between expected and unexpected, which is precisely the livingness in life, and this applies too to the living God. The God of surprises also knows what it is to be surprised by joy. This in no way implies an imperfection on

14. Ibid., 138.

15. Baelz, *Prayer and Providence*, 66.

16. Buber, *I and Thou*, 127.

17. Brook, *The Empty Space*, 119.

18. Ibid., 95.

God's part, as classical theology imagined. On the contrary, it is precisely God's freedom in this regard that constitutes God's perfection. Surprise is also related to the way in which the implausible scenes in Shakespeare's plays—Orsino's sudden decision to marry Viola, Hermione's statue coming to life—nevertheless move us. When considered on paper they do not work; they are self-evidently absurd. But here we know that the merely analytical lets us down. Brook found that the only way to *understand* these scenes was to *play* them, when somehow they made perfect sense: "the illogical breaks through our everyday understanding to make us open our eyes more widely."[19] A similar principle seems to run behind Jesus' parables and indeed through the New Testament narrative as a whole. When people used to tell George Macleod about "coincidences" he used to reply, "If you think that's a coincidence you must lead a very dull life!" There is something about the surprising fullness of everyday life to which theatre points us.

Sixthly, according to Brook, the art of direction is recognizing that there is a right time for everything: a time for waiting, a time for silence, a time for pushing, a time for repletion, a time for freedom, a time for discipline. Love is supremely inventive and it is God's inventiveness together with God's patience that constitutes God's true infinity. There is no almighty tyrant but there is divine director, in among the actors, endlessly resourceful in creativity, full of humor, compassion, and himself the truth at the heart of "holy theatre." Brook observes how Antoine Artaud railed against the sterility of theatre before the war, "describing from his imagination and intuition another theatre—a Holy Theatre in which the blazing center speaks through those forms closest to it. A theatre working like the plague, by intoxication, by infection, by analogy, by magic; a theatre in which the play, the event itself, stands in the place of the text itself."[20] Here is the rapprochement between theatre and the Platonic idea of attraction, according to which the ultimate force in the universe is the attraction of beauty or, according to John, the love shown on the cross. As such, we might also suggest that Christian mission properly understood works only by "intoxication, by infection, by magic." This is, of course, a different sense of magic than that which Ivan Karamazov castigates. That is magic as hocus pocus, which Brook tells us he was attracted to as a young man, going to introduce himself to Alistair Crowley. But the magic

19. Ibid., 101.
20. Ibid., 55.

Artaud has in mind is the magic of *The Tempest*: the magic of imagination, vision, love, creativity, and forgiveness. Liturgy and mission should
have this magic; mission understood as crusade, and liturgy as a dull,
repetitive performance is deadly theatre in every sense of the word.

Lastly, Brook gives an importance to the notion of limits. The purpose of exercises in rehearsal is to increase resistance by limiting alternatives and then to use this resistance in the struggle for true expression.[21]
In the rehearsals for *A Midsummer's Night's Dream*, Brook insisted that
each actor find their own way to say their lines, but he did so with rigor.
For Brook the director is not a puppet master; does not "let be," but on
the other hand he or she increases resistance to limiting attributes and
uses this resistance in the struggle for true expression.[22] This suggests
that the limits involved in creation may be the most positive vehicle for
both divine and human creativity. So providence works through the
acceptance of limits, and to understand that is to accept limits as a gift.
Providence in that sense is opposed to Prometheanism.

Brook talks not only about holy theatre but also about rough theatre, the theatre improvised from the back of a cart or in an upstairs
room, the theatre where the audience joins in and answers back. Creation
and human history are both the holy and the rough theatre of God, for
ultimately rough and holy theatre cannot be separated. The world and its
history, Rahner writes,

> are the terrible and sublime liturgy, breathing of death and sac-
> rifice, which God celebrates and causes to be celebrated in and
> through human history in its freedom, this being something
> which he in turn sustains in grace by his sovereign disposition.
> In the entire length and breadth of this immense history of
> birth and death, complete superficiality and folly, inadequacy
> and hatred (all of which "crucify") on the one hand, and silent
> submission, responsibility even to death in dying and in joyful-
> ness, in attaining the heights and plumbing the depths, on the
> other, the liturgy of the world is present. . . . [This liturgy] must
> be interpreted, "reflected upon" in its ultimate depths in the cel-
> ebration of that which we are accustomed to call liturgy in the
> most usual sense.[23]

21. Ibid., 56–57.

22. Ibid., 56.

23. Rahner, "Considerations on the Active Role of the Person in the Sacramental
Event," 169.

And also, I think Brook would say, in theatre.

There are moments, says Brook, when a performance becomes a total experience, when the divisions between the deadly, rough, and holy theatre become nonsense. "At these rare moments, the theatre of joy, of catharsis, of celebration, the theatre of exploration, the theatre of shared meaning, the living theatre are one." But then he goes on: "The moment is gone and it cannot be recaptured slavishly by imitation—the deadly creeps back and the search begins again."[24] This is a parable of both the Christian life and the life of the church, which is always, as Alan Ecclestone has said, a matter of having the courage to begin again.[25] Is it not clear that the work of the Holy Spirit is resistance to deadly theatre, again signified parabolically by what happens again and again to the church's liturgy? But "deadly theatre" is part and parcel of life: the routines into which relationships get trapped, the sanctification of traditions within cultures, and time-honored norms in law and politics all can be forms of deadliness. Life only exists where the search begins again, and this is as true for God as for the creature. Jesus offers "life in all its fullness" (John 10:10) because the possibilities of exploration within the divine reality— which is love—are literally infinite. There is no end to the possibilities of exploration within God. To think of God in terms of the theatre director, therefore, is to think of one who evokes talents, skills, and capabilities the creature (the actor) did not know it had. It gives God a supremely active and creative role in leading creation while being alongside it, but it does not destroy the autonomy of the creature. It is creative without being manipulative. Of course, it is the very nature of analogy to be partial and limited. It points, but does not explain. With those caveats in mind we can recall that Brook said the director's role is like God. But perhaps the reverse is true, and we can think of God in terms of Brookian direction, or what I take to be not so very different, in terms of the actor-playwright in Shakespeare's theatre.

Bibliography

Baelz, Peter Richard. *Prayer and Providence: A Background Study*. London: SCM, 1968.

Brook, Peter. *The Empty Space*. Harmondsworth, UK: Penguin 1972.

———. *There Are No Secrets*. London: Methuen 1993.

24. Brook, *Empty Space*, 151.
25. Ecclestone, *Yes to God*, 7.

Buber, Martin. *I and Thou*. Translated by Walter Kaufmann. Edinburgh: T. & T. Clark, 1970.

Collier, Jeremy. *Mr. Collier's dissuasive from the play-house; in a letter to a person of quality, occasion'd by the late calamity of the tempest*. London: Richard Sare, 1703.

Ecclestone, Alan. *Yes to God*. London: Darton, Longman and Todd, 1975.

Fiddes, Paul. *The Creative Suffering of God*. Oxford: Oxford University Press, 1988.

Gorringe, Timothy. *God's Theatre: A Theology of Providence*. London: SCM, 1991.

Jourdain, Sylvester. "Discovery of the Bermudas." In *The Tempest*, edited by Frank Kermode, 141. London: Methuen, 1964.

Rahner, Karl. "Considerations on the Active Role of the Person in the Sacramental Event." In *Theological Investigations*, translated by David Bourke, 14:161–84. London: Dartman, Longman and Todd, 1976.

Schama, Simon. *The Embarrassment of Riches: Interpretation of Dutch Culture in the Golden Age*. London: HarperCollins, 1987.

Selbourne, David. *The Making of Midsummer Night's Dream*. London: Methuen 1982.

Strachey, William. "A True Reportory of the Wracke and Redemption of Sir Thomas Gates, Knight." In *The Tempest*, edited by Frank Kermode, 135–40. London: Methuen, 1964.

Talbot, William. *A Sermon preach'd before the Lords spiritual and Temporal in Parliament assembled*. London: Printed by W. S. for T. Bennet, 1704.

5

In Praise of Empty Churches

SHANNON CRAIGO-SNELL

EMPTY CHURCHES ARE MAKING a lot of Christians nervous.[1] Church membership is stagnating or declining in many places, and more and more people are describing themselves as having no religious affiliation. For people involved in church ministry or theological education, the specter of an empty church portends a grim future. However, there is a kind of emptiness that is vital to church. This emptiness comes into view when we begin to think of church not as an institution or even a community, but rather as a performance. I understand church as a disciplined performance of relationship with God in Jesus Christ, mediated by Scripture, in the hope of the Holy Spirit. This is a long and dense description, but in this essay I focus on the notion of church as performance. This is, of course, a particular play on the analogies between theatre and church that have been part of Christian traditions for centuries. However, instead of using metaphors between church and theatre to assign roles and match players, I use the basic analogy as an invitation into conversation with unexpected dialogue partners. In particular, I bring together the field of performance studies, theologian Karl Barth, and theatre director Peter Brook. The resulting conversation highlights emptiness—of a particular sort—as a practice of hope in the Spirit, vital to performing church.

---

1. Portions of this essay appear in *The Empty Church: Theatre, Theology, and Bodily Hope.*

88

Performance

Performance studies is an eclectic field that incorporates work in several disciplines, including anthropology, sociology, linguistics, ritual studies, and theatre studies. Scholars from these various backgrounds debate and discuss exactly what performance is and how it ought to be studied. While that sounds quite chaotic, it is also productive, and I glean from this discussion three basic contours of performance.[2]

First, a performance is an *event* that takes place in a specific time, location, and community. Because it is an event instead of a static entity, interpreting and analyzing a performance requires paying attention to its context. The context is both a producer and a part of the performance. Performances are not permanent, but rather temporal, transitory, and somewhat fleeting.[3]

Second, a performance is an *interaction*. It is deeply relational. There are many relations at play in any given performance. One of these is between the performer and the audience. The audience may be a group of theatergoers in red-upholstered seats, a few coworkers one is trying to impress, or even one's own self. Another relation at work in performance is between the performance, the performer, and the larger culture that surrounds them. A performance is both a manifestation of, and a response to, the culture in which it is produced.[4]

A third element of performance is *doubleness*. An action that is performed is "placed in mental comparison with a potential, an ideal or a remembered original model of that action."[5] An actor performing a role attempts to embody a character deeply imagined but not identical to himself; an athlete tries to live into a better version of herself by attaining a personal record; and a young woman, newly married, steps into the role of daughter-in-law by cleaning the apartment before her in-laws visit. In each case, there is a model for the action performed. Marvin Carlson refers to this as "the peculiar doubling that comes with consciousness

2. I have written more extensively elsewhere about contested definitions of performance and my focus on these three contours. See Craigo-Snell, "Theology as Performance."

3. See Schechner, *Performance Studies*, 1, 24.

4. See Carlson, *Performance*, 13.

5. Ibid., 5. Here Carlson is summarizing a point made by Richard Baumann in his entry for "Performance" in the *International Encyclopedia of Communication*.

and with the elusive other that performance is not but which it constantly struggles in vain to embody."[6]

In colloquial terms, performance often means doing something for show or pretending to be something (or someone) you are not. Yet in performance theory, doubleness does not necessarily suggest pretense in this way. Often doubleness points to a quality of our most mundane behaviors, as it highlights the ways in which our patterns of daily living consist of repeating bits of behavior that we have seen before, done before, or been taught. A performance has doubleness in that it is made up of elements we have already performed or learned from someone else. Theorist Richard Schechner calls this "restored behavior."[7] He writes, "the everydayness of everyday life is precisely its familiarity, its being built from known bits of behavior rearranged and shaped in order to suit specific circumstances."[8]

The idea of doubleness is not about pretence in another, related way. The concept of performance does not necessarily support a static view of identity in which there is a clear, prior self that then pretends to be something different than it naturally or originally is. Indeed, the idea of performance is often used to indicate the ways in which how someone performs in the world constitutes her identity on a profoundly deep level.[9]

This broad stroke description of performance—an interactive event of restored behavior—might lead to a sense that everything is a performance. If everything *is* a performance, then clearly the term "performance" loses descriptive value. However, the growing use of "performance" in academic circles is not about defining things as much as it is about focusing questions. The determination of what *is* a performance is made according to cultural standards.[10] In the West we agree that a

6. Carlson, *Performance*, 5. Emphasis his.

7. Schechner writes, "restored behavior is 'out there,' separate from 'me.' To put it in more personal terms, restored behavior is 'me behaving as if I were someone else,' or 'as I am told to do,' or 'as I have learned.' Even if I feel myself wholly to be myself, acting independently, only a little investigating reveals that the units of behavior that comprise 'me' were not invented by 'me.'" Richard Schechner, *Performance Studies*, 28.

8. Ibid., 23.

9. See Carlson, *Performance*, 24, 44–45. See also the work of Jacques Derrida and Judith Butler. Butler's work, especially "Performative Acts and Gender Constitution" and *Gender Trouble*, has contributed significantly to the analysis of "performativity." The concept of performativity is often used within contemporary discussions of the social construction of the self. For a brief overview, see the "Introduction" by Madison and Hamera.

10. See Schechner, *Performance Studies*, 30.

production of Macbeth *is* a performance. What the field of performance studies invites us to do is to interpret or analyze a much broader spectrum of events *as* performance.[11] This simply means analyzing them in a particular way. It encourages attention to the things I have just mentioned in my description of performance—to event, interaction, and doubleness; to the relationship with culture and the formation of identity.

It is not difficult to view church as performance in this way. It is easy to point to event and interaction in church, and doubleness as well. We are not what we are called to be. Actual churches are communities of fallen people, performing badly in a broken world. Across centuries and continents, Christian churches have perpetrated enormous harm. Christian communities have visions of what church should be, visions that vary but carry common themes of faith, hope, love, hospitality, and service. We fall far short of these visions. It would be inaccurate to describe church simply as a place of welcome and care, a community of faith and hope. At the same time, it would be theologically inaccurate to define church simply by giving an exact description of all church activities. The vision of what church ought to be is part of its identity, constitutive of church in a very real way. There is doubleness between what we are called to be and what we concretely enact, and a clear view of this doubleness is key to understanding who we are.

Let me return to the description of church with which I began. Church is the disciplined performance of relationship with Jesus Christ, mediated by Scripture, in hope of the Holy Spirit. Just because it is possible to see church as performance in this more technical sense does not mean it is a good idea. In this next section, I present a significant challenge to this view from within the traditions of Christian theology by focusing on the work of Karl Barth.

Karl Barth

There is ample reason to believe Barth would have serious reservations about my proposal. Beginning with the second edition of his commentary on Romans, Barth was consistently critical of the tendency of liberal Protestant theology to start with and to focus upon the human. I have

11. See ibid., 30, 32. Schechner also notes that in a contemporary society of webcams and reality television, performative understandings of gender and sexuality, and increasing technological mediation of everyday life, the boundaries between what *is* and *is not* performance are often blurry. Ibid., 42.

clearly started with the human in describing church as a performance of relationship with Jesus Christ. Barth says a human starting point reverses the proper order of theology by making God a predicate of our knowledge or experience. At best, we create a false god amenable to our own self-understanding. At worst, we have no norm by which to reject divine pretensions, whether in ourselves or in others. Either way, we are not addressing the reality of the God of Jesus Christ, God who is subject and not object, God who is "wholly other" than human beings.

Barth connects beginning with humanity and natural theology as promoted by liberal Protestantism. He contends that many theologians, such as Friedrich Schleiermacher and Emil Brunner, falsely imagine that there is a natural point of contact between God and humanity. Such a point would allow humans to know something of God on our own steam, or at the very least would enable us to discriminate among various revelatory sources. This is a form of arrogance that breeds idolatry and denies the "infinite qualitative distinction" between God and humanity.[12] In other words, it nearly guarantees that we will invent gods to support our own ideas and comforts, rather than being confronted by the God of Jesus Christ who overwhelms and masters us.

Barth offers a challenge to my ecclesiology regarding both method and content. My inquiry begins with the activity of humans, engages in dialogue with other disciplines (performance and theatre studies), and argues that human activity is theologically significant and constitutive of church. Given the scope of disagreement, it seems wise to look more closely at the rationale behind Barth's position. Perhaps there is a word of caution here that should be heeded.

Commentary on Romans

Barth's commentary on Paul's letter to the Romans was written for readers familiar with war. He says, "When I first wrote it . . . it required only a little imagination for me to hear the sound of the guns booming away in the north."[13] In this context, Barth compares the life of Jesus Christ with "the crater made at the percussion point of an exploding shell, the void

---

12. Barth, *Epistle to the Romans*, 10.
13. Ibid., v.

by which the point on the line of intersection makes itself known in the concrete world of history."[14]

Barth's emphasis on Jesus goes hand in hand with his rejection of natural theology. His definition of the gospel undercuts many traditional ways of speaking about the church in service of God or the world. He offers, instead, a disturbing vision of the community living in the aftermath of an explosion.

> [T]he activity of the community is related to the Gospel only in so far as it is no more than a crater formed by the explosion of a shell and seeks to be no more than a void in which the Gospel reveals itself. The people of Christ, His community, know that no sacred word or work or thing exists in its own right: they know only those words and works and things which by their negation are sign-posts to the Holy One. If anything Christian(!) be unrelated to the Gospel, it is a human by-product, a dangerous religious survival, a regrettable misunderstanding. For in this case content would be substituted for a void, convex for concave, positive for negative, and the characteristic marks of Christianity would be possession and self-sufficiency rather than deprivation and hope.[15]

Church must remain empty in response to the grace of God and in recognition that grace comes from God alone and not from human efforts. Both divine revelation and human faith are gifts of God. Barth focuses on the activity of God to such a degree that obedient human activity is rendered in negative terms. Being faithful includes the readiness "to accept the void" and "tarry in negation."[16] He writes, "Depth of feeling, strength of conviction, advance in perception and in moral behavior, are no more than . . . unimportant signs of the occurrence of faith. And moreover . . . they are not positive factors, but . . . stages in the work of clearance by which room is made in this world for that which is beyond it."[17]

When human efforts to know God are rated more highly, there emerges what Barth terms "the criminal arrogance of religion."[18] Whenever we presume to possess knowledge of God, whenever we assume that

14. Ibid., 29.
15. Ibid., 36.
16. Ibid., 42.
17. Ibid., 40.
18. Ibid., 37.

God needs something from us, or whenever we assign to God the most exalted place within our human-centered framework, we are creating a "No-God."[19] This is not the God of Jesus Christ, the God whose explosive grace undoes our human possibilities. When we view ourselves in such near proximity to God, our worship becomes a form of self-adulation. Barth writes, "Secretly we are ourselves the masters in this relationship. . . . And so, when we set God upon the throne of the world, we mean by God ourselves. In 'believing' on Him, we justify, enjoy, and adore ourselves."[20]

Barth rails against all the ways in which churches substitute a visible God of their own creation (a no-god) for the incomprehensible, invisible God of Jesus Christ. He writes: "The invisibility of God seems to us less tolerable than the questionable visibility of what we like to call 'God.'"[21] Church communities are set up for this structurally, for they attempt to make God visible and comprehensible, "attempt to humanize the divine."[22] This always fails. Either the failure is straightforward or it appears successful by partaking of idolatry, trading a visible no-god for the invisible God of Jesus Christ.

When it fails honestly, Barth claims, religion is the highest human possibility. "Religion compels us to the perception that God is not to be found in religion."[23] This is not an excuse to abandon religion and to sleep in on Sundays, for religion is not a consumer good to be chosen or rejected in aisle seven. He states, "Religion is not a thing to be desired or extolled: it is a misfortune which takes fatal hold upon some men, and is by them passed on to others."[24]

This low evaluation of religion and church in Barth's text is an important element of his rejection of natural theology as well as an admonition of triumphalist views of church. Pleasant pictures of the role of churches go hand in hand with optimism about human efforts to reach God. Barth critiques them both. In doing so, he outlines a vital role for religion—as religion acknowledges its own failure, it rejects natural theology and triumphalism. While Barth repeatedly emphasizes that God is the only one who can cross the immeasurable distance between God and

19. Ibid., 44.
20. Ibid.
21. Ibid., 47.
22. Ibid., 332.
23. Ibid., 242.
24. Ibid., 258.

humanity, there are indications that we can play some part in this clearance, even if it is only to recognize that we cannot reach God on our own. Barth says that the church is constituted by the Word of God, for which we must wait. He relies, again, on wartime imagery to describe its power.

> The Word is nigh unto us. Wherever we cast our eye, the dynamite is prepared and ready to explode. But if there is no explosion, or if something less final takes place, can we not take just the smallest risk which is, in fact the greatest? Are we always to prefer a thousand other days to one day in the outer courts of the Lord? Shall we never permit our hands to be empty, that we may grasp what only empty hands can grasp?[25]

There is a positive note about emptiness here, an affirmation of its value. Declaring the futility of human action in accessing God on nearly every page, Barth still affirms that emptiness, and our awareness of it, can play a role as we await the Word of God.

Church Dogmatics

Barth's later writing on church, scattered throughout *Church Dogmatics*, yet remarkably consistent, moves from an apophatic to a kataphatic tone.[26] Most notably, his mature ecclesiology is profoundly Christocentric. The community is the body of Christ, not because of its own character or of its own accord, but rather due to the "awakening power" of the Holy Spirit, which continually "refound[s]" the church.[27] The refounding and awakening that constitutes the community as the body of Christ is an "event."[28] The event that is church is the act of the Holy Spirit; the acting subject of church is God.[29] Of course, there are many ways in which the human participants are "the obvious subjects" of the activities of church. Yet what constitutes church as church—that is, as the body of Christ—is the event of the Holy Spirit awakening people to faith, the event of the Holy Spirit gathering the community.[30]

25. Ibid., 380–81.

26. Buckley, "Christian Community, Baptism, and Lord's Supper," 200.

27. Barth, *Church Dogmatics*, IV/1, 661, 647.

28. Ibid., 652.

29. See ibid., 694. Here, Barth discusses specifically that God is the subject who gives church its holiness.

30. "To be awakened to faith and to be added to the community are one and the same thing." Ibid., 688.

It might be tempting, given Barth's emphasis on church as event, to think that he is offering a performative view of church in which God is the performer. The church would be the interactive event in which the Holy Spirit awakens the community to become the Body of Christ. But it won't work to think of God as performing in Barth's theology, if "performance" is understood in a technical, rather than metaphorical, sense. There is event, there is interaction, but there is no doubleness in God's act.[31]

God is not repeating an act God has learned from someone else or has been taught by society. God's behavior is not restored. God is not trying to meet an ideal or attempting to fulfill a social role.[32] Barth would surely reject the idea that God strives in vain to embody something. God fully embodies Godself, magnificently succeeding in God's salvific act of love in Jesus Christ! That the God who acts to create, redeem, and consummate is triune does not mean that doubleness is a characteristic of these acts.[33]

Barth's rendering of church as event and his emphasis on God's act provide a strong temptation to performance language, but ultimately such language does not fit his ecclesiology. God acts, but does not perform. We perform, but our performance is not constitutive of church.[34]

Barth offers not a model of performative ecclesiology but some valuable insights and important cautions. The insights include a strong realism regarding God as "other" than humanity and regarding human sinfulness.

God reveals Godself to humanity. Given the magnificence and mystery of God, such revelation does not become knowledge that humanity

31. Barth's own work implies a metaphorical sense of performance by referring to the "drama of Jesus Christ." See *CD* III/1, 387.

32. Jesus surely performed by engaging in everyday restored behaviors. He performed the social roles of son, carpenter, teacher, and so forth. However, the concept of performance does not apply to the first or third persons of the Trinity, or to the Godhead. One could perhaps argue that Barth subsumes all activity of God into the "act" of Jesus (drawing on texts such as *CD* 111/4, 441) in such a way that it could be seen as performance, but I think this does harm to his doctrine of the Trinity in order to make Barth's theology fit a technical description of performance that did not exist when he wrote.

33. Fodor and Hauerwas attempt to use the Trinity as a way to conceptualize God's acts as performance. However, this does not fit within an analytical understanding of performance that includes doubleness.

34. Joseph L. Mangina explores the dynamic interplay between human and divine agency. See Mangina, "The Stranger as Sacrament," 339.

possesses. Often, we would prefer a smaller god, more amenable to our own agendas and less likely to spark transformation, more comprehensible and therefore less frightening. One danger of religion is to begin worshiping a no-god of our own creation, who sanctifies our own views and strivings, who becomes visible at our command. Barth guards against such no-god, a vigilant gatekeeper against human pretensions. He demands emptiness in which God's revelation can be both perceived and hoped-for. In Barth's wartime imagery, this emptiness is a result of God's explosive revelation. There is a valuing of emptiness here and suggestions that the Christian life in community might at least point to its own emptiness in a work of clearance. Yet given his larger theological framework and commitments, Barth cannot develop this. He cannot articulate the ways in which emptiness is a discipline that humans can practice.

Peter Brook

To learn about the discipline of emptiness, I turn to British theatre director Peter Brook, particularly his first book, a theatre classic entitled *The Empty Space*.[35] This slim volume is a typology of theatre, yet it can also be read as an unintentional, but no less brilliant, typology of church.

Holy Theatre

The first type of theatre that Brook describes is Holy Theatre, which is "The Theatre of the Invisible-Made-Visible." To communicate what he means by this, Brook offers an assortment of images and stories, from which he then draws a few markers for identifying theatre that is Holy. The first image is that of the conductor of an orchestra.

> We hear that trumpets destroyed the walls of Jericho, we recognize that a magical thing called music can come from men in white ties and tails, blowing, waving, thumping and scraping away. Despite the absurd means that produce it, through the concrete in music we recognize the abstract, we understand that ordinary men and their clumsy instruments are transformed by an art of possession. We may make a personality cult of the

---

[35] This text has been a resource for several ethicists and theologians. See Gorringe, *God's Theatre*; Vanhoozer, *The Drama of Doctrine*; Hart and Guthrie, eds., *Faithful Performances*. I have written about Brook in Craigo-Snell and Monroe, *Living Christianity*.

> conductor, but we are aware that he is not really making the mu-
> sic, it is making him—if he is relaxed, open and attuned, then
> the invisible will take possession of him; through him, it will
> reach us.[36]

Brook takes it as a given that his readers will know what he means, that this invisible will be familiar. He states, "many audiences all over the world will answer positively from their own experience that they have seen the face of the invisible through an experience on the stage that transcended their experience in life."[37] This assumption—that we will recognize what he is talking about—is vital to Brook's argument in *The Empty Space*. He does not provide a philosophical argument for why theatre is important or what vital role it plays. Neither does he provide sociological or anthropological accounts of the role of theatre in particular cultures. Instead, Brook gives a theological rendering of theatre based on the assumption that his readers will recognize what he is talking about based on their own past experience.

Brook states that the invisible is always in the visible. However, it cannot be seen "automatically," but only under "certain conditions." Holy theatre, then, "not only presents the invisible but also offers conditions that make its perception possible."[38] Thus Brook offers a picture of Holy Theatre that looks something like this: there is a reality deeper than what we commonly apprehend in daily life. Sometimes this invisible is made visible in theatre. When this happens, it is not the achievement of the players involved, for it happens by a sort of possession. At the same time, the work of the company and the audience is vital, as it contributes to the conditions in which the invisible—which is always in the visible—can actually be perceived.

Deadly Theatre

This picture of Holy Theatre, however, is not Brook's ideal of what theatre ought to be. Indeed, he is very clear that attempting to create a purely holy theatre does not work. When we aim solely for the holy, we quickly become concerned with the gravity of our own work and the importance of our own traditions. This easily devolves into what Brook calls the Deadly

36. Brook, *The Empty Space*, 42.
37. Ibid.
38. Ibid., 56.

Theatre. Imagine a professional production of one of Shakespeare's plays. The actors are in period costume, the sets are elaborate, and the diction is elevated. Couples in fancy dress arrive in time to see their colleagues and, perhaps more importantly, be seen by them as well. The audience knows what Shakespeare is supposed to look like. To the extent that the production fulfills their expectations, they are bored; to the extent that it varies from their expectations, they are disappointed.[39] This is Deadly Theatre.

This movement from an ideal of Holy Theatre to a reality of Deadly Theatre can often be seen in productions of Shakespeare.[40] Yet Shakespeare's writing also provides a clue for Brook regarding how to avoid this movement. He writes that Shakespeare's "aim continually is holy, metaphysical, yet he never makes the mistake of staying too long on the highest plane. He knew how hard it is for us to keep company with the absolute—so he continually bumps us down to earth. . . . We have to accept that we can never see all of the invisible. So after straining towards it, we have to face defeat, drop down to earth, then start up again."[41]

Rough Theatre

Bumping back down to earth is the work of Rough Theatre. This is theatre of dirt and profanity, popular theatre that happens in a barroom or an attic, theatre created on the cheap and enjoyed by the locals. According to Brook, "it is most of all dirt that gives the roughness its edge; filth and vulgarity are natural, obscenity is joyous: with these the spectacle takes on its socially liberating role, for by nature the popular theatre is anti-authoritarian, anti-traditional, anti-pomp, anti-pretense."[42] The energy of Rough Theatre is the energy of liberation, both the liberation of laughter and political liberation.[43] It is the "energy that produces rebellion and opposition."[44] It is powered by "the wish to change society."[45]

In many ways the Holy and the Rough are truly antagonistic to one another. "If the holy makes a world in which a prayer is more real than a belch, in the rough theatre, it is the other way round. The belching then,

---

39. Ibid., 10–11, 22.
40. "The Deadly Theatre takes easily to Shakespeare." Ibid., 10.
41. Ibid., 62.
42. Ibid., 68.
43. Ibid., 69, 85.
44. Ibid., 70.
45. Ibid.

is real and prayer would be considered comic."[46] While Holy Theatre "deals with the invisible," Rough Theatre "deals with men's actions."[47] Rough Theatre also has its temptations to excess: "The defiant popular theatre man can be so down-to-earth that he forbids his material to fly. He can even deny flight as a possibility, or the heavens as a suitable place to wander."[48]

Brook's ideal is a theatre that brings Rough and Holy together. This is shown by his repeated remarks that Shakespeare—who is Brook's admitted model[49]—combined Rough and Holy in illuminating juxtaposition. Brook examines Shakespeare's mingling of Rough and Holy in *Measure for Measure*, signaled clearly by the use of prose and verse, respectively. "If we follow the movement in *Measure for Measure* between the Rough and the Holy we will discover a play about justice, mercy, honesty, forgiveness, virtue, virginity, sex and death: kaleidoscopically one section of the play mirrors the other, it is in accepting the prism as a whole that its meanings emerge."[50]

While Brook's desire for a theatre both Rough and Holy is apparent in his elevation of Shakespeare's technique, he does not fully articulate why these two antagonistic elements should be held together. However, there are some indications to follow, particularly in his discussions of Brecht and Beckett. He writes of Beckett's tragic imagery:

> There are two ways of speaking about the human condition: there is the process of inspiration—by which all the positive elements of life can be revealed, and there is the process of honest vision—by which the artist bears witness to whatever it is that he has seen. The first process depends on revelation; it can't be brought about by holy wishes. The second one depends on honesty, and it mustn't be clouded over by holy wishes.[51]

Brook's ideal theatre includes both inspiration from the Holy and honest accounting of the Rough. Humanity looks different in holy light, and acceptable social arrangements suddenly become less acceptable. Holiness demands new honesty about roughness.

46. Ibid., 71.
47. Ibid., 70.
48. Ibid.
49. Ibid., 95.
50. Ibid., 88, 89.
51. Ibid., 58.

Empty Space

If we accept the ideal of a Holy/Rough Theatre, how do we go about it? What is needed? The opening lines of *The Empty Space* set the stage for this question: "I can take any empty space and call it a bare stage. A man walks across this empty space whilst someone else is watching him, and this is all that is needed for an act of theatre to be engaged."[52] All that is needed is an empty stage, but it turns out an empty stage is rather hard to come by. The rest of the book is, in a sense, an extended essay about how to keep the stage empty, during which it becomes clear that Brook is referring to a particular, metaphorical type of emptiness. Recall the conductor in Brook's anecdote about Holy Theatre. "[I]f he is relaxed, open and attuned, then the invisible will take possession of him."[53] Effort on the part of the players cannot force the invisible to become visible. That is a moment of inspiration. However, the work of the theatre company is still vital. The conductor must be "relaxed, open and attuned." The musicians must be highly skilled, the players must know their lines and staging, the audience must be amenable to the possibility of holiness. This is all part of the emptiness needed for theatre, emptiness that is part of the conditions that make the perception of invisible-made-visible possible. Of course, even the relaxation of the conductor could be "God-sent" or "god-given," but this small element of emptiness can also be "brought about by work."[54]

Brook identifies the ways in which theatre gets filled up even before the play begins with such things as audience expectations. Perhaps we come to the theatre expecting high culture and the experience of something "nobler-than-life":[55] red velvet, elaborate costumes, and perfect enunciation. Perhaps we come to the theatre sure that holiness does not exist anymore, that there is no deeper reality, that any glimpse of magic must be a trick of the light.

Something else that clutters the stage is tradition. Theatre companies have patterns of how they do things, how they were taught, and long-standing conceptions of what good theatre ought to be. Those traditions can fill up the theatre, with everyone so invested in abiding by tradition that tradition itself takes center stage. Another form of theatrical clutter

52. Ibid., 9.
53. Ibid., 42.
54. Ibid., 105, 109.
55. Ibid., 10.

is repetition. A stage can be filled with the effort to repeat yesterday's performance, or with the dead weight of rote memorization. These three things—expectation, tradition, and repetition—fill the stage and prevent the emptiness that Brook desires.

Yet theatre itself requires each of these. If the audience truly had no expectations, they might enter the theater and sit on the stage, jump up and join the fight scene, or at the very least answer rhetorical questions. Expectations about what theatre is and what our roles are within it are necessary. Likewise, tradition is what allows theatre to grow and develop, to be something more than "hey kids, let's put on a show!" Tradition grants depth and richness to theatre, pushing us beyond the childish impulse to strut our stuff. Finally, repetition is a basic building block of theatre; it is necessary for remembering lines, rehearsing scenes, and re-enacting events on stage. In Brook's analysis, therefore, some of the basic structural elements of theatre can also prevent emptiness, cluttering the stage. They are necessary and cannot simply be pitched. Yet they must not be allowed to become clutter. That fine line marks the difficult work of keeping the stage empty.

Immediate Theatre

Brook offers no manual or handbook for emptiness; to do so would be a contradiction. Setting things in stone or believing we know how theatre ought to be done is a source of Deadly Theatre, antithetical to the emptiness Brook desires.[56] Instead, he offers an ad hoc, autobiographical collection of approaches and techniques to be used as a starting point. He calls this Immediate Theatre. It is not the ultimate goal of theatre, but a description of some of the ways Brook attempted to create the emptiness needed for theatre that is both Holy and Rough.

In response to the Deadly tendencies of expectation, tradition, and repetition, Brook suggests more, not less. Theatre needs to undertake the work of teaching audiences to expect more from theatre than a night out in fancy dress. We must learn to expect the invisible to become visible in surprising and new ways. Brook is wary and critical of tradition, for its normative connection to the past is a natural ally of the Deadly. However, he writes with admiration of Noh actors who communicate meaning from

---

56. "The Deadly Theatre approaches the classics from the viewpoint that somewhere, someone has found out and defined how the play should be done." Ibid., 14.

generation to generation,[57] and he intimates that even the normative role of tradition can be central in the search for an empty stage. Brook writes that a company called The Living Theatre,

> exemplary in so many ways, has still not yet come to grips with its own essential dilemma. Searching for holiness without tradition, without source, it is compelled to turn to many traditions, many sources—yoga, Zen, psychoanalysis, books, hearsay, discovery, inspiration—a rich but dangerous eclecticism. For the method that leads to what they are seeking cannot be an additive one. To subtract, to strip away can only be effected in the light of some constant.[58]

Tradition can be the constant that allows for experimentation and prevents open expectations from devolving into spiritual tourism. In a certain way, more repetition is also needed to increase the range of possibilities open to a performer. Brook writes that actor Lawrence Olivier "repeat[ed] lines of dialogue to himself again and again until he condition[ed] his tongue muscles to a point of absolute obedience—and so gain[ed] total freedom."[59] Olivier no longer had to think about remembering the lines, and therefore he could think about their meaning again in new and changing ways. To prevent expectation, tradition, and repetition from turning Deadly, however, we need help. We require assistance. For Brook, the audience renders this assistance, helping to keep meaning ever present and not relegated to the past.

Through all of this, it is clear that emptiness is a discipline for Brook. It is hard work, and it is not sufficient. It ultimately cannot generate the Holy/Rough theatre he desires. Nonetheless, the discipline of emptiness still matters. All the rehearsal and repetition, creativity and tradition, expectation and experimentation can help to create the conditions in which we might perceive the invisible-made-visible, present in and among the dirt of our human lives.

Holy Church

Although Barth and Brook are radically different authors, there are echoes and resonances throughout their work. Both men have a sense

57. Ibid., 12. Cf. 103.

58. Ibid., 63.

59. Ibid., 138.

of something beyond humanity and human culture that reveals itself. Barth identifies this in Jesus Christ, in Scripture, and in church. For Barth, the event of church is when the Spirit awakens human awareness to God's reconciling and redeeming work in Jesus Christ. When the Spirit awakens faith in this way, church becomes the body of Christ. Brook is speaking in an entirely different genre, about a different form of event. Yet he claims that in Holy Theatre, the invisible becomes visible under conditions in which it is possible to perceive it. There are a number of similarities between Barth and Brook here, including, I believe, a strong realism regarding the source of inspiration. Holiness in theatre depends upon something more than human culture and personal excellence.[60]

At the same time, Brook goes much farther than Barth regarding the role of human beings. Recall Brook's initial metaphor of the conductor. It presupposes long hours of training and rehearsal on the part of the musicians. The conductor himself must be "open, attuned, and relaxed." And then Brook uses the language of possession; something beyond the conductor steps in. Finally, he notes that the conductor "is not really making the music, it is making him."[61] Brook is neither a theologian nor a philosopher, and his words are appropriately more evocative than rigorously precise. Yet he points to something subtle and important. The effort of the conductor does not make the invisible visible, but neither is it beside the point. The hours of rehearsal form the conductor so he could be taken up in such a way. His discipline readies him for possible possession.

While Brook's use of the term "possession" serves to emphasize the otherness of the Invisible he spies in Holy Theatre, it might be more precise to speak of partnership, for the agency and efforts of the conductor are not lost but empowered in this event. The conductor does something for which he has trained extensively. The Invisible makes far more of the conductor's actions than they could be on their own. What the conductor does and what the Invisible does are not in conflict or competition. The formation of the conductor readies him for partnership in this particular way. The Invisible does not possess a gymnast and use her to conduct an orchestra, nor possess a conductor to do flips across the stage. It is the whole-personed discipline of the conductor that allows him to be open to

---

60. Brook does not explain precisely what he means by the Invisible in *The Empty Space*. Max Harris attempts to identify what Brook could mean in a way that would be compatible with Barth's theology in the book, *Theater and Incarnation*. Harris, *Theater and Incarnation*, 123.

61. Ibid., 42.

the Invisible in this way. His intellect grasps the subtleties of the score and the strengths of the musicians, his emotions access the spirit of the music, his will spurs on the discipline in desire for a Holy performance, and his body has developed the particular musculature necessary for artful wielding of the baton. All of this does not guarantee a Holy performance, but rather serves as an invitation to the Invisible. It is the cultivation of an environment amenable to possession, or better still, an openness to partnership. This is true not just of the conductor, but of every member of the orchestra.

I would also push Brook's choice of words regarding the phrase "invisible-made-visible." This sight-oriented, cognitive language emphasizes that we perceive what the Invisible is up to in our midst. Yet Brook's example of the conductor implies much more. The conductor not only perceives what the Invisible is doing, he gets to be in on the action. Beyond this one metaphor, such participation is implied throughout Brook's text. He is writing for members of the theatre company who work in hope of the visible becoming visible precisely in their performances. The company Brook envisions is not hoping just to see the invisible; they are hoping to participate in its visibility. They have a role to play.

Brook does not attempt to pin down exactly how Holy Theatre is possible or define its contours. Instead, he relies on his readers' memory of past experiences. In Christianity, we have a long collective memory of interactions with God. Creation itself is funded by God's desire to be in relationship with humanity. The relationship that God intends is not one in which our role as human beings is simply to perceive, see, or know what God is up to. Such a cognitive account would suggest that God's relationship with us does not involve our whole selves—body, intellect, emotions, and will. Yet Scripture overflows with collective memories of ways in which God has invited us not only to see what God is doing, but to be in on the action. We are invited to participate and to partner with God. Of course, it is a wildly unequal partnership, yet it still involves the activity of both parties. They are not inversely proportional. It is not the case that the more God is active, the less we are. Instead, the more God is active, the more empowered our own activity becomes.

Our church performance is, I contend, embodied hope for partnership with God. In church, we learn the stories and language of Scripture, the repertoire of sacraments, and the affections of faith. This is a whole-personed discipline that forms us as possible partners, as fit players who can be taken up and allowed in on the drama of God's activity in the world.

Deadly Church

Humanity is in the odd position of both longing for relationship with God and being scared to death of it. Our impulse is to control it. We want it to come at our beck and call, and when it arrives we want it to condone our actions and bless our aspirations. Thus our various performances in both church and theatre often invoke the Holy in ways that simultaneously secure us against it.

NB

It takes little effort to picture Deadly Church. It is one where the congregation gathers without any real expectation that they might interact with God during worship. Some people come in expectation of fulfilling a societal norm or in the hope of providing a good ethical grounding for their children. Several come to church to pray, but none expect an answer. Meanwhile, the minister has prepared the service carefully. The theme of the psalm is echoed in the hymns, the bulletin includes a detailed mission statement, and the responsive readings are clearly marked for seamless congregational participation. The sermon begins with a humorous story, ends on an uplifting note, and includes a bit of sober wisdom in the middle. The entire service is well crafted and there is very little silence. It is almost as if we are saying to God, "Don't worry, we have this covered. Your presence is not needed today." Demonstrating just the right mix of repentance and commitment, we leave little room for God to reveal Godself. In fact, such revelation might disrupt our lives far more than we desire, so we secretly prefer a worship service that is boring and predictable.

This illustration assumes a mainline Protestant worship service, but in fact Deadliness can encroach in any church tradition, high or low. Intricate liturgies, rich in tradition and repetition, can seem a particularly easy target. Yet Deadliness can dwell just as comfortably in low-church settings. Spontaneous responses can also be scripted, in the sense that there are cultural norms and expected roles to follow. Even the nearly-literal empty space of a Quaker meeting involves a great deal of expectation, tradition, and repetition. These can become static over time, cherished forms of protection from the unruly revelation of God.[62] Any church can become Deadly.

62. See Selleck, *Gentle Invaders*, 180. Selleck notes that during Reconstruction,

Barth and Brook agree that aiming strictly for the Holy produces Deadliness and that the Holy and the Deadly are antagonistic to one another. Barth leaves it at that. The Holy Church is what God does, when the Spirit awakens, and the Deadly theatre is what we do, creating our visible no-god. Brook, however, takes a different path, introducing the Rough Theatre.

Rough Church

It is the makeshift, profane, rebellious, and dirty theatre that provides Brook a way forward from the Holy/Deadly impasse. In strictly theatrical terms, Rough Theatre gives Brook an anti-authoritarian element to fight against the conservative and traditionalist forms of theatre that try so hard to be Holy. Within Christian theology, we can take Brook's insights further still. There is an incarnational sensibility to Brook's writing. The Holy and the Rough are intertwined because God chooses to be in relation with humanity. This is clearest in the incarnation. In Jesus Christ, fully human and fully divine, God gets dirty. God is present—bodily present—in and to the roughest realities of human life. God belches and bleeds, intimately experiences the harms we can do to one another. The Holy is present in the Rough.[63] In the sending of the Spirit at Pentecost, the founding of church, God invites us into partnership, to be in on the action by performing with the Spirit in consonance with Jesus Christ. The Rough is called to be with the Holy.

In church as in theatre, the Rough upsets the Deadliness that results from aiming entirely at the Holy. An honest account of human reality, including our own brokenness, guards against Deadly tendencies. Repetition is disrupted by pain expressed. A clear view of the all-too-human realities of tradition—crafted in conflict and susceptible to selfish manipulation—strikes against our pretension. Finally, expectation can be honed by real need. In Rough Church we bring our whole selves—in all our dirt and brokenness, desperation, and confusion—into performance of relationship with Jesus Christ. We do not leave parts of ourselves behind, such as those bodies of which we are not too fond, or those thoughts

---

some white Quakers were reluctant to welcome African-American Christians into worship, for fear that they would sing.

63. Max Harris identifies Brook's ideal of Holy/Rough theatre as incarnational, arguing that its roots lie "in the Christian drama of the Middle Ages." Harris, *Theater and Incarnation*, 101.

that we know should be more generous, or those shameful memories and scary emotions. The nerve to do this, to bring our whole selves into the performance, derives from the historical memory of God's persistent intent to be in relationship with humanity, from God's Holy/Rough incarnation in Jesus Christ and from the Spirit's willingness to partner with us.

From this perspective, the lack of the Rough in Barth's ecclesiology seems problematic. Barth's appreciation of the finitude and sinfulness of humanity leads him to a relentless focus on Jesus Christ. Yet can one do justice to Jesus without an appreciation of dirt? Avenues of incarnational thinking are cut off by Barth's refusal to value the Rough. Paradoxically, Barth's Holy-only attempts at a profoundly christological view of church prevents his ecclesiology from fully appreciating the incarnation, which is so vital to Barth in other moments within his theology.[64]

Within the framework of Barth's theology, assigning any significant import to the work of the people—liturgy—risks imagining that God is at humanity's disposal, to be summoned by our effort and at our whim. Max Harris, a theologian deeply influenced by Barth and Brook, articulates the difficulty. Having argued that theatre and incarnation are deeply connected, Harris writes, "it is one thing to suggest that God chose a 'theatrical' mode of self-revelation and quite another to propose that human art may conjure up an incarnation in the theater."[65] Harris addresses this worry by specifying that the "invisible" that is made visible in theatre is not God. "Theater may well bear a likeness to that sensory mode of self-revelation attested in the classic texts of the Christian faith. But, at least for the Christian, the theater will not move beyond likeness to rival, claiming to emulate the Incarnation by summoning spirit or universal will to inhabit its material signs."[66] Theatre may bring hidden insights of the human predicament into "greater clarity," but it cannot make God visible through its own efforts.[67] Harris's text does not address ecclesiology directly, but I infer there are similar limitations upon church. As I understand Harris, it is not the case that theatre deals with humanity and church deals with God, such that theatre cannot conjure an incarnation

64. Harris's *Theater and Incarnation* emphasizes the incarnation within a theological framework deeply influenced by Barth and a theatrical framework deeply influenced by Brook. However, he does not specifically take up Barth's ecclesiology, which defines church as the activity of God in the Holy Spirit, so he does not address the degree to which church is, or ought to be, incarnational.

65. Harris, *Theater and Incarnation*, 112.

66. Ibid., 128.

67. Ibid.

but church can. Rather, incarnation does not come about through human efforts, but only through divine grace.

Empty Church

Learning from Barth without being entirely beholden to him, I suggest a different approach to this quandary. Human performance cannot conjure incarnation nor summon God. Perhaps, however, we can foster emptiness. God does not require our efforts in order to become visible. Yet our discipline of emptiness might contribute to the conditions in which the invisible-made-visible could be perceived. We might unclutter the stage a bit, as a work of clearance and an act of invocation. Our performance of church does not force the Spirit's hand. Rather, as a community, we remember that God has partnered with us in the past and hope in God's Spirit for the present and future. This hope is an embodied performance, a discipline that prepares us for partnership with God.

Immediate Church

Brook's words on repetition, tradition, and expectation can be useful in our efforts to foster emptiness in church. In Immediate Church, we would study Scripture repeatedly, so often that the muscles of our tongues remember words of faithfulness. Through repeated study, we could know the Bible so well that it goes past being familiar and seems always new. Likewise, we would learn Christian traditions well and regard them not as precious heirlooms from the past but useful instruments for the present, intended for everyday use. Finally, in Immediate Church we would come to church services expecting to get caught up in the reality of God. I do not mean the kind of commodified expectation that pervades our culture: "I expect to get what I paid for!" In this attitude, any mediocre sermon or lengthy service could generate disappointment and frustration. Rather, I mean openness to the surprising newness of God. The God of Jesus Christ is constantly thwarting our sensibilities about where God ought to be. Look for Jesus in the palace and he's in the manger; look for him with the poor and he's with the tax collectors; look for him with the Pharisees and he's with the prostitutes. God is surprising. *Reliably* so. It is possible to cultivate an expectation of having our expectations undone.

The theological term for this is humility, and it is a virtue that requires practice.

The part of Brook's discussion of Immediate Theatre that does not correlate easily with church is about assistance. For Brook, the assistance that enables theatre to move away from the Deadly and towards his Holy/ Rough ideal comes from the audience. However, insights from performance theory suggest that the audience for any particular performance can be fluid and multiple.[68] Insights from influential theatre directors such as Augusto Boal suggest that overcoming strict divisions between actors and audience is key to theatre that is liberating rather than oppressive.[69] And close theological reading of liturgical practices suggests that Christians move between and among various roles during any given worship service and throughout the liturgical year. We are all actors, audience, and stage crew. We are each repentant sinner, beloved child, believer, doubter, recipient of grace, and minister to others. For all these reasons, I resist the impulse to assign roles.

While I do not follow Brook in looking to the audience, I do follow Brook's recognition that assistance is needed.[70] The real question is, "whence cometh our help"? The assistance needed for church comes from the Holy Spirit. The Holy Spirit empowers and enables our performance from its earliest beginnings. It is the action of the Spirit into which we hope to get caught up. Our performance is disciplined in order to help us become sensitive to the workings of the Spirit in a whole-personed way, to get in on the action and participate in what the Spirit is doing in the world.

The Holy Spirit is always and everywhere present and active in the world. Most of the time, we do not notice. The discipline of church performance does not guarantee that we will be aware of the Spirit, but it is a performance of hope that we might be. Our performance is embodied hope *for* the Spirit and *in* the Spirit—hope that our whole-personed selves will be taken up in the movement of the Spirit of God.

For over a hundred years, scholars and clergy have been lamenting the decline of mainline Protestant churches in Europe and America. The church is empty, they declare. With Brook and Barth in mind, I can't help thinking: "I hope so. We are trying!" In our best moments we know

68. See, for example, Goffman, *The Presentation of Self in Everyday Life*.

69. See Boal, *Theatre of the Oppressed*.

70. At one point Brook writes, "there is a similar relation between actor and audience to the one between priest and worshipper." Brook, *The Empty Space*, 60.

that our task is not to keep the pews full but to keep the altar empty. Our performance of hope should be a performance of emptiness, expecting the Spirit. It should be concave, not convex. It should make a void visible. Living in hope means cultivating a discipline of emptiness that awaits and appreciates the movement of the Spirit of God. This requires a self-critical stance within the church, such that the performance is always provisional, ongoing, and open to further inspiration. It requires trusting that the Spirit will come again.

The Gospel of Mark tells us that "When the Sabbath was over, Mary Magdalene, Mary the mother of James, and Salome brought spices" and went to where the crucified Jesus had been laid in a tomb (Mark 16:1–2). The body was not there. Instead, the grace of God appeared in an unexpected way, with a young man telling them that Jesus had been raised. The women who went to the tomb that morning handed down that emptiness to us. They told their tale in such a way that we hear they were too afraid to speak it, and when they did no one believed them. They handed over to us not the record of their eloquent success, but the emptiness in which the grace of God appeared. The church of the risen Christ began in an empty tomb, and at our best, we are still there. Like the women who saw the empty tomb, we come with expectations, repeating actions called for by our traditions. These expectations, traditions, and repetitions are what bring us to the moment when all three are overwhelmed and upended by the surprising newness of God.

Bibliography

Barth, Karl. *Church Dogmatics*, IV/1. Translated by G. W. Bromiley. Edited by G. W. Bromiley and T. F. Torrance. Edinburgh: T. & T. Clark, 1956.

———. *Epistle to the Romans*. Translated by Edwyn C. Hoskyns. London: Oxford University Press, 1933.

Baumann, Richard. "Performance." In *International Encyclopedia of Communication*, edited by Erik Barnouw et al., 262–66. New York: Oxford University Press, 1989.

Boal, Augusto. *Theatre of the Oppressed*. Translated by Charles A. and Maria Odilia Leal McBride. New York: Theatre Communications Group, 1979.

Brook, Peter. *The Empty Space*. New York: Atheneum, 1987.

Buckley, James J. "Christian Community, Baptism, and Lord's Supper." In *The Cambridge Companion to Karl Barth*, edited by John Webster, 195–211. New York: Cambridge University Press, 2000.

Butler, Judith. *Gender Trouble: Feminism and the Subversion of Identity*. New York: Routledge, 1990.

————. "Performative Acts and Gender Constitution: An Essay in Phenomenology and Feminist Theory." In *Performing Feminisms: Feminist Critical Theory and Theater*, edited by Sue-Ellen Case, 270–82. Baltimore: Johns Hopkins University Press, 1990.

Carlson, Marvin. *Performance: A Critical Introduction*. 2nd ed. New York: Routledge, 2004.

Craigo-Snell, Shannon. "Theology as Performance." *The Ecumenist* 16.4 (2008) 6–10.

Craigo-Snell, Shannon, and Shawnthea Monroe. *Living Christianity: A Pastoral Theology for Today*. Minneapolis: Fortress, 2009.

Fodor, James, and Stanley Hauerwas. "Performing Faith: The Peaceable Rhetoric of God's Church." In *Rhetorical Invention and Religious Inquiry: New Perspectives*, edited by Walter Jost and Wendy Olmsted, 381–414. New Haven: Yale University Press, 2000.

Goffman, Erving. *Presentation of Self in Everyday Life*. New York: Anchor, 1959.

Gorringe, T. J. *God's Theater: A Theology of Providence*. Valley Forge, PA: Trinity, 1991.

Harris, Max. *Theater and Incarnation*. Grand Rapids: Eerdmans, 1990.

Hart, Trevor A., and Steven R. Guthrie, eds. *Faithful Performances: Enacting Christian Tradition*. Burlington, VT: Ashgate, 2007.

Hauerwas, Stanley. *With the Grain of the Universe: The Church's Witness and Natural Theology*. Grand Rapids: Brazos, 2001.

Madison, D. Soyini, and Judith Hamera. "Introduction." In *The Sage Handbook of Performance Studies*, edited by D. Soyini Madison and Judith Hamera, xiii–xx. Thousand Oaks, CA: Sage, 2006.

Mangina, Joseph L. "The Stranger as Sacrament: Karl Barth and the Ethics of Ecclesial Practice." *International Journal of Systematic Theology* 1.3 (1999) 322–39.

Schechner, Richard. *Performance Studies: An Introduction*. New York: Routledge, 2002.

Selleck, Linda B. *Gentle Invaders: Quaker Women Educators and Racial Issues during the Civil War and Reconstruction*. Richmond, IN: Friends United Press, 1995.

Smith, Ted A. *The New Measures: A Theological History of Democratic Practice*. Cambridge: Cambridge University Press, 2007.

Vanhoozer, Kevin J. *The Drama of Doctrine: A Canonical-Linguist Approach to Christian Theology*. Louisville: Westminster John Knox, 2005.

6

Play It Again

Kierkegaard's Repetition *as Philosophy and Drama*

GEORGE PATTISON

Introduction: Theatre in Kierkegaard's Life and Work

IN THIS CHAPTER, I will look at Kierkegaard's relation to theatre, leading to a discussion of the role of theatre in his *Repetition*, together with
some reflections on my own experience of adapting this work for theatrical performance. As we shall see, theatre is by no means marginal
to Kierkegaard's authorship, but is a constant presence in it, as it was in
his life.

In a short, posthumously published book entitled *The Point of View
for My Work as an Author*, Kierkegaard attempted to explain the rationale
behind what many readers experienced as the mystifying complexity of
his pseudonymous authorship. In this "report to history," as he called it,
he said that when he wrote *Either/Or* (the first of his great pseudonymous works), he was already in the monastery.[1] Among other things,
this meant that he had renounced the prospect of marriage, as well as
the pursuit of an academic or church career. But his was an odd kind of

1. See Kierkegaard, *The Point of View*, 31 (*Søren Kierkegaards Skrifter*, 16:20).

monastery. For, as he tells us, he made sure every day to make short visits to the theater during the period of writing *Either/Or*, arriving late in the evening and staying for five to ten minutes, just long enough to be seen. He explains that the aim of this ruse was to ensure the pseudonymity of the 800-page book he was working on, so that his contemporaries would be unable to imagine that a "lounger" who had time to go to the theater every evening could possible be the author of what one reviewer would describe as a "monster" of a book.[2]

We would completely misinterpret this cunning plan, however, to think that Kierkegaard merely used the theater as a ploy in one of his social maneuvers: quite the contrary. Theatre was a central and abiding passion of his life; *Either/Or* itself contains two big essays dedicated to theatrical works: Mozart's *Don Giovanni* and A. E. Scribe's comedy *The First Love*. The former is a general discussion of the work without reference to any particular performance, but the latter gives us a very direct glimpse of the theatrical world with which Kierkegaard was familiar, since it is a review of a performance at Copenhagen's Theater Royal. It is not entirely accidental that it was a play by Scribe that caught Kierkegaard's attention, since his work was regularly presented in Copenhagen, in translations by J. L. Heiberg, himself an eminent dramatist, critic, and promoter of Hegelianism, who was campaigning to redirect the Danish theatre away from German traditions and toward French ones. Although largely forgotten today, Scribe was the most successful of all contemporary French dramatists, said to have earned more in one year than all the rest of the dramatists in France (and I believe Europe) put together. Heiberg not only translated this work and many others, but his wife Johane Luise, the diva of the Danish stage, starred in it. Later, she would be the dedicatee of Kierkegaard's most renowned piece of writing about the theatre, "The Crisis and a Crisis in the Life of an Actress," which in a manner entirely favorable to the actress, compared her début performance as Juliet in her teenage years to a reprise of the same role in her thirties. *The First Love* also starred Joachim Ludvig Phister, another actor who was a particular favorite of Kierkegaard, and to whom he would also dedicate an extensive article, which would not be published, however, during Kierkegaard's lifetime.[3] *Either/Or* also included a long essay on Antigone, which despite not referring explicitly to any actual produc-

---

2. Ibid., 58–62 (*Søren Kierkegaards Skrifter*, 16:39–44).

3. Both these articles will be discussed further below.

tion, seems most likely to have been inspired by the production staged in Berlin at the time of Kierkegaard's arrival in that city in October 1841.[4] The production had music by Mendelssohn and was widely reported in the press, while the translation was the one used by Kierkegaard in the notes that gradually developed into his own essay on *Antigone*.

The theatrical pieces included in *Either/Or* and the essays devoted to Mme Heiberg (to whom Ibsen also dedicated a rather dismally bad poem) and Herr Phister by no means exhausted Kierkegaard's writing on theatre. In 1845 he published a short critical note on an 1845 production of *Don Giovanni* at the Theater Royal. His short, novella-like work *Repetition* included an extensive discussion of a Berlin production of the farce *The Talisman*, by the Austrian Johan Nestroy, prefaced by some general remarks about the nature of theatrical art. A further "literary" pseudonymous work, *Stages on Life's Way*, ends with a set of reflections about tragedy and comedy in the context of modernity. These reflections relate back to issues broached in the essay on *Antigone* and include a discussion of whether *Hamlet* can be considered a Christian drama.[5]

Although these works comprise Kierkegaard's major writings about theatre (and, if collected, would add up to a reasonably sized book), they by no means exhaust the manifold references to dramatic works and theatrical performances that appear throughout his works, sometimes in the form of merely fugitive remarks, sometimes in fuller allusions or brief discussions. Sophocles, Shakespeare, Molière, Lessing, and Goethe are amongst the "greats" who figure in his writings, alongside Danes such as Holberg, Adam Øhlenschlæger, Henrik Hertz, J. L. Heiberg, and now forgotten personalities such as Scribe and Vernoy de St. Georges. These theatrical allusions also include references to ballet—specifically to the great reformer of the Danish ballet, August Bournonville—as well as to opera, notably *Don Giovanni*.

4. At the same time, Kierkegaard was reading Hegel's *Aesthetics* in which Antigone plays a significant role. In his *Philosophy of History*, Hegel goes so far as to call her "the heavenly Antigone, the most glorious figure that has ever appeared on earth . . ."(Hegel, *Geschichte der Philosophie* I in *Werke*, 18:509). As George Steiner has demonstrated, Hegel was by no means alone in his estimation of both play and heroine. On the contrary, he seems here to express a view widely held from the late-eighteenth through to the middle of the twentieth century (Steiner, *Antigones*, 1–19). Steiner discusses Hegel's view of *Antigone* on pages 19–42 and Kierkegaard's on pages 51–66. See also my *Kierkegaard and the Quest for Unambiguous Life*, 142–70.

5. Ziolkowski, *The Literary Kierkegaard*, 183–212. The "Shakespearean" theme in this "Letter to the Reader" also includes thoughts about Romeo, Juliet, and the modern (i.e., post-Romantic) devaluation of romantic love.

The fact that Kierkegaard himself was lampooned in at least one contemporary play and, in that sense at least, also *appeared* on stage, merely underlines the extent to which dramatic literature, theatre, and those associated with it were utterly integral to his life. As we have seen, he would also venture to the theater when abroad, but there is little doubt that the Danish Royal Theater was at the center of his theatrical experience. He knew and was known to several of the main writers, directors, and actors, however slightly. Not least significant of these was J. L. Heiberg himself who, though only named Director of the Theater in 1849 (relatively late in Kierkegaard's career), had been an active and influential figure in its complex artistic politics since at least 1831 and was married to the diva of the Danish stage, Johane Luise Heiberg, applauded by Kierkegaard, Ibsen, and many others. Given Heiberg's preference for French over German theatre, it is perhaps paradoxical that he was also one of those chiefly responsible for introducing Hegelianism to Denmark and attempting to popularize it, even writing a "speculative comedy" performed on the King's birthday in 1838. In this role, he would become the object of some of Kierkegaard's most bitter philosophical barbs, although as the tribute to Mme Heiberg was in part intended to show, Kierkegaard had also greatly admired him as a man of the theatre and the witty and stylish author of a string of successful musical comedies or vaudevilles.[6]

Theatre in 1830s and 1840s Copenhagen

But what was the theatrical life in Copenhagen, in which Kierkegaard took such a keen interest?[7] It was certainly very different from the theatrical life of London then or any contemporary European capital today. The Theater Royal was the only proper theater in the city, although there

6. Heiberg's role in the culture of the Golden Age has been foregrounded in a number of translations and edited collections by Jon Stewart. See, e.g., Stewart (ed.), *Johan Ludvig Heiberg;* Stewart (ed.), *The Heibergs and the Theater.* The present author takes a more negative view of Kierkegaard's early attitude to Heiberg's idea of the application of the dramatist's "controlled irony" to existential and theological questions. See my *Kierkegaard, Religion and the Nineteenth-Century Crisis,* 96–115. In addition to Johane Luise, Heiberg's mother, Thomasine Gyllembourg, was a significant literary figure whose work was much praised by Kierkegaard, and he was also responsible for publishing *Clara Raphael,* generally regarded as one of the first feminist novels in Scandinavia. On these women see Katalin Nun, *Women of the Danish Golden Age.*

7. The following discussion of life at the Theater Royal is dependent on Peter Tudvad's definitive treatment in his *Kierkegaards København,* 214–91.

was also a range of entertainments such as Pierrot and Pantomime shows, put on at venues such as the Tivoli Gardens (from 1843), or at open-air events such as the summertime "Deer Park" fair. But if Copenhagen had only one main theater, the range of performances on offer more than compensated for this numerical limitation. In the 1831 season, from September 1 to May 31, the Theater Royal performed approximately one hundred different productions, from across the whole range of theatrical genres, including works by "the greats" and contemporary light entertainment. Performances were held on Sundays and public holidays, with rest days only on Christmas Day, Easter Day, and Whit Sunday. A Copenhagen resident such as Kierkegaard, therefore, could soon build up a rather rich stock of theatrical experiences.

When did Kierkegaard's own theater-going begin? Children under ten were not legally allowed in the theater until 1849, and the Danish writer Peter Tudvad consequently guesses that since Kierkegaard was born in 1813 and came from a rather conservative family, it is unlikely that he attended the theater until the late 1820s, possibly having seen Mme Heiberg's reputation-making performance as Juliet in the 1828–29 season when he was sixteen years old. The first clear reference to a contemporary performance is from September 1834—among the earliest of all Kierkegaard's journal notes—again to a comedy by Scribe, *Fra Diavolo*. Starting from here, Tudvad has trawled through the Theater Royal's calendar right through to 1855, the year of Kierkegaard's death, noting the manifold possible allusions found in Kierkegaard's published and unpublished works to any productions he might have seen.

In a small way, I suggest, this does change our view of Kierkegaard's own creative writing process. To take one example among many: a journal note from November 1834 (among the very earliest of Kierkegaard's surviving notes) contains references to yet another play by Scribe, to Goethe's *Egmont*, and a comedy by Holberg. One might have assumed that these references would have been based on reading—he was also a prolific reader—but, since Tudvad shows these plays were performed earlier in the year, Kierkegaard is as likely as not drawing on his memories of live theatrical performances.[8] Kierkegaard, in other words, is not

8. The note (Kierkegaard, *Journals and Papers*, vol. 1: entry 118; *Søren Kierkegaards Skrifter*, vol. 27, 102:1) also, interestingly, has a distinct theological import. Kierkegaard writes: "Doubtless the most sublime tragedy consists in being misunderstood. For this reason the life of Christ is the supreme tragedy, misunderstood as he was by the people, the Pharisees, the disciples, in short, by everybody, and this in spite of the most exalted ideas which he wished to communicate. This is why Job's life is

just sitting in the library reading books: he is out there in the theater and writing not just on what he has read but *on what he has seen*.

Kierkegaard's Theory of Theatre

That theatre is something *seen* is a key to Kierkegaard's understanding of theatre and of the limits of theatrical art in relation to religious existence. Danish, like German, speaks of theatergoers as "spectators" rather than the English "audience" (i.e., listeners) and the "stage" itself is referred to as a "show-place." But whether or not Kierkegaard is being guided by the built-in metaphors of his native language, his theory of theatrical art is explicitly developed in relation to what was then a standard distinction between plastic and musical forms of art. The former portray their subject matter in terms of non-temporal spatial representation whereas the latter are arts of time. This distinction is already found in Lessing, with whose *Hamburg Dramaturgy* Kierkegaard was familiar, and became normative for the aesthetic theories of German Idealism, including Hegel's. This was not conceived as a simple divide, however, with architecture, sculpture, and painting on the one hand and music, poetry, and other forms of literature on the other. According to Hegel and others, poetry too—including dramatic poetry—had a visual dimension. In fact, the whole sphere of the aesthetic, as Hegel conceives it, is bounded by the definition of art as representing the idea in a form commensurate with sensuous immediacy. What art—any art, including poetry—gives us is an image, an imaginative representation of the idea that is, in itself, beyond image and representation. It is the pure productive freedom of the divine, comprising both the divine freedom of God and the finite freedom of the human being. This definition suggests both the power, necessity, and limits of the aesthetic. In fact, Hegel's *Lectures on Aesthetics* both begin and end by drawing attention to these limits and arguing that, in an important sense, the age of art is past. Namely, while art will continue to be made and enjoyed and will serve the education of both the human race and its individual members (in the sense of *Bildung* or "formation" current at the time), it can no longer be regarded as the "highest" interest of humanity, which, for Hegel, is now science or knowledge.

---

tragic; surrounded by misunderstanding friends, by a ridiculing wife, he suffers." This is followed by the illustrative examples taken from Scribe, Goethe, and Holberg. It is also more than a little striking that this kind of "tragedy" is, at many subsequent points in his career, just what Kierkegaard feels he himself had suffered.

Kierkegaard adopts much of this Hegelian approach.[9] He too sees art as presenting the idea in sensuous form. This basic definition, however, bears manifold nuance. Thus, in his eulogy of Mme Heiberg, he argues that the role of Juliet demands more than a pretty young actress who, in her person as well as in her art, shows us a pretty and innocent young girl (even if that is all that many of the public want to see). At the time of her own debut, Mme Heiberg—Miss Pätges as she was then—had herself been a ravishing, nineteen-year-old beauty. But Kierkegaard's question is whether, as an artist, she understands the *idea* of Juliet, the *idea* of female innocence. This question is only answered when, as Kierkegaard puts it, she undergoes the metamorphosis from being a girl to being a mature woman. A successful metamorphosis is one in which it becomes clear that she has indeed grasped the idea and, by virtue of the freedom this gives her, is able to play Juliet just as well in her thirties as she did in her teens. The performance is still a matter of sensuous representation—she *shows* us Juliet—but the sensuousness of the representation is now subordinated to the freedom of the idea.[10]

Nevertheless, as this example also suggests, such sensuous representation is only possible in relation to ideas that are, in and of themselves, appropriate to it. In this respect, Kierkegaard seems, like Hegel, to have believed that he was living in the age of "the end of art," although against Hegel he sees ethics and faith rather than science or knowledge as the highest interest of humanity. As he puts it in *Stages on Life's Way*, "If the age of poetry is past, the task is to seize the religious. Nothing in between will do."[11] Art, the sphere of the aesthetic, takes us so far, but cannot finally give adequate representation to the trials of spiritual life in and through which human beings come to develop the heart of their God-relationship. As opposed to the Hegelians, however, he does not see science, knowledge, or citizenship as adequate to living out all that spiritual life implies. Even religion is problematic, and a further twist in Kierkegaard's "end of art" theme, is that he comes to see public religion as no less "aesthetic" than the world of art and literature. Church itself has become a kind of theatre and the preacher a kind of actor. In the last year of his life he attacked the idea of church establishment in a series of highly satirical articles and pamphlets in which he made just this point,

9. For a full discussion of Kierkegaard's relation to Hegelian aesthetics see my *Kierkegaard: The Aesthetic and the Religious*, 1–62.

10. See Kierkegaard, *Christian Discourses*, 301–26.

11. Kierkegaard, *Stages on Life's Way*, 415 (*Søren Kierkegaards Skrifter*, 6:384).

commenting that the clergy never seem to think that the traditional ban on burying actors in consecrated ground applies to them. Preachers, like poets, have come to see their task in terms of offering pictorial images of spiritual doctrines, and instead of calling their congregations to faith and action they offer them "quiet hours" in which to contemplate the soothing images that their preaching conjures forth.[12] (As an aside, we may note that this was indeed just what contemporary homiletic theory said should be the preacher's task.)

Theatre in *Repetition*

Unlike many religious iconoclasts, however, Kierkegaard does not see the end of art as requiring the burning of books or the closing of theaters. As long as it remains within its proper limits and does not seek to become a substitute religion (as Kierkegaard and many others saw happening in Romanticism), art has a good, proper, and even necessary role in human life. His short, pseudonymous book *Repetition* contains one of the clearest passages in his work regarding this positive evaluation of the continuing role of art, a passage that may justly be called a celebration of theatrical art. The argument is rather straightforward but has significant connections to the entire network of Kierkegaard's major philosophical and theological themes and, in this respect, provides an exceptionally helpful perspective on these themes.

Through the pen of his pseudonym Constantin Constantius, Kierkegaard argues that theatre has a special affinity to the stage of life that we would, perhaps, call adolescence. We have already seen that in Kierkegaard's own lifetime there was some debate as to what was an appropriate age at which to allow young people to start attending the theater. In this context, Kierkegaard's argument seems to favor a liberal approach. Theatre is not only permissible for young people: it is extremely desirable. Why? Because while theatrical representation appeals directly to the sensuousness that is the dominant element of their lives as children, it also gives them, via their sympathetic identification with the *dramatis personae* of the stage, an anticipatory experience of the multiplicity of possible roles that will become open to them as adults. Moreover, precisely because these are merely theatrical representations,

---

12. For a discussion of how this relates to the Danish homiletics of the time see my *Kierkegaard and the Theology of the Nineteenth Century*, 172–79.

they do not fall under the aegis of morality or ethics. For the time of the theatrical performance, there is no moral damage in identifying oneself with the robber chief or even Richard III or Lady Macbeth. These are all possibilities, but the fact that we entertain them as spectators does not mean that we accept or would accept them as actualities. The sphere of the ideal is, as a whole, the sphere of possibility—a point that would be central in Kierkegaard's criticism of Hegelian claims to base knowledge of God on the structure of human ideation. Such knowledge can never give more than possibility. Possibility is crucial. It is the dawn of freedom in the human spirit. But it is not, in this sense, the actuality of spirit. It must be actualized or made real through freedom and decision. But back to the theatre: by trying out the broadest possible multiplicity of roles— and we have seen how many roles the Theater Royal offered its audiences every year—the young person is educated in possibility and, in this way, educated in freedom. As the passage concludes, there comes a time when we must leave the theatre behind, the shadows of the stage flee away, and we are faced with the cold light of everyday, bourgeois reality in which we must learn to be who we are. Yet our lives as citizens and even, perhaps, as religious persons, will be all the more serious the more we realize that our task as adults is, precisely, to be the roles we choose for ourselves. Theatre teaches us just what it means to be in role, but we have then to choose our role and step forth in it onto life's stage.

In *Repetition*, the eulogy of theatre is contextualized in a discussion of the farces performed at Berlin's Königstädter Theater. As the text makes clear, this is not the kind of theatrical experience that theorists of high art usually spend much time discussing. But it is not accidental that just this genre is the focus of our discussion here.

But what is this passage doing in this extraordinary book, that is a bit like a novella and a bit like a work of philosophy? If *Repetition* is "about" anything, it is about time and the relationship between time and eternity. It begins with the question of whether motion is possible. As it soon becomes clear, this implies the further question regarding the meaning of that particular kind of motion that is a human being's existence in time. Does this mean, as Heraclitus suggested, that we are handed over to a chaotic flux of unrepeatable experiences, or is it possible for us to develop a coherent and sustainable identity through time, to develop a self, or in nineteenth-century language, to exist as spirit? Constantin does not attempt to argue the issue philosophically, but sets up a series of experiments. Perhaps the most serious of these—with obvious connections to Kierkegaard's own current life crisis—is whether it is possible for a young man who has broken off his engagement to get back together with his jilted lover. But this primary "repetition" is illustrated more humorously when Constantin takes a trip to Berlin to see if he can relive his past experiences in that city—including the experience of farce at the Königstädter. The significance of farce emerges if, keeping in mind Heraclitus' saying that we cannot step twice into the same stream, we attend to Constantin's account of the effect farce has on him.

> Thus did I lie in my box, discarded like a swimmer's clothing, stretched out beside the stream of laughter and unrestraint and applause that ceaselessly foamed by me. I could see nothing outside the space of the theater, hear nothing but the noise in which I was living, only emerging now and again, seeing Beckmann and laughing myself weary till I once more sank back, exhausted, beside that foaming stream.[13]

Precisely because farce lacks the structure of tragedy and more conventional forms of comedy, it is the purest possible theatrical representation of sheer flux, the pure flow of time itself. Therefore, it is the genre best suited to test the question: is repetition possible?

Here, as in his other experiments, Constantin's attempt ends in failure. The young man doesn't get his fiancée back and he himself is not moved to laughter as he was on the occasion of his last visit to the Königstädter. In his view, this demonstrates that repetition is not possible and that human beings are delivered over to the sheer flux of becoming and thrown towards death, as his twentieth-century reader Martin Heidegger would put it. He ends the first part of the book with a eulogy of the post-horn, which, as he says, is incapable of blowing the same note twice. It should be mentioned that this is not Kierkegaard's own position. Nevertheless, it does serve him to point us to where exactly the issue of faith lies. Are we, in the end, just products of time and no more, or are we creatures who live by virtue of a relation to the Eternal, to God?

Conclusion

Kierkegaard's pseudonymous writings are an attempt to address such questions in ways that shake us out of the too-easy conventions of academic discourse on religion. They include works that, like *Repetition*, are

---

13. Kierkegaard, *Repetition*, 166 (*Søren Kierkegaards Skrifter*, 4:40–41).

novel-like in structure and form, works of satire, and works that frankly are virtually impossible to classify. Yet, interestingly, Kierkegaard never published any dramatic work. He had, as a student, written an Aristophanic satire on the Hegelian fad to which many of his fellow students had succumbed, and his journals contain a number of short dialogues, mostly of a comic or satirical nature.[14] As has been mentioned, one of the most substantial pieces of theatrical writing he wrote was a study of the actor J. L. Phister in the role of Captain Scipio, written in 1848. Captain Scipio serves in the Papal Police and therefore represents the dignity of a uniform that has both political and ecclesiastical elements. Yet his job also involves the very undignified task of looking after the drains, and what gives the character particular comic effect is that he is constantly tipsy, balanced at the very edge of being drunk without ever actually being so. It is his mastery of expressing these comic contradictions that Kierkegaard finds so impressive in Scipio's performance.[15] Yet, if Kierkegaard's writings belie his reputation as "the melancholy Dane" by their fascination with the comic and the many funny passages they contain, even at times using brief dialogue forms, he always stops short of fully dramatized comedy.[16]

Yet I have long been convinced that his own writing was deeply shaped by his experience of theatergoing. Furthermore, in terms of his own aesthetic theories, he is seeking, like the dramatist, to *show* us just what the various possible positions vis-à-vis the decision of faith look like when taken out of theology textbooks and "staged" in life. In a well-known article from the 1920s, Martin Thust compared Kierkegaard's authorship with a puppet theatre in which each pseudonym enacted a very particular and definite role.[17] Whether or not the analogy entirely fits, it does flag up both the appeal and the limits of reading Kierkegaard under the rubric of "theatricality." On the one hand, Kierkegaard insists on showing what the ideas at issue in his works might look like if they are adopted by individual personae and lived out as real human possibilities. On other hand, he simultaneously treats each idea as somehow complete and finished in itself; although his characters and ideas interact

14. On the "cult" of Aristophanes in the early nineteenth century, see Ziolkowski, *The Literary Kierkegaard*, 55–86.

15. See Kierkegaard, *Christian Discourses*, 327–44 (*Søren Kierkegaards Skrifter*, 16:126–43).

16. On Kierkegaard's use of the comic, see Lippitt, *Humour and Irony*.

17. See Thust, "Das Marionettentheater."

or, at least, get juxtaposed, they do not essentially develop through this interaction and their scope is strictly defined from the start.[18] It is this, I think, that Thust is aiming at by talking of a puppet-theatre rather than drama as such.

In 2013, I directed an adaptation of *Repetition* that was performed at John's College, Oxford, on April 25 and 26. If this practical theatrical experience is allowed to be fed back into our reflections on Kierkegaard's own text, it soon became clear during rehearsal that, precisely as *dramatis personae*, figures such as Constantin Constantius and the Young Man of *Repetition* have the potential for development and transformation that a strict application of Kierkegaard's own principles might not allow.[19] That is to say, they have more breadth, depth, and credibility than the surface of the text at first seems to allow. They are less ciphers and more the germs of fully rounded existential characters.[20] Perhaps, being more informed by his own theater-going than he may have known, Kierkegaard's authorship is, despite everything, an essay in a kind of dramatic art.

Bibliography

Hegel, Georg Wilhelm Friedrich. *Philosophie der Geschichte* I. In vol. 18 of *Werke*. Frankfurt am Main: Suhrkamp, 1970.

Herman, Wladimir. *Kierkegaards Sidste Dage*. Publication details unknown. Performed at Bellevue Theatre, Copenhagen, 1982.

Kierkegaard, Søren. *Christian Discourses/The Crisis and a Crisis in the Life of an Actress*. Translated by Howard V. Hong and Edna H. Hong. Princeton: Princeton University Press, 2009.

———. *Fear and Trembling/Repetition*. Translated by Howard V. Hong and Edna H. Hong. Princeton: Princeton University Press, 1983.

———. *Journals and Papers*. 2 vols. Bloomington, IN: Indiana University Press, 1967, 1970.

18. In one early journal entry, for example, he objects to Lenau's Faust committing suicide, an act, he says, which doesn't fit with the essential idea of Faust; namely, that Faust represents doubt but not despair. See Kierkegaard, *Journals and Notebooks*, AA: 38, 44 (*Søren Kierkegaards Skrifter* 17, AA: 38, 44); references are to journal entry not page numbers.

19. Other adaptations of Kierkegaard's works or aspects of his life for the stage include Piper, *The Seducer*; Herman, *Kierkegaards Sidste Dage* (*Kierkegaard's Last Days*); Nagy, *The Seducer's Diary* (in *Hungarian Plays: New Drama from Hungary*); Poole, *All Women and Quite a Few Men are Right*.

20. The same can be said of other personages from the pseudonymous works. See the continuation of the story of Assessor Vilhelm in my *Kierkegaard and the Quest for Unambiguous Life*, 171–93.

———. *The Point of View.* Translated by Howard V. Hong and Edna H. Hong. Princeton: Princeton University Press, 1998.

———. *Søren Kierkegaards Skrifter.* Edited by Niels Jørgen Cappelørn et al. Copenhagen: Gad, 1997–.

———. *Stages on Life's Way.* Translated by Howard V. Hong and Edna H. Hong. Princeton: Princeton University Press, 1988.

Lippitt, John. *Humour and Irony in Kierkegaard's Thought: Climacus and the Comic.* Basingstoke, UK: Macmillan, 2000.

Nagy, Andras. *The Seducer's Diary.* In *Hungarian Plays: New Drama from Hungary.* Edited by László Upor. London: Hern, 1996.

Nun, Katalin. *Women of the Danish Golden Age: Literature, Theater and the Emancipation of Women.* Copenhagen: Museum Tusculanum Press, 2013.

Pattison, George. *Kierkegaard: The Aesthetic and the Religious: From the Magic Theatre to the Crucifixion of the Image.* London: SCM, 1998.

———. *Kierkegaard and the Quest for Unambiguous Life. Between Romanticism and Modernism.* Oxford: Oxford University Press, 2013.

———. *Kierkegaard and the Theology of the Nineteenth Century.* Cambridge: Cambridge University Press, 2013.

———. *Kierkegaard, Religion and the Nineteenth-Century Crisis of Culture.* Cambridge: Cambridge University Press, 2002.

Piper, Myfanwy. *The Seducer.* London: Duckworth, 1958.

Poole, Roger. *All Women and Quite a Few Men Are Right.* Unpublished. Performed at the Netherbow Arts Centre, Edinburgh Festival, 1986.

Steiner, George. *Antigones.* Oxford: Clarendon, 1984.

Stewart, Jon, ed. *The Heibergs and the Theater: Between Vaudeville, Romantic Comedy and National Drama.* Copenhagen: Museum Tusculanum Press, 2012.

———, ed. *Johan Ludvig Heiberg: Philosopher, Littérateur, Dramaturge, and Political Thinker.* Copenhagen: Museum Tusculanum Press, 2008.

Thust, Martin. "Das Marionettentheater Sören Kierkegaards." *Zeitwende* 1 (1925) 18–38.

Tudvad, Peter. *Kierkegaards København.* Copenhagen: Politiken, 2004.

Ziolkowski, Eric. *The Literary Kierkegaard.* Evanston: Northwestern University Press, 2011.

7

The Play of Christian Life

When Wisdom Calls to Wisdom

Jim Fodor

Introduction

THEATRE AND THEOLOGY MEET in play. Just exactly what that means, of course, needs some elaboration and defense. In what follows I wish to substantiate this claim by showing how theatre and theology are analogically related by virtue of play. One important implication of demonstrating the cogency and coherence of this thesis is that it opens up the prospect that theatre and theology, by attending to each other's respective "playful" engagements, are poised perhaps to enter more fully into a mutually illuminating and reciprocally productive dialogue. It is part of my task to sketch out how a potentially fruitful relationship between theatre and theology can be appropriately discerned through a theologically informed, hermeneutical, and aesthetic approach to play. My contention is that at least some forms of theology are intrinsically theatrical and dramatic. Conversely, at least some forms of theatre can be better understood and appreciated when seen as presupposing and drawing upon theological concepts and frameworks.

It hardly bears repeating that the extant literature on theology and theatre is enormous.[1] One way to delimit such a vast undertaking is to concentrate on an area receiving attention in the recent past, namely, the focus on liturgy (understood as a kind of theatre) as a source of theological renewal. This will serve as my point of entry into theological and theatrical conceptions of play.[2]

In *The Spirit of the Liturgy*, Joseph Cardinal Ratzinger (now Pope Emeritus Benedict XVI) regards play as the essence of liturgy. He is not alone in this, nor is he the first to characterize liturgy in this way. In the 1920s, leaders of the Liturgical Movement—of whom Romano Guardini was a key spokesperson[3]—suggested that liturgy be understood in terms of "play." The point of the analogy was that games have their own rules and set up their own worlds, which remain in force from the inception of play until its termination. Moreover, while games and plays are meaningful, they do not have a purpose—which accounts for their liberating, and in some cases therapeutic, power. "Play takes us out of the world of daily goals and their pressures and into a sphere free of purpose and achievement, releasing us for a time from all the burdens of our daily world of work."[4]

There is a further and significant connection between play and childhood. We understand "child's play" as activities that, because they are carefree and unencumbered by the seriousness that marks the adult world, tend to be characterized by delight, ease, grace, and exuberance. As Ratzinger explains,

> Children's play seems in many ways a kind of anticipation of life, a rehearsal for later life, without its burdens and gravity. On this analogy, the liturgy would be a reminder that we are all children, or should be children, in relation to that true life toward which we yearn to go. Liturgy would be a kind of anticipation, a rehearsal, a prelude for the life to come, for eternal life, which St. Augustine describes, by contrast with life in this world, as a fabric woven, no longer of exigency and need, but of the freedom of

1. The range and variety of works in this area is truly daunting. However, two good sources to consult for broad overviews are Balthasar, *Theo-Drama*, vol. 1, and Dox, *The Idea of the Theatre in Latin Christian Thought*.

2. It is important to clarify that my aim is *not* to try to reduce either theatre or theology to a single concept, but rather to show how the analogical uses of "play" illuminate vital aspects of both.

3. Guardini, *The Spirit of the Liturgy*.

4. Ratzinger, *The Spirit of the Liturgy*, 13.

generosity and gift. Seen thus, liturgy would be the rediscovery within us of true childhood, of openness to a greatness still to come, which [even in adult life remains unfulfilled].[5]

In Ratzinger's eyes, the most theologically appropriate name to give to the play of children is hope. For in all its modes, play expresses a most fundamental human and indeed Christian disposition, a particular orientation to life:

> [play] lives in advance the life to come, the only true life, . . . the life of freedom, of intimate union with God, of pure openness. . . . [Play thus effectively] imprint[s] on the seemingly real life of daily existence the mark of future freedom . . . [it breaks open] the walls that confine us, and let[s] the light of heaven shine down upon earth.[6]

Ratzinger suggests three promising analogies between play and liturgy that cry out for theological appropriation. First, play "sets up its own world" according to its own rules and in that sense it is an activity that is, to use a technical expression, "autotelic." It has a *telos* or end internal to its own movement and is thus defined by no other measure than itself. *Play is valued for its own sake.* Second, insofar as the meaning of play is not determined by or directed to any external purpose, it thereby affords a kind of escape or release from our everyday work-world. Engaging in play liberates us from a world otherwise dominated by instrumental forms of rationality. *Play is liberating, therapeutic, and healing.* Third, by virtue of its anticipatory structures and future orientation, play inculcates hope. Hope is, moreover, authenticated and elevated by the distinctive qualities of liturgical play, namely, the play of Wisdom of which Scripture speaks. Indeed, without this crucial sapiential or wisdom dimension, analogies between the ordinary world of play and liturgical play do not finally hold. In short, absent a consideration of the God of Wisdom, play is—from a theological point of view—finally robbed of hope. *Rehearsing life in play and worship fosters hope.*

These insights call for deeper and more extensive theological elaboration. One way the analogical relations between play and theology might be qualified and deepened is through a more thoroughgoing

5. Ibid.

6. Ibid. Unquestionably, a great deal can be gleaned from the theological reflections of Ratzinger and Guardini, but also the work of play theorists within the disciplines of anthropology, psychology and cultural studies: Johan Huizinga, Roger Caillois, Mihaly Csikszentmihalyi, and others.

engagement with the performing arts generally and with theatre in particular. Theatre is especially germane not only because of the long and intimate (one could say "congenital") relation between theatre and the liturgy,[7] drama and religious ritual, but also because the Christian faith as a whole evinces an overarching dramatic form.[8]

In what follows, I propose to explicate the analogies between play and theology, the world of theatre and the world of wisdom-play or liturgy. First, I consider the way in which theatrical performance throws important light on the dynamics of play and playfulness. I argue that actors read plays playfully and the audiences receive plays playfully. Second, because acting and reading are so thoroughly intertwined, there is an important hermeneutical dimension to play and to dramaturgy, one which leads me to the work of Hans-Georg Gadamer. Play is at the heart of Gadamer's philosophical hermeneutics not simply as a universal feature of human culture but more radically as a fundamental ontological structure of human being. Gadamer's work is helpful preparation for and in sympathy with (even if finally insufficient for) a full and properly *theological* account of play. For this I turn, in the third part, to a key Scripture passage in the wisdom literature of the Christian Old Testament—Proverbs 8—and using this as a grounding text, consider several features of this passage that have profound implications for theology and for theatre. In the course of this exposition of the distinctive aspects of wisdom play, I engage David Ford's recent work, *Christian Wisdom*, which I think importantly supplements, but also corrects and qualifies, the insights of Cardinal Ratzinger. I close by drawing out several ways in which the world of theatre and the world of theology offer each other mutually helpful and reciprocally illuminating insights regarding their respective spheres of interest.

7. Accounts of the liturgy as "sacred drama" are so common as to warrant only a brief comment. For a helpful overview of the literature and the state of the scholarship in this area, see Hardison, *Christian Rite and Christian Drama in the Middle Ages*, especially chapter 2, "The Mass as Sacred Drama," 35–79; Cf. Kinghorn, *Medieval Drama* and Harris, *Medieval Theatre in Context*.

8. See the work of Quash, *Theology and the Drama of History* and Vanhoozer, *The Drama of Doctrine*.

Theatrical Play: Audiences and Actors

Audiences

For an Audience is the title Paul Thom gives to a general philosophy of the performing arts. One of his arguments is that all works of art "are made to be viewed, listened to, or read."[9] In other words, they are intended "for an audience." Second, if artworks are to become "objects of aesthetic contemplation and enjoyment," they need to be accessible in specific ways to sense perception.[10] Third, the apprehension and appreciation of an artwork—as with any object or event—always entails an interpretive act, a "seeing as" or "hearing as."

The point is common enough: we register an object in our perceptual field not first as a set of raw sensory data upon which we later impose our interpretation. Rather, we construe meaning concurrently and from the very outset as we holistically apprehend an object or event by our sensory apparatus.[11] Thus audiences are always and inescapably active, contributing to the meaning of the art form not so much as consumers but in a way as coproducers. Whether viewing a play, listening to an orchestra, or reading a piece of literature, the audience exhibits a particular kind of activity that Thom characterizes as play and playfulness. "This playfulness bestows certain freedoms on the beholder, whose attention can 'play back and forth' over the work, dwelling selectively on particular aspects of the work and wandering from one strand in the work to another."[12] Indeed, this "playful beholding" or "playful reading" is not limited to an audience but extends to the actors and performers as well. "This playful reading and re-reading of dramatic, musical, and dance works is done both by those who are *preparing* a performance of such a work and by those who *witness* the performance."[13] On Thom's account, therefore,

9. Thom, *For an Audience*, 191.

10. Ibid., 31.

11. Sensory perception is imbued with meaning from the outset. As Joel Weinsheimer puts it, "we do not hear pure sounds but always a car in the street, a baby crying; we do not see pure colors and shapes but always a face, a knife, a wreath of smoke." Weinsheimer, *Gadamer's Hermeneutics*, 94. Similarly, Gadamer: "mere seeing and mere hearing are dogmatic abstractions." *Truth and Method*, 82.

12. Thom, *For an Audience*, 31.

13. Ibid. As he writes elsewhere in the book, "works for performance . . . are made for playful beholding" (75), and this is because playfulness is an integral feature of the kind of attention that the beholder is supposed to bestow on the work insofar as it

"openness to playful beholding" or "attending playfully" to a work of art is the distinguishing feature of *both* its production *and* its reception.[14]

In sum, Thom's argument is that theatre is constituted by these different layers of attention, thereby enriching the audience's experience aesthetically but also intellectually and emotionally. To witness a play is thus not merely to be a passive spectator, but to perform the activity of "playful beholding." This is perhaps most notable in forms of interactive or participatory theatre in which the audience interacts with the performers by consciously breaking both physically and verbally the "fourth wall" that traditionally separates the performers on stage from the audience. But even in traditional theatrical presentation, an audience's attention is always "playful."[15] It is the variety and openness of this "playful reading" that challenges the view that a work of theatrical art is in itself complete, a finished product or object, which the actors deliver to an audience. On the contrary, a play calls for substantive interpretation on the part of the audience who contribute to its meaning (in ways different from but no less significant than the playwright, the director, and the actors) by means of an integrating act of apprehension that "holds together" the disparate elements configured by the exercise of playful attention.

Actors

Actors are no less part of this "playful attending" than audiences. To be sure, actors contribute in much more overt and direct ways to a play's performance. At first blush this may seem to preclude them from the kind of "playful beholding" that characterizes the audience's role. Indeed,

---

belongs to "the teleology of all [art] works, not just of a privileged subclass of them" (28).

14. Ibid., 186.

15. Thom identifies several types of playful attention "whose possibility is implicit in the very nature of artistic performance" (ibid., 205). First, because performing is a process that unfolds over time, an audience's attention can play between the performers' present actions and recollected past actions or anticipated future ones. Second, because performances normally involve several performers, an audience's attention can play between one performer and another. Third, because a work can receive several performances, an audience's attention may play between an earlier performance and later performance of the same work. Fourth, because the play is for an audience, the audience's attention can play between aspects of the performance and aspects of their own lives. Fifth, because performances are given in performance spaces and such a space has an outside, audience attention can play between what occurs inside the performance space and what has occurred or may occur outside it.

one might expect actors to develop a much more focused kind of attention, a disciplined concentration. However, this turns out not to be the case. Even though their contributions are distinct from the audience's, actors likewise exhibit forms of "playful beholding." They clearly attend to the appearance of their own actions, which is one of the key features of—and reasons for—rehearsing a play before performing it in front of a live audience. "Because of the 'twice-done' nature of their actions, performers can become distanced from these actions."[16] Thom calls this "divided awareness," by which he means the kind of attentiveness actors possess "of both the *content* of what they are doing and its *appearance*." Consequently, "the performers' awareness thus includes a reference to an audience"[17] insofar as actors have a sense—even if only a projected and highly revisable one—of how their performance will appear to an audience. Part of what it means to be an actor, then, is learning to anticipate how audiences will likely respond to the staged actions and to adjust and modify them accordingly. Indeed, trying to develop a sense of how the audience will receive the actors' staged movements and gestures is a large part of rehearsal and performance preparation.[18] Actors help one another by "pointing out how things will look and sound," a role which falls to the director in a special way.

From the actor's or performer's point of view, divided awareness or "aesthetic distancing" correlates with and in some sense mirrors the attention of the audience. If an audience engages in "playful beholding" (the ability to orchestrate and hold together in some coherent fashion multiple forms of attention), then the corollary for actors is to engage in a kind of playful reading.

David Cole, a playwright and a theorist of drama, advances a compelling argument for seeing acting as a form of reading. His argument converges with, but also enhances and augments, Thom's analysis of "playful beholding." Cole contends that "the lost physical of reading" is best appreciated when seen through the lens of theatrical performance. Reading, in other words, is an intrinsic and continuous feature of theatrical play, an ineradicable feature of acting from start to finish, not merely

16. Thom, *For an Audience*, 162.

17. Ibid., 163; emphasis added.

18. For a more detailed and nuanced account, see Richard Schechner's analysis of the staging of a play in terms of a three-phase process: a proto-performance, the performance itself, and an aftermath. Schechner, *Performance Studies*, 191.

a preliminary "phase or aspect of the acting process" that happens when the actor first receives the script and does an initial read-through.[19]

> Acting is a physicalization of . . . reading [insofar as] . . . the act of reading which acting physicalizes was itself originally—had its origins in—a bodily process. In acting, then, what was once physical [in reading but which is now largely suppressed and forgotten] becomes physical once more. *Acting is the recovery of a "lost" physical of reading.*[20]

From the audience's perspective, it may seem like the script should "disappear" when the actors come on stage. It appears that the actors' time with the script has ended, being fully assimilated, internalized, and committed to memory through rehearsal and repeated readings. But to think that reading has ceased altogether for the actors would be a mistake.

> *Insofar as the "disappearance" of the book in performance refers to acting's "going beyond" reading into physicality, performance represents a return to the (original) condition of reading itself. . . . [T]he physical dimension that acting seems to "add" to reading is in fact no addition but, rather, a restitution. Acting restores to reading . . . a "lost" physical dimension that reading has had to forgo in order to become [modern] reading.*[21]

That the physical aspects of reading—its orality, its bodily enactments, its corporality and other performative dimensions—have been largely forgotten or concealed in the modern West is not an argument for its absence. While muted, these bodily aspects are present nonetheless. They persist, albeit in latent and subtle ways.[22]

The person who has been most instrumental in our day in bringing to conscious awareness the way in which reading is "the essence of the acting process" is Constantin Stanislavski. In Stanislavski, Cole believes, one discovers precisely why it is that reading cannot be viewed as "a mere preliminary to acting but as already part of the acting process."[23]

---

19. Cole, *Acting as Reading*, 1.

20. Ibid.

21. Ibid., 18.

22. For an account of the extensive ways that the body is involved in reading, even in modern reading practices, see chapter 3, "The Lost Physical of Reading," in Cole, *Acting as Reading*, especially 31–33.

23. Ibid., 8.

Stanislavksi notes how in rehearsal, in listening to the play being read aloud, the actors are already in motion.

> [T]hey are carried away by the reading. They cannot control the muscles of their faces, which oblige them to grimace or mime in accordance with what is being read. They cannot control their movements, which occur spontaneously. They cannot sit still, they push closer and closer to the person reading the play.[24]

Reading and acting coinhere, then, in a way that is neither exclusively active nor entirely passive. Rather they are correlated in a complex nexus of activity and passivity, self-projection and self-surrender. In other words, both reading and acting exhibit a passive "intake" dimension and an active element of "taking in." For to take in is to receive, incorporate, and *take* in, yet in a way that also does not preclude a kind of surrender to the role, to directorial intent, and to one's own impulses.[25] Reading is present at the origins of acting but it is also present as its eventual goal. "All theatrical performance is the performance of reading."[26]

Paul Thom's reflections on how audiences participate in the construction of the meaning of staged dramas by means of "playful beholding," and David Cole's ruminations on how acting and reading stand in for cognate descriptions of the same bodily rooted, performative processes intersecting both actors and audiences, leads one to contemplate how these two approaches might be transposed into higher levels of philosophical explication and theological appropriation. With regard to philosophical explication, I draw on the work of Hans-Georg Gadamer. With respect to theological appropriation, the recent work of David Ford on "wisdom theology" I find highly suggestive.

24. Stanislavski, *Creating a Role*, 5.

25. This description anticipates Gadamer's account of play (outlined below) insofar as it lays bare "the ontological status of works of art," especially the reproductive or performance arts. For neither actors nor audiences are related to these works as detached or disinterested spectators, but as players who participate in the play in their own way.

26. Cole, *Acting as Reading*, 18. Conceiving theatergoing as reading is primarily the view of semioticians, for whom a theatrical production is a "text," composed of "signs," and therefore requiring to be "read." Two representative semiotic approaches to theatre are Ubersfeld, *Reading Theater* and Alter, *A Sociosemiotic Theory of Theatre*.

Extending the Play: Gadamer and
Philosophical Hermeneutics

One of the most distinguishing features of Gadamer's philosophical hermeneutics is the central role he accords to play.[27] Indeed, play not only serves as the key organizing principle of his magnum opus, *Truth and Method*, but it reappears in his later works, underscoring its ongoing relevance in Gadamer's evolving hermeneutical philosophy.[28] What follows is a brief sketch of Gadamer's understanding of play in order to grasp how his hermeneutical project might consolidate the insights of Paul Thom and David Cole by setting them within a wider framework of a philosophical anthropology and ontology.[29]

A main preoccupation in Gadamer's work has been to challenge the longstanding philosophical prejudice regarding art's relation to truth. The charge—going back to Plato—is that art has nothing to do with truth and that beauty, while the object of human desire, does not lead to genuine knowledge. As a result, the arts have been relegated to mere expressions of personal taste and idiosyncratic preference. Notwithstanding Kant's valiant attempt to give sound epistemological standing to the arts by showing how aesthetic judgments do in fact rest on firm philosophical foundations, the prejudice against the intrinsic filiation of art and truth remains as firmly intact as ever. Ironically, one reason why this prejudice is so hard to dislodge is due to the efforts of Kant himself. For the price Kant paid to establish the epistemological soundness of aesthetic judgment was a thoroughgoing "subjectivization" of aesthetics.[30] The result of Kant's critique of judgment, in other words, is an aesthetics deeply entrenched in human subjectivity (albeit communal subjectivity), which

27. Gadamer gives extensive attention to play in two principal places: *Truth and Method* and *The Relevance of the Beautiful*.

28. I am very much in agreement with Richard Bernstein's contention that play is at the heart of Gadamer's hermeneutical philosophy of dialogue. "As we explore Gadamer's understanding of philosophical hermeneutics, we will see just how central this concept of play is for him; it turns out to be the key or the clue to his understanding of language and dialogue." Similarly: "If we are truly dialogical beings—always in conversation, always in the process of understanding—then the dynamics of the play of understanding underlie and pervade all human activities." See Bernstein, *Beyond Objectivism and Relativism*, 121, 122, 137. The same assumption animates the work of Vilhauer, *Gadamer's Ethics of Play* and "Beyond the 'Fusion of Horizons': Gadamer's Notion of Understanding as 'Play.'"

29. I am indebted to Bernstein's account in much of what follows.

30. See Kant, *The Critique of Judgement*.

thus easily leads down the path to relativism. Gadamer believes it is possible to overcome this "radical subjectivization" of art bequeathed to us by Kant and his followers.

In order to overcome this radical subjectivity in aesthetics and properly establish the philosophical and ontological grounding of works of art, Gadamer discovers in the concept of play an important clue.[31] Indeed, Gadamer contends that play is irreducibly basic: it is "an elementary phenomenon," "a universal structure of human existence."[32] And more specifically—with reference to theatre and the performing arts—play is "the mode of being of the work of art itself."[33] Gadamer rejects the way the concept of play has been construed in recent history, namely, "subjectively" and affectively, as a matter exclusively of human consciousness.

For Gadamer, "Play fulfills its purpose only if the player loses himself in his play,"[34] which is his way of indicating the need to overthrow the hegemony of human subjectivity. Play is key, not the consciousness of the player. Rightly grasping the essence of play thus precludes regarding the player as one who behaves toward play as a subject towards an object.[35] The to-and-fro movement that belongs to play itself—its internal buoyancy, so to speak—is fundamentally a "happening" that includes but at the same time outstrips the subject.[36]

> Play clearly represents an order, in which the to-and-fro motion of play follows of itself. . . . The structure of play absorbs the player into itself, and thus frees him from the burden of taking the initiative, which constitutes the actual strain of existence. This is seen also in the spontaneous tendency to

31. As Gadamer elaborates, "I wish to free this concept [play] of the subjective meaning that it has in Kant and Schiller and that dominates the whole of modern aesthetics and philosophy of man." Gadamer, *Truth and Method*, 101.

32. Gadamer, *Relevance of the Beautiful*, 123, 124. Gadamer argues that "play is so elementary a function of human life that culture is quite inconceivable without this element." Ibid., 22.

33. Gadamer, *Truth and Method*, 101.

34. Ibid., 102.

35. In other words, play "is not to be understood as something a person does." Gadamer, *Truth and Method*, 104.

36. "To say that the game takes over, or plays, the player is not to imply that an object takes over where the subject leaves off. Quite the contrary, the subject loses itself precisely when it does not stand over against an object in itself, when it no longer treats the game as an object but as something it joins, gets caught up in, and finally belongs to." Weinsheimer, *Gadamer's Hermeneutics*, 103.

repetition that emerges in the player and in the constant self-renewal of play . . ."[37]

Play's power to absorb the player into itself but also to sustain its dynamic in "the constant self-renewal of play" means that all playing is at the same time a being-played. Indeed, part of the fascination and attraction that games have "consists precisely in the fact that the game masters the players." Even in games where one tries to perform tasks that one has set oneself, there is a risk that they will not "work," "succeed," or "succeed again," which is the allure of the game. Whoever "tries" is in fact the one who is tried.[38]

Take, for example, the child "who counts how often he can bounce the ball on the ground before losing control of it."[39] Here the child himself sets the rules; he chooses to play *this* game and not another. The rules that the child sets, moreover, are entirely non-purposive; they are autotelic in the sense that they serve no other end or goal than the game itself.[40] Not surprisingly, the child will be "unhappy if he loses control on the tenth bounce and proud of himself if he can keep it going to the thirteenth."[41] Paradoxically, even though the child chooses to play, he has no determinative "say" about the distinctive character of the game for the simple reason that "the ball is freely mobile in every direction, appearing to do surprising things of its own accord."[42] It is "the game itself" rather than the player that constitutes the game's real subject. As Gadamer remarks, the game "holds the player in its spell, draws him into play, and keeps him there."[43] Contrary to the received way of thinking of play, which regards it primarily as the expression of human subjectivity, it is more accurate phenomenologically to regard its mode of being as nothing other than pure "presentation" of play. On this view, "players are not the subjects of play; instead play merely reaches presentation (*Darstellung*) through

---

37. Gadamer, *Truth and Method*, 104–5.

38. Ibid., 106.

39. Gadamer, *Relevance of the Beautiful*, 23.

40. As Gadamer explains, "the child gives itself a task in playing with a ball, and such tasks are playful ones because the purpose of the game is not really solving the task, but ordering and shaping the movement of the game itself." Gadamer, *Truth and Method*, 107.

41. Gadamer, *Relevance of the Beautiful*, 23.

42. Gadamer, *Truth and Method*, 106.

43. Ibid., 106.

the players."[44] Play has its own essence, correlated with, but nonetheless independent of the consciousness of those playing.

The main emphasis of Gadamer's account, then, is the primacy of the play itself quite apart from, and indeed prior to, human consciousness. Gadamer highlights two further features of play critical to understanding theatre and the world of drama. The first is the analogy between play and language (dialogue). Entering into play is to be filled with the spirit of play—its buoyancy, freedom, and the joy of success. Play "fulfills" the players.[45] What Gadamer means by play "fulfilling" the players is structurally related to entering into dialogue, where one soon discovers that one is carried further not by individual interlocutors but by the dialogue itself. Vital to human encounter and exchange, therefore, is the play of the subject matter itself, more so than the will of individual speakers.[46] The structure of the dialogue, like that of the game, is such that what the players experience is always "a reality that surpasses" them. The upshot of Gadamer's philosophical analysis is this: play in its primordial sense is best described neither subjectively nor objectively but "medially," as "a process that takes place 'in between.'"[47]

The second distinctive feature of play relevant to theatre is the distinction Gadamer draws between the autotelic character of games on the one hand—the distinguishing character of which is "*self*-presentation"—and the intentionality of play in its representative function on the other—the chief characteristic of which is the play's "presentation for an audience." The autotelic character of play means that the game presents *itself*, plays itself, with no end other than playing it. The child's game of bouncing the ball is a clear illustration of the autotelic character of play. But to play something is also to represent it,[48] which further differentiates play into those types that are intended for an audience and those types that are not.[49]

44. Ibid., 106, and Gadamer, *Relevance of the Beautiful*, 23.

45. "[P]lay does not have its being in the player's consciousness or attitude, but on the contrary play draws him into its dominion and fills him with its spirit." Gadamer, *Truth and Method*, 109.

46. An analogous process occurs in interreligious dialogue. For an engaging exposition, see Higton and Muers, *Text in Play*.

47. Gadamer, *Truth and Method*, 109. On the "medial" role of play, see ibid., 103, 104, 105, 109, 117.

48. This is true at least potentially, if not in fact. "All presentation is potentially a representation for someone." Ibid., 108.

49. For a differentiated typology and classification of games see Callois, *Man, Play, and Games*.

All types of play form "closed worlds." This is true right across the spectrum of play, including children's games of "bouncing the ball" or "playing house,"[50] athletic contests and professional sporting events, religious ceremonies and liturgical services, and musical and theatrical performances. Only those types of play that are intended "for an audience" exhibit, for Gadamer, "the characteristic feature of art as play."[51] This sets up an interesting paradox: while plays, concerts, and religious rituals are all "closed off from those in attendance"—an audience or a congregation—they nonetheless "exist completely for [the audience]."[52] But the other side to the paradox is equally revealing: not only does the play exist entirely for the audience, but without the audience's contribution and participation there is no chance for the play becoming a closed world. Gadamer puts it as follows:

> However much a religious or profane play represents a world wholly closed within itself, it is as if open toward the spectator, in whom it achieves its whole significance. The players play their roles as in any game, and thus the play is represented, but the play itself is the whole, comprising players and spectators. In fact, it is experienced properly by . . . one who is not acting in the play but watching it. . . . A complete change takes place when play as such becomes a play. It puts the spectator in the place of the player.[53]

The closure of the world of play is only brought about if an audience is present. Drama theorists often speak of the closed world of theatre as letting down its fourth wall to allow access by the audience. But this is not quite right, according to Gadamer, who argues that it is the fourth wall *of the audience* that effectively closes—in the sense of "makes whole" or "completes"—the play world of the staged drama.[54] What this image

50. The element of make-believe or pretense that is integral to children's games and to theatre is treated extensively and with insight by Walton, *Mimesis as Make-Believe*. I am indebted to Ivan Khovacs for drawing this important work to my attention.

51. Gadamer, *Truth and Method*, 108.

52. Weinsheimer, *Gadamer's Hermeneutics*, 106

53. Gadamer, *Truth and Method*, 109.

54. See Ibid., 108 n. 204. One might say that "the closure of the play is curiously the condition of the play's possibility and accessibility, its being a play for us." But it may not be all that curious if, taking the image of the fourth wall, one sees the audience's role as not only *constructing* the fourth wall but *pulling it down* behind them, so to speak, so as to be inside rather than outside the enclosed world of the play. There are, admittedly, imperfections with this analogy. Perhaps one of the most important is the sense in

of wall-building (or wall-lowering, as it may be) suggests is that a work of art is not a self-contained and self-enclosed object that stands over against a spectator or audience.[55] There is, rather, a dynamic interaction or transaction that occurs between a theatrical performance and the audience whose very participation in the play is so intimate and extensive as to be nothing less than co-constitutive of its meaning.

A theatrical play is thus essentially open, in the sense that it requires an interpreter.[56] And the interpreter, moreover, is not someone who is detached from the work of art but is someone upon whom the work of art makes a claim. What this means is that the audience must become present to the work of art by "participating" in the play, interpreting it, and by making sense of it.

If it is the case that an audience is as deeply involved in the onto-logical event of a theatrical performance as Gadamer suggests, it follows that the work of art is fully realized only when it is performed for an audience. Meaning is therefore not self-contained and simply "there" to be discovered; meaning rather comes to realization in and through the "happening" of understanding.

For Gadamer, play helps define what is distinctively human about human beings. Play has ontological significance. "The fundamental givenness of human play and its structures" shows itself in "the to and fro of constantly repeated movement."[57] It is a motion that is endless and self-renewing because "neither pole of the movement represents the goal in which it would come to rest." Further, there is a certain "leeway" to play, a freedom distinguishable by virtue of its "self-movement," "the most fundamental characteristic of living beings," according to Aristotle.[58] What

---

which the stage on which the actors perform their roles is "off limits" to the audience during the play. As Joel Weinsheimer puts it, "it is also true that a wall has been let down on the stage: the closed world of the stage is also open, is for an audience, even though the open space between auditorium and stage is impregnable. The play is gone . . . the moment that openness is transgressed." Weinsheimer, *Gadamer's Hermeneutics*, 106.

55. "Openness toward the spectator is part of the closedness of the play." Gadamer, *Truth and Method*, 109.

56. The openness of a play is fully compatible with its (relative) completeness. For it is true to say that each performance of a play is complete when it comes to a close, just as any game is complete when it ends. But this does not preclude it from being performed again an unlimited number of times. My thanks to Wes Vander Lugt for making this distinction clear.

57. Gadamer, *Relevance of the Beautiful*, 22.

58. Ibid., 23.

distinguishes human self-movement from the self-movement of other living forms is the way human play exhibits itself in our reason, namely as "that uniquely human capacity which allows us to outplay this capacity for purposive rationality."[59] Because human play is devoid of intrinsic purpose—except the aims set according to the rules, order, and self-discipline of reason itself—it displays what Gadamer calls "a phenomenon of excess, of living self-presentation."[60] In other words, precisely because human play is "a movement that is not tied down to any goal"[61] it is potentially open to any and every goal.

In sum, we can identify several key implications of Gadamer's philosophical reflections on play for our understanding of theatre. First, the demonstration of the ways in which play is ontologically human clearly elevates the status and importance of the arts generally, and the performing arts in particular. Second, Thom's ruminations on the ways in which plays are "for an audience" receives not only support from Gadamer but also a deeper, more philosophical grounding. For Gadamer shows why theatrical play is not only a type of play intended "for an audience" but also why such plays remain open and invite completion by an audience. Thom can find philosophical corroboration in the way that Gadamer shows how theatre plays are both "*for* an audience" and "*by* an audience." Indeed, Gadamer takes up Thom's observations about the role of "playful beholding" on the part of both audiences and actors, exhibiting how playful attention is essential and integral to its mode of being—the very play of plays. Third, although the argument cannot be fully developed here, Gadamer's arguments about the interpretive process generally, and the practice of reading in particular, support David Cole's claim that acting is a kind of reading. Gadamer is in accord with the centrality of reading to theatre; that it is a constant, ineradicable feature of acting from start to finish and not simply a preliminary rehearsal technique. Moreover, he would agree that acting is a "physicalization" of reading, a recovery or restitution of the lost bodily aspects of reading. By grounding reading, like playing, ontologically as the constitutive mode of human being, Gadamer confirms and strengthens Cole's thesis regarding the inextricable relation between reading and theatrical performance.

Gadamer gives us the philosophical insight that play is not simply a cultural phenomenon but the fundamental mode of being of all works

59. Ibid.
60. Ibid., 22.
61. Ibid.

of art, including theatre. What awaits clarification is how to articulate a distinctively *theological* understanding of play and then to ask the question: "How does a theological understanding of play relate to theatre?"

The Play of Wisdom: Toward a Christomorphic Performative Faith

A properly theological account of play, as indicated at the outset, allows play to assume the shape of Wisdom as displayed in Christian liturgy. Perhaps no other Scripture passage is more defining and determinative in this regard than Proverbs 8, where the personified figure of Lady Wisdom appears. She invites her listeners to heed her call, receive her instruction, and acquire her riches, the end of which is life rather than death.[62]

> 1 Hear how wisdom calls
> and understanding lifts her voice.
> 2 She takes her stand at the crossroads,
> by the wayside, at the top of the hill;
> 3 beside the city gate, at the entrance to the city,
> at the approach by the portals
> she cries aloud:

Then Lady Wisdom speaks at length in her own name; her address is public and universal. Her first claim is the honesty and integrity of her message. Wisdom propounds truth and justice (8:7–8). Her instruction is beyond price (8:10–11). The description continues, enumerating the noble qualities that Lady Wisdom communicates: prudence, knowledge, and aversion to anything evil. Indeed, the attributes of counsel, strength, and understanding impeccably establish her credentials as one worthy to offer instruction for life. Then comes the remarkable passage about Wisdom's origins (8:22–31).

---

62. Numerous commentators and exegetes have written on this profound passage. I have benefited from their many insights, especially those of Roland E. Murphy on this passage and on Proverbs generally. See his "Proverbs and Theological Exegesis"; "The personification of Wisdom"; and *The Tree of Life*. Other important sources consulted include Whybray, *Wisdom in Proverbs*; Cox, *Proverbs*; Scott, "Wisdom in Creation"; Yee, "The Theology of Creation in Proverbs 8:22–31"; Crenshaw, *Old Testament Wisdom*; von Rad, *Wisdom in Israel*; Perdue, "Cosmology and The Social Order in the Wisdom Tradition"; Hadley, "Wisdom and the Goddess." All quotations from Proverbs 8 below are from the Revised English Bible.

22 The Lord created me the first of his
    works long ago, before all else that he made.

23 I was formed in the earliest times,
    at the beginning, before the earth itself.

24 I was born when there was yet no ocean,
    when there were no springs brimming with water.

25 Before the mountains were settled in their place,
    before the hills I was born,

26 when as yet he had made neither land nor streams
    nor the mass of the earth's soil.

27 When he set the heavens in place I was there,
    when he girdled the ocean with the horizon,

28 when he fixed the canopy of clouds overhead
    and confined the springs of the deep,

29 when he prescribed the limits for the sea
    so that the waters do not transgress his command,
    when he made earth's foundations firm.

30 Then I was at his side each day,
    his darling and delight,
    playing in his presence continually,

31 playing over his whole world,
    while my delight was in mankind.

There are many noteworthy features of this remarkable passage. First, it is simply astounding that Lady Wisdom claims that she is "born" of God.[63] Second, it is amazing that Wisdom would, in declaring that she is "before" all creation, ascribe to herself such unequalled antiquity and cosmic precedence. Third, Wisdom's medial role relating God and humanity, heaven and earth, is also striking. Fourth, there is an enigmatic quality to Wisdom. On the one hand, she "is not to be found, because she is with God," yet on the other hand, "human beings are encouraged to fall in love with her, to pursue her and attain her as gift from God."[64] Fifth,

---

63. To be sure, there is a good deal of controversy and discussion about how best to translate the Hebrew term (*qānānī*) in this context, as it is also variously translated "acquired," "possessed," "created," and "begot." The term is translated "born" in other places in Scripture where metaphors of birthing and gestation are in evidence. For more on this see Yee, "The Theology of Creation in Proverbs 8:22–31," 89–91.

64. Murphy, "The Personification of Wisdom," 232.

there is no personification in Scripture comparable to that of Wisdom.[65] *Hokmāh*, the Hebrew term for wisdom, is a feminine noun, and there are of course many female personifications in the Bible (e.g., "Daughter of Zion"). However, it is only in Prov 8:35 that we find Wisdom being given a voice resembling God's voice: "whoever finds me finds life." That Wisdom turns toward and relates to humanity not as an "It"—a set of abstract teachings or a catalogue of laws and statutes—but in the form "of a person, a summoning 'I,'" is no doubt also significant.[66] The potential theological implications that issue from the personification of Lady Wisdom in Proverbs 8 have made this text into a *crux interpretationis* in the Christian tradition.

Theologians have debated whether a mere literary device can do justice to the figure of Lady Wisdom, given how great is the extent and significance of the literary personification. Are we dealing with more than a literary character? Some are reluctant to make this text carry too great a theological load, and the question whether there is something more than personification here is an ongoing debate (largely between exegetes and theologians). But it is worth pointing out that within Scripture the Greek word "hypostasis" is used very broadly to refer to an extension of divine attributes, or to certain communications of God—such as spirit, word, or *Shekinah* (the divine presence in the world)—suggesting the immanence of the transcendent one. Proverbs 8 has proven to be an immense wellspring for the development of Christian doctrine, especially the doctrines of creation, Christology, and the Trinity.[67] Clearly this is a vast topic much too complex to consider here. For our purposes it suffices to focus on what this passage says about Wisdom and play.

> 30 Then I was at his side each day,
>   his darling and delight,
>   playing in his presence continually,
> 31 playing over his whole world,
>   while my delight was in mankind.

As Roland Murphy points out, "due attention should be given to the significant repetition of 'delight' and 'playing.'"[68] "There is more emphasis

---

65. Ibid.

66. Von Rad, *Old Testament Theology*, 444. Cited in Murphy, *The Tree of Life*, 138.

67. Proverbs 8 plays a central role in the history of theology, serving as a source in the Arian controversies of the early church. For a succinct summary and evaluation, see Young, "Proverbs 8 in Interpretation (2)."

68. There is no consensus among text scholars on how best to translate the

on joy and play than on any other activity of Wisdom."[69] "Delight" is perhaps the most distinguishing characteristic of Wisdom in this context. Indeed, the delight seems to resound in all directions: it is clearly associated with the idea of "playing" before God on the face of the earth; the LXX renders Wisdom as "all delight" (Prov 8:30), and the implication is that both God and humanity take delight in Wisdom's play.[70] The echoes and allusions to the creation account in Genesis 1 are too copious to escape notice.

Might there be a sense that Wisdom represents both a *development* of the divine blessing bestowed upon humans in the creation account (Gen 1:28—"Be fruitful and increase in number; fill the earth and subdue it") and, reciprocally, an *amplification* of what "dominion" or "mastery" entails: a playful participation in the created order marked by sheer delight, overwhelming joy, and wonder? Gadamer's description of "the constant self-renewal of play" is, it seems to me, a strikingly apt translation of Wisdom continuously playing in God's presence (Prov 8:30). Indeed, the adverbs describing Wisdom's joyful activity—"day after day," "each day," "continually"—suggest a created order that is dynamic, not a finished product but a happening in which humanity is invited to participate. By heeding Wisdom's call and following in her ways, we join this ongoing movement whereby we are allowed to "play our part" in bringing creation's meaning towards completion.[71]

Play helps us recognize that the created order we inhabit and sustain is not necessary. It is contingent, sheer gift, which is another way of speaking of God's non-purposive activity and hence God's sheer delight in play. Wisdom's delight—as we see so vividly and graphically in Proverbs 8—is play that is "before" but also "for" an audience, an audience that comprises at once God and humanity.

---

enigmatic Hebrew term '*mwn* in verse 30 (variously rendered as "cherished or favorite child," "nursling," "protégé," "craftsman," "architect"). The Hebrew term is ambivalent not because of its form—which consists of three Hebrew consonants—but because of the lack of clarity concerning how it ought to be vocalized (Murphy, *Tree of Life*, 136). This is further reinforced by the literary structure of the text. Yee remarks on how in Proverbs 8:31, "The strophe is chiastically structured in the interplay between 'delight' and 'playing'" (Yee, "The Theology of Creation in Proverbs 8:22–31," 93).

69. Murphy, *Tree of Life*, 120.

70. Ibid., 136.

71. See Yee, "The Theology of Creation in Proverbs 8:22–31," 94.

In *Christian Wisdom*, David Ford explores further the character of "the 'good pleasure' of God—what delights God's heart."[72] He asks the question, "How is 'good pleasure' related to fearing God 'for nothing'?"[73] Ford notes that the Hebrew term translated "'for nothing' is *hinnam*, meaning gratuitously, for no purpose, without cause, . . . [simply] 'as a gift.'"[74] He therefore concludes that to speak of God's good pleasure, God's delight, is nothing short of referring to the way "God generates and celebrates creation 'for naught', for its own sake."[75] If we relate to God and to God's world in the same way that God relates to his creation, we would be—to paraphrase the expression "fearing God for nothing"—responding to God and to God's world playfully. For to play in a non-purposeful manner means refusing to see either God or creation "in terms of human utility, control or even comprehensibility."[76] The ability to engage in autotelic play is one and the same with the capacity to recognize that "[C]reation has a dignity, freedom, beauty, mystery and intense life of its own."[77] In short, "fearing God for nothing" amounts to relating to God for God's own sake, and that—according to Proverbs 8—is nothing short of mirroring Wisdom's delightful, exuberant, autotelic play.

Concluding Thoughts

By way of conclusion, allow me to sketch three mutual benefits of relating theology and theatre that follow from the lines of analysis that have been developed above. I wish to suggest that theatre has something vital to offer theology, and vice versa. Moreover, the exchange is reciprocal and mutually illuminating because receiving what the other offers requires an active "taking in" and transformation, which is at that same time a deepening of one's own practices and possibilities.

72. Ford, *Christian Wisdom*, 23.

73. Ibid., 100.

74. Ibid., 113.

75. Ibid., 114.

76. Ibid., 113.

77. Ibid., 114.

Re-reading is a "core practice" of both theology and theatre

Reading and acting are internally related, as we have seen from David Cole's analysis, with acting exhibiting the "physicalization" and restoration of the "lost" bodily dimensions of reading. But reading—and especially the reading of Scripture in liturgy, in devotion, and in prayer—is also an essential practice of Christian faith. More precisely, it is the *re-reading* Scripture that constitutes Christianity's core practice for two reasons. First, we are never Scripture's first readers but always find ourselves entering into an ongoing tradition of reading. Second, even if we could be Scripture's first readers, Christians simply do not read Scripture once, as if its meaning is determined once for all. In the same way, actors do not perform a play only a single time on the presumption that its meaning could be exhausted or determined once and for all. In these ways, the practices of reading Scripture and performing plays are alike: they both present themselves as open to repeat performances. Given their multiple, recurring renditions, and given the way in which modes of "playful beholding" invariably mark their production as well as their reception, re-reading Scripture and repeatedly performing a play result in an overwhelming proliferation of meaning within the tradition of its production and reception.

Wisdom itself provides a guide to actors and readers, audiences and spectators, on how to negotiate the vast range of possible meanings. David Ford helpfully speaks of the two-fold character or dialectic between the "wisdom of ramification" and the "wisdom of reserve." On the one hand, the capacity to discern more than a single 'voice' speaking in Scripture, or entertaining in a passage more than one possibility of meaning, implies a certain "ramification of meaning." The benefit of this "wisdom of ramification" is that it allows for "the scriptures and other elements to be endlessly improvised upon and related to new people, ideas, practices and situations." It acknowledges "a diverse flowering of meanings" that well up from multiple readings and re-readings, and it enables us continually to be "open to an abundance of meaning." But left to its own, ramifying wisdom tends to overwhelm and confuse. This calls for, on the other hand, a "wisdom of reserve" that recognizes that "the ramification [of meaning] has many dangers and requires even greater discernment." A "wisdom of reserve" is not so much a brake or check on a "wisdom of ramification" as it is a capacity "to discern what is most essential without overspecifying." While it is careful not "to overdefine something inexhaustibly rich," a "wisdom of reserve" is also cognizant of the need to offer direction and limitation given the contingent world of play that we inhabit. The challenge is to learn how "to combine wisely the disciplines of reserve with ramifying improvisations."[78]

The ways we are addressed by and concomitantly respond to the play of Wisdom include but also exceed our verbal capabilities

Although the practices of re-reading and re-playing are integral to both theatre and theology, theatre offers theology a timely reminder not to limit itself to what can be verbalized and articulated linguistically. There is a tendency and a temptation on the part of theology simply to trade in texts.[79] A theologian's craft is honed by reading, whether Scripture, commentaries and sermons on Scripture, mystical treatises and devotional texts, philosophical works, and books on social theory, history, literature, and so on. Theologians are also very good at continually producing more and more texts. The danger is for theology to develop into a text-centered practice that minimizes, neglects, and eventually suppresses altogether the performative aspects of reading. And here is where drama and theatre contribute a welcome and salutary antidote to an exclusively text-centered theology.

Given that reading is itself a kind of performance and thus truly a kind of acting, theology must deepen and broaden its understanding of what it means to read. Thankfully, the world of acting and theatrical plays reminds all of us, but theologians especially, of the overtly physical dimensions of reading. Drama demonstrates palpably how reading is unavoidably a bodily process, thereby helping restore a breadth and fullness it always had but which is now largely forgotten.[80] But in a complementary move, Ford offers Cole's thesis an important "wisdom" qualification.

78. All quotations in this paragraph are from Ford, *Christian Wisdom*, 83, 67, 88, 84, 67, 68.

79. For more on the way developments in post-Renaissance theatre led to the play script assuming a relatively independent status as a text of literature, see Barry, "Shakespeare with Words" and Voss, "Printing Conventions and the Early Modern Play."

80. The work of Anne Fliotsos is instructive here. She attempts to develop a set of bodily kinesthetic explorations of the script in an effort to break the stranglehold of an intellectual approach to the script, which, in her judgment, still dominates in modern theatre. See Fliotsos, "From Script Analysis to Script Interpretation" and Fliotsos, *Interpreting the Playscript*.

Ford calls attention to the "core connection" between the practice of reading and the cries of wisdom. In particular, he differentiates "the cries *for* wisdom" on humanity's part and "the cries *by* the personified biblical wisdom." Emblematic of the cry *for* wisdom is the account of the disciples on the road to Emmaus in Luke's Gospel (Luke 24:13–53). Here the disciples' "eyes" (understanding) are opened not through Jesus' exposition of the Scripture but in the breaking of bread. This leads Ford to conclude that "[t]here is here a wisdom about the limits of verbal wisdom—even when it is taught by Jesus—and *a fortiori* about the limits of textually conveyed wisdom." Ford's point is that linguistic signs alone (and their verbalization) are not sufficient but need supplementation by gesture and enactment—in this case, the breaking of bread, the sharing of a meal. One may say that this is quite in accord with David Cole's argument about how acting helps retrieve and restore the "lost physical" of reading. But there is more to it than that. There are also the cries *by* wisdom—in this case Wisdom incarnate in Jesus. The Gospel accounts of the crucifixion of Jesus call theologians to reflect on the diverse ways by which Wisdom resounds with passionate cries. First and foremost, they are cries of anguish, lament, and dereliction, and the exclamations of affliction and pain; but Wisdom is also registered beyond words, in enacted wisdom, or even in silence. As Ford puts it, "*Theology is called to be ceaselessly attentive to these cries—articulate, inarticulate, or even silent—and to exercise discernment while being gripped by them . . .*"[81]

The mode of play that characterizes theology and theatre alike is one that always calls for an audience

Wisdom's delight, as vividly and graphically displayed in Proverbs 8, is a kind of play that occurs not only "before" time and creation, but "within" time and space and for an audience. The original audience is God but it also extends to humanity. Both the play of theology and the play of theatre are for an audience; both are open to and invite participation in the play of Wisdom's world. Hence the task that falls to an audience is one of completing the play's meaning. Gadamer's analysis of play in terms of games and sporting contests, but also as forms of theatre drama, music and dance, shows how play constitutes the fundamental mode of human

---

81. All quotations in this paragraph are from Ford, *Christian Wisdom*, 4, 37, 37, 51 [italics original].

being. Although works of art and ball games constitute "closed worlds," paradoxically they exhibit a modality of play that calls for an audience. Indeed, transitory arts and performing arts—including theatre, and by analogy religious rituals, liturgical dramas, and theology itself—are all forms of play that, absent an audience, would be unintelligible. An audience is essential if these modalities of play are to attain their rightful unity and meaning through a "closure" of the play's fourth wall.

Lady Wisdom's continual playing in God's presence, with unending delight over God's whole world, is a profound emblematic figure of a kind of ontological participation that is at the heart of what it means to be a human being. Beginning with Proverbs 8, theology can offer to theatre a way of "grounding" what it does at its most fundamental level—that is to say, ontologically and theologically. Theological reflection of the kind I have argued for here shows dramatists, actors, playwrights, performers, and others that the performing arts are rooted in and authorized by a *sapiential* structure of play that is inherently part of God's good created order. As such, the writing, rehearsal, preparation, and execution of a play deserve the dignity and honor, but also the sheer delight and joy, accorded it by Wisdom. Since Wisdom authenticates play, delights and rejoices in it for its sheer being, actors, performers, and audiences can better appreciate their respective roles as participants in the play of the world. To what higher calling can theatre aspire? Indeed, is it not the same calling whereby theologians might begin again to hear, through theatre, Wisdom calling to Wisdom?

Bibliography

Alter, Jean. *A Sociosemiotic Theory of Theatre.* Philadelphia: University of Pennsylvania Press, 1990.

Balthasar, Hans Urs von. *Theo-Drama: Theological Dramatic Theory.* Vol. 1, *Prolegomena.* Translated by Graham Harrison. San Francisco: Ignatius, 1988.

Barry, Jackson G. "Shakespeare with Words: The Script and the Medium of Drama." *Shakespeare Quarterly* 25 (1974) 161–71.

Bernstein, Richard. *Beyond Objectivism and Relativism.* Philadelphia: University of Pennsylvania Press, 1983.

Callois, Roger. *Man, Play, and Games.* Translated by Meyer Barash. New York: Free Press, 1961.

Cole, David. *Acting as Reading: The Place of the Reading Process in the Actor's Work.* Ann Arbor, MI: University of Michigan Press, 1992.

Cox, Dermot. *Proverbs: With an Introduction to Sapiential Books.* Wilmington, DE: Glazier, 1982.

Crenshaw, James L. *Old Testament Wisdom: An Introduction.* Rev. ed. Louisville, KY: Westminster John Knox, 1998.

Csikszentmihalyi, Mihaly. *Beyond Boredom and Anxiety: Experiencing Flow in Work and Play.* San Francisco: Jossey-Bass, 1975.

Dox, Donnalee. *The Idea of the Theatre in Latin Christian Thought: Augustine to the Fourteenth Century.* Ann Arbor, MI: University of Michigan Press, 2004.

Fliotsos, Anne. "From Script Analysis to Script Interpretation: Valorizing the Intuitive." *Theatre Topics* 19.2 (2009) 153–63.

———. *Interpreting the Play Script: Contemplation and Analysis.* New York: Palgrave Macmillan, 2011.

Ford, David F. *Christian Wisdom: Desiring God and Learning in Love.* Cambridge: Cambridge University Press, 2007.

Gadamer, Hans-Georg. *The Relevance of the Beautiful and Other Essays.* Edited by Robert Bernasconi. Cambridge: Cambridge University Press, 1986.

———. *Truth and Method.* 2nd ed. Translated by Joel C. Weinsheimer and Donald G. Marshall. New York: Crossroad, 1990.

Guardini, Romano. *The Spirit of the Liturgy.* Translated by Ada Lane. London: Sheed and Ward, 1937.

Hadley, Judith M. "Wisdom and the Goddess." In *Wisdom in Ancient Israel: Essays in Honour of J. A. Emerton,* edited by John Day et al., 234–43. Cambridge: Cambridge University Press, 1995.

Hardison, O. B. *Christian Rite and Christian Drama in the Middle Ages: Essays in the Origin and Early History of Modern Drama.* Baltimore: Johns Hopkins University Press, 1965.

Harris, John Wesley. *Medieval Theatre in Context: An Introduction.* London: Routledge, 1992.

Higton, Mike, and Rachel Muers. *Text in Play: Experiments in Reading Scripture.* Eugene, OR: Cascade, 2012.

Huizinga, Johan. *Homo Ludens: A Study of the Play Element in Culture.* Boston: Beacon, 1955.

Kant, Immanuel. *The Critique of Judgement.* Translated with analytical indexes by James Creed Meredith. Oxford: Oxford University Press, 1952.

Kinghorn, A. M. *Medieval Drama.* London: Evans Brothers, 1968.

Murphy, Roland E. "The Personification of Wisdom." In *Wisdom in Ancient Israel: Essays in Honour of J. A. Emerton,* edited by John Day et al., 222–33. Cambridge: Cambridge University Press, 1995.

———. "Proverbs and Theological Exegesis." In *The Hermeneutical Quest: Essays in Honor of James Luther Mays on His Sixty-Fifth Birthday,* edited by Donald G. Miller, 87–95. Allison Park, PA: Pickwick, 1986.

———. *The Tree of Life: An Exploration of Biblical Wisdom Literature.* New York: Doubleday, 1990.

Perdue, Leo G. "Cosmology and the Social Order in the Wisdom Tradition." In *The Sage in Israel and the Ancient Near East,* edited by John G. Gammie and Leo G. Perdue, 457–78. Winona Lake, IN: Eisenbrauns, 1990.

Quash, Ben. *Theology and the Drama of History.* Cambridge: Cambridge University Press, 2005.

Rad, Gerhard von. *Wisdom in Israel.* London: SCM, 1972.

Ratzinger, Joseph Cardinal. *The Spirit of the Liturgy*. Translated by John Saward. San Francisco: Ignatius, 2000.

Schechner, Richard. *Performance Studies: An Introduction*. London: Routledge, 2002.

Scott, R. B. Y. "Wisdom in Creation: The 'ĀMÔN of Proverbs 8:30." *Vetus Testamentum* 10.2 (1960) 213–23.

Stanislavski, Constantin. *Creating a Role*. Translated by Elizabeth Reynolds Hapgood. Edited by Hermine I. Popper. New York: Theater Arts Books, 1961.

Thom, Paul. *For an Audience: A Philosophy of the Performing Arts*. Philadelphia: Temple University Press, 1993.

Tydeman, William. *The Theatre in the Middle Ages: Western European Stage Conditions, c. 500–1500*. Cambridge: Cambridge University Press, 1979.

Ubersfeld, Anne. *Reading Theater*. Translated by Frank Collins. Edited by Paul Perron and Patrick Debbèche. Toronto: University of Toronto Press, 1999.

Vilhauer, Monica. "Beyond the 'Fusion of Horizons': Gadamer's Notion of Understanding as 'Play.'" *Philosophy Today* 53.4 (2009) 359–64.

————. *Gadamer's Ethics of Play: Hermeneutics and the Other*. Lanham, MD: Lexington, 2010.

Vanhoozer, Kevin J. *The Drama of Doctrine: A Canonical-Linguistic Approach to Christian Theology*. Louisville: Westminster John Knox, 2005.

Voss, Paul J. "Printing Conventions and the Early Modern Play." *Medieval and Renaissance Drama in England* 15 (2003) 98–115.

Walton, Kendall L. *Mimesis as Make-Believe: On the Foundations of the Representational Arts*. Cambridge: Harvard University Press, 1990.

Weinsheimer, Joel C. *Gadamer's Hermeneutics: A Reading of Truth and Method*. New Haven: Yale University Press, 1985.

Whybray, R. N. *Wisdom in Proverbs: The Concept of Wisdom in Proverbs 1–9*. Naperville, IL: Allenson, 1965.

Williams, Gary J. et al., eds. *Theatre Histories: An Introduction*. London: Routledge, 2006.

Yee, Gale A. "The Theology of Creation in Proverbs 8:22–31." In *Creation in the Biblical Traditions*, edited by Richard J. Clifford and John J. Collins, 85–96. Washington, DC: Catholic Biblical Association of America, 1992.

Young, Frances. "Proverbs 8 in Interpretation (2): Wisdom Personified. Fourth-Century Christian Readings: Assumptions and Debates." In *Exegesis and Theology in Early Christianity*, 102–15. Variorum Collected Studies Series. Farnham, UK: Ashgate, 2012.

8

Doing God's Story

Theatre, Christian Initiation,
and Being Human Together

Todd E. Johnson

Prolegomena

As a Christian I believe the fullness of our humanity is found by entering into the life of the triune God who was ultimately revealed in the dying and rising of Jesus of Nazareth, fully human yet fully divine. This is possible through the anointing of the Holy Spirit, the same anointing Jesus received when he began his ministry on earth. Tertullian famously said that Christians are made, not born. Indeed, we must be formed into being Christ's disciples by processes of initiation and formation that allow us to grow over time into the roles we play within the body of Christ through the giftedness of the Holy Spirit. Another early Christian leader, Saint Irenaeus, said it this way: "The Glory of God is a human being fully alive, and to be alive consists in beholding God."[1] This essay is about becoming fully alive.

There are three sets of assumptions on which I will build my argument. The first has to do with meaning and communication. Saint

1. Irenaeus, *Adversus Haereses* (Against the Heresies) 4.20.7.

153

Augustine was fascinated by a question: How is it that one could have an idea in their head and get that idea into the head of another person? How can one communicate what they are thinking to another person? Augustine believed that before humanity's fall from grace through sin, we were able to communicate directly with one another and with God. But since the fall we have been incapacitated by our sinful state and now are limited to the confines of our bodies. Hence, all we have to communicate are signs, words, gestures, and sounds. Augustine, in his early treatise *On the Teacher,* raised this question as a matter of how one teaches and how one learns.[2] In this way, Augustine is stretching his rhetorical training and its emphasis on words and broadening language to include more than just words, but symbols, gestures, and music as well, all of which are vehicles for communication between human beings and between humanity and God.

Augustine mused that God might be able to communicate to us directly, but has chosen to operate within the limits of our sinful nature. For this reason, God spoke through events (burning bushes), visions (Jacob's vision of a stairway to heaven), people (prophets), and finally, through God's incarnation in Jesus Christ. In each of these ways God has chosen to communicate using verbal and nonverbal means, engaging the entirety of our humanity.

This has some very practical applications as it addresses the nature of our everyday communication. For example, if I wanted to communicate to you "hot fudge sundae," I could give you a hot fudge sundae and then you would know exactly what it was I had in mind. But what if I were unable to do that? As in this case, you are reading an essay by someone you have never met and who has no way of delivering a hot fudge sundae to you. I could include a picture of a hot fudge sundae in this essay, but then you would only know what it looks like and even then, only from one perspective. If I was with you in person, I could gesture with my hands the size and shape of this dessert. But as it is, I only have those symbols known as words, and their agreed upon meaning, and the hope for shared experiences of ice cream, hot fudge, whipped cream, and so on. So I write using words that describe the cream-white color of the ice cream, the bittersweet smell of the hot fudge being poured over the ice cream, the size of the crushed peanuts sprinkled on the steaming fudge,

2. Augustine also explored this question in terms of music. In *On Music,* a treatise written about the same time, Augustine argued that music, particularly rhythm, is the grammar of sound, giving it structure and meaning.

the sound of whipped cream spritzing out of a can onto the ice cream, and the sight of the glistening long-stemmed cherry on the very top of this delightful mound of calories.

To communicate thoughts and feelings—to communicate any-thing—we are dependent upon signs, words, and gestures to transport meaning. We learn the meanings of these signs, words, and gestures to understand and be understood. But this understanding is not complete. Along with content comes context. In an attempt to avoid life becoming a sequence of random events, each with a meaning in and of itself, we connect the events together through narrative logic. We interpret most events through their narrative context, even if we have to create it our-selves. I invite you to consider how many choices you make based on an assumption of your life's story, where it has come from, where it currently is, and where you hope it to go. Moreover, our lives fit into larger narra-tives of family, nation, and ethnicity. And for many of us, we understand our lives by the narrative of our religion. But in any case, placing your life in a larger narrative for self-understanding, intention, and purpose in life is an act of faith, trusting that this narrative framework offers value and meaning to our lives.

My second assumption has to do with theatre. Theatre is an art form in which actors use signs, words, and gestures to communicate meaning. In most cases this meaning takes a narrative form. Theatre is a medium through which people—the actors—tell stories by becoming the story. Characters are created by actors who invite us to suspend belief and trust that their characters are real, if only temporarily. The thoughts they have, the relationships in which they are engaged, and the emotions they ex-press are real, at least as long as the house lights are down and the stage lights are up. These stories reflect upon the meaning or meaninglessness (or both) of life and are offered to audience members who believe that giving themselves to the stories and these storytellers will be of value. The storytellers offer their story persuaded that it is of value to the audi-ence. It may be a light comedy, a heavy tragedy, or a profound drama, but they trust it will delight if not enlighten the audience. And this mutual exchange is an act of faith.

My last premise has to do with faith itself. People are born with faith. This is because people are not octopi. Let's take a peek at the life cycle of an octopus to understand this contrast. Imagine a pair of octopi have grown rather fond of each other and head off to some romantic coral reef or other aquatic equivalent of Niagara Falls or Las Vegas. The female octopus is impregnated and begins gestating scores of eggs within her. The father, however, is dead shortly after mating. The mother will return to her lair, often a cave, where she will hang a sack of the preemie octopi she has birthed. She will lie beneath them, circulating seawater around them using her siphon and keeping a vigilant and protective eye on the very dangerous world at the sea bottom. After some months, the mother octopus will take a big gulp of seawater and blow her little octopus larvae out into the ocean. This may be her last breath, as she will die shortly after sending her children out into the world. These newly hatched octopi will float above the sea bottom in clouds of plankton, feeding on other larvae, such as starfish and crab. They will gain weight quickly and soon drift down to the bottom of the sea. Within a year or so the survivors of the brood will repeat the cycle.

This is not a human life cycle. If a mother and father were to die immediately after giving birth and leave a newborn child alone in the world, the child would soon be dead. A newborn does not inherit a genetic code that will guide her through life, a sort of owner's manual hardwired into her brain. Instead, a child is born with faith: faith that someone will care for and nurture her; faith that someone will protect and instruct her; faith that someone will model for her how to be human. This is because human beings are hardwired at birth to be imitators. We learn by imitation, mimesis. This is how we learn to communicate, learn to fit into our social systems, learn how to become human.

The late liturgical and ritual scholar Mark Searle explored the practice of infant baptism as a means of initiating and forming the baptizand into a Christian disciple. He balked at the idea that baptism infuses faith. Faith is a given, even in the infant who cannot be called a believer. Searle writes, "The question then is less one of whether a child can 'have' faith than it is a question of the kind of faith it comes in fact to exercise in the first weeks and months of life."[3] Faith, in this perspective, is not an act of rational cognition. Instead, in this case, faith is an integrated, holistic, almost pre-rational sense of how one is in relationship to the world. Therefore, the question is not whether or not a baptized child will have faith, but whether or not the child's faith will become a Christian faith.

Building upon this understanding of faith, Searle continues, "Thus it is not so much that baptism infuses faith into a child as that baptism is the deliberate and conscious insertion of the child into the environment

3. Searle, "Infant Baptism Reconsidered," 41.

of faith, which faith is the faith of the Church, which is in turn the faith of Christ himself."[4] In this understanding, Christian faith is the way one "leans into life," the way one interprets the signs, words, and gestures of their world, the way one discovers the reality of knowing God and being known by God. Faith is the very way that one has grown to understand the world and chooses to put their life into the ongoing story of God's redemption in the world and to play the role of a Christian disciple. This is not an *act* of faith, but an ongoing *life* of faith.

The Redeeming Story

Robert Webber began his last book, the culmination of a lifetime of study of Christian worship, with this story. "Some time ago a pastor friend of mine looked me in the eye and asked, 'What is worship? Give me a one-liner that will solve my confusion.' I shot back with the four words of this chapter title: 'Worship does God's story!'"[5] Please note the verb "to do." Worship does not primarily tell God's story (though it does), nor does it primarily celebrate God's story (though it does). Worship *does* God's story. It enacts it. It embodies it. Worship puts flesh and blood on God's story of salvation—the ongoing story of God's faithfulness—and the promises that define the vision of the future of God's story. It creates a space for God's story to inhabit and invites us to place our lives into that story. As God's story becomes our story, we become the story by our day to day living of the gospel.

Worship, as I have argued elsewhere, along with the entire life of the Christian disciple, is not the performance of our faith. Instead, it is the rehearsal of our faith. Our life will never fully reflect the triune life of God as it has been revealed over time. Instead our life of faith is an arc—a trajectory of growth—across which we seek to embody kingdom principles and grow closer in our approximation of our imitation of Christ as a fully human life.[6] Our faith is an organic process, not a static "thing." Our story is part of a larger whole, and we tell this story by becoming the story.

4. Ibid., 43.

5. Webber, *Ancient-Future Worship*, 29.

6. For example, see Johnson and Savidge, *Performing the Sacred*, 94; and Johnson, "Redeeming Performance," 20–21.

Though not all would agree. Liturgical scholar Lester Ruth pursued a taxonomy of Christian worship that is descriptive without being prejudiced or pejorative and without reducing liturgical categories to those of style, such as contemporary and traditional. Ruth came up with three sets of questions with which to describe the substance of worship. One of those questions is "whose story is told?" Ruth offers a range of possible answers to this question situated between two poles. At one end of the spectrum there are "cosmic story" churches whose worship focuses on the acts of God in salvation history, from creation, through covenant and redemption, to the promise of God's eschatological consummation. At the other end are "personal story" churches, whose worship focuses upon the story of the individual woman or man coming to faith in Christ.[7]

Though no pure form of either church strictly exists, churches that lean strongly toward one end of the spectrum or the other are not hard to find. I find this dichotomy helpful in understanding the distinction between sacraments and ordinances. Returning to the theme of initiation, the point of ritual efficacy differs greatly within the personal and cosmic understandings of initiation. For example, in a sacramental understanding of baptism, water is consecrated, which sets it apart from ordinary water. The traditional prayer said over the water (appropriately enough referred to as the "Water Prayer") begins with God's Spirit moving over the waters of creation, and continues with references to Noah and his family saved from the waters of the flood, the Israelites being saved by safe passage through the waters of the Red Sea and the Jordan, and finally to Jesus' baptism in the same Jordan River. The prayer concludes by asking the Spirit to use the water to bring the baptizand to new life in Christ. The water is set apart—made sacred—by placing it into the narrative of God's use of water in God's work of salvation. By baptizing in this water, the person and their life is placed into God's story of salvation.

This is not the case with an ordinance understanding of baptism. Here the ritual moment that makes the baptism efficacious is the personal testimony of the baptizand. Their testimony of having made the choice to accept God's offer of salvation is what is necessary to be baptized, and the rite of baptism concretizes those themes of having died and risen with Christ, having been buried with Christ in baptism (Rom 6:3–5). This ordinance view of baptism can easily be understood as a personal story orientation to faith rather than a cosmic story orientation.

7. Ruth, "A Rose by Any Other Name," 47–48.

It primarily celebrates the individual's choice. The sacramental understanding is more of a cosmic story approach, where people literally place their stories into the larger narrative of God's salvation history.

Though both views fit within the paradigm of salvation by grace through faith (Eph 2:8), they understand faith differently. For a sacramental, cosmic story understanding, "Faith" is the objective revelation of God in history. It is the truth that exists outside of individuals into which they place their life. For the ordinance, personal story understanding, "faith" is the individual's subjective response and personal assent to the larger Christian Faith. It would be a caricature to say that in the personal story orientation, one places God's story into one's own personal story. However, recent studies have shown that this is in fact a belief held by a number of contemporary Christians.[8]

If my premises can be accepted for the sake of argument, then both "faith" and "Faith" are part of the faithful response to God's saving grace, but one's personal faith is understood as the act of placing one's life narrative within the larger narrative of the Christian Faith. It is the larger story of Faith that defines and corrects the individual's story of faith, even for personal story churches. Or, to use a different metaphor, we do not become the body of Christ individually; rather, member by member, we become the body of Christ in which the whole is greater than the sum of its parts (1 Cor 12:7–27).

The roots of this understanding of faith and Faith, personal and cosmic, subjective and objective run deep. They can be found in the Jewish understanding of prayer and its foundation established upon God's revelation in human history. This is particularly evident in two primary forms of prayer found in the Hebrew Scriptures. One prayer, the *berakah*, is an excellent example of this. *Berakah* comes from the root *barak*, which means to bless. A *berakah* prayer is one that addresses God indirectly ("Blessed be the God of Israel, who . . ") and then recounts God's saving acts in history. It may not seem much like a prayer to us, as it neither intercedes for anyone nor petitions God for anything. It simply recounts God's saving acts. God's people have been blessed by these acts and God's nature has been revealed in these acts. And God is blessed when humans recount these divine saving acts.[9] *Berakah* has a sort of creedal quality

---

8. See Luhrmann, *When God Talks Back*.
9. Bradshaw, *Two Ways of Praying*, 46–51.

to it, which gives insight into why early Christians understood that they prayed the creeds. By praying, they were *doing* the story of God.

However, there is more to the Jewish understanding of prayer than just this. A complementary form of Jewish prayer before the Christian era was the *hodayah*, which is derived from the root *hodah*, which means to thank, acknowledge, or confess. This form of prayer is different than the *berakah* as it begins with a direct address ("Blessed are you, O Lord . . .") and then recounts saving acts of God. The prayer continues, however, with a subjective response asking God to act in the present as God has acted in the past. This seems more like a prayer to most of us, as it has that intercessory or petitionary quality we commonly associate with prayer.[10]

A concrete example of the two would look like this. On the one hand, a *berakah* prayer praising God for the exodus might be, "Blessed be the God of Israel, who heard the cries of His people in bondage, brought them out from under the oppressive rule of Pharaoh, and led them into the Promised Land. Thanks be to God!" On the other hand, a *hodayah* prayer rooted in the same theme could be, "Blessed are you, our God, who heard the cries of His people in bondage, brought them out from under the oppressive rule of Pharaoh, and brought them into the Promised Land. Now hear our prayer, Lord, and bring us out from under the oppressive rule of Nebuchadnezzar and return us to the Promised Land." In both cases, the prayers begin with the objective statement of what God has done in history (Faith), but the *hodayah* continues with the subjective response of asking God to act now as God has acted before. In both cases, the cosmic story of God's redemption is primary and the subjective response is grounded in objective revelation.

Paul Bradshaw draws this to a fine point. Suggesting that we have lost touch, at least in part, with our biblical heritage of prayer and worship, he offers this summary of his proposed corrective: "Recalling to mind what God has done, we are interpreting our human experience in religious terms; we are making our creedal confession of faith; we are proclaiming our gospel to the world; we are restoring ourselves and all creation to a relationship of holiness to God; and all this is not for ourselves but so that God may be glorified."[11] In the terms we have been

10. Ibid., 51–53.

11. Ibid., 55. Bradshaw also notes that the *berakah* and *hodayah* prayers were synthesized into a hybrid prayer form, the *birkat ha-mazon*, which became a common Jewish meal prayer. All three forms of prayer serve to reinforce the point that our heritage of Christian prayer is rooted in the story of God's saving acts, before it moves to subjective response, if in fact that shift is made.

working with, we have found a narrative framework into which we place our lives, a framework that provides the perspective from which we now view all of the world and its history.

This sets the stage for our next consideration: how do we glean from the wisdom of theatre in order to "do" God's story? Moreover, how can we be more attentive to the story told, as those who hope to live into it? All this is to be done that we might become more like Christ and become more fully human, and in the process glorify God.

Making the Story Present

Now we shift gears a bit and turn to theorists who examine and interpret ritual and theatre. Some, as we will see, treat them as similar if not identical phenomena. Others see them as related but necessarily distinct. The latter is the direction this essay will go. What will hold them together, I will conclude, is the potential for transformation they both contain. This will lead necessarily into a discussion about how we understand what a performance is, both on stage and in life, as well as how we embody the roles we play. This section will conclude with how all of this informs what it means to be and become a human person.

Transforming Narrative

Theatre, like life, is dynamic and active. In theatre, real people act in real ways to communicate what is most almost always a fiction. Still, theatre is an event, a performance, a phenomenon. Bert States, in his extended essay on the phenomenology of theatre, begins by suggesting that theatre has two components: imitation and action.[12] Imitation implies that there is something beyond the play that is being imitated, while action implies that there is something real—true, if you will—happening on stage in the moment. Theatre is simultaneously presentational and representational, having both an internal and an external referent. It is only in considering theatre phenomenologically that both of these components can be attended to simultaneously.

Following States's line of logic, theatre is an art form. Art, seen phenomenologically, removes elements of life from their normal context and puts them in a new framework, giving those elements a fresh viewing,

---

12. States, *Great Reckonings in Little Rooms*, 5.

enabling them to be seen in a new way. Art serves to move us away from what we expect and know, to perceive the ordinary in new and even evocative ways. Andy Warhol's soup cans, for example, invite us to see a can of Campbell's soup, along with all of our commercial society, in a new way. In a similar but different way, Irving Berlin's "White Christmas" allows us to see Christmas differently. In both of these cases, this new way of seeing has now become so familiar that it is in fact part of our experience of the objects themselves in everyday life. But a painting is not a can of soup, and a song is not Christmas. In theatre, however, this distinction is not as firm.

As States points out, a semiotic perspective on theatre reduces theatre to signs, and the stage becomes linked symbolically to those things to which it is referring. But the sign and the signified seem to collapse when seen from a phenomenological perspective. States observes, "we tend generally to undervalue the elementary fact that theater—unlike fiction, painting, sculpture, and film—is really a language whose words consist to an unusual degree of things that *are* what they seem to be. In theater, image and object, pretense and pretender, sign-vehicle and content, draw unusually close. . . . Put bluntly, in theater there is always a possibility that an act of sexual congress between two so-called signs will produce a real pregnancy."[13]

This intensely real, human quality makes theatre a volatile art form. In film, one does not expect anything to go wrong. Mistakes are edited out and only the best takes are used. But on stage a mistake could occur at any time, bringing attention to itself as an actual human event in time and space, though pretending to be something else. Viewing the theatrical event phenomenologically can lead to a blurring of the categories "real" and "fiction." Victor Turner addresses this in his study of ritual and theatre. A number of scholars, Turner contends, deem using the terms performance and drama to describe ritual as problematic. But Turner points out the porous membrane between theatre and ritual in his use of the term "social drama," a state caused by a disruption of normative social behavior resulting in social crisis, creating drama in real life events. Further theatrical practices established by Richard Schechner in his Performance Group seemed to be as much ritual as they were theatrical.[14]

---

13. Ibid., 20.
14. Turner, *From Ritual to Theatre*, 91–93.

Following Schechner's lead, Turner suggests a distinction between ritual and theatre. Theatre, he argues, happens when a separation between performer and audience is created in what was originally a ritual context. In ritual, there may be priests or other ritual leaders, but there is no distinction between those who are participants and those who facilitate their participation.[15] What holds them together, however, is the performative quality of a narrative. A narrative, in part or whole, is embodied in space and time by living people, inviting people to engage in the event either as audience, in theatre, or as participants, in ritual. But in both cases, a narrative is provided on the basis of which they can reflect upon their life experiences. In theatre, we have the potential to gain new insights into ourselves and our world by engaging the story performed. In ritual, we have the potential to participate and invest ourselves in the narrative world of the ritual.

In a similar vein, Richard Schechner, in his major work *Performance Theory*, addresses at length what he calls the "poetics of theatre," as well as the difference between "social drama and aesthetic drama." Relying heavily upon the work of Victor Turner, he identifies the efficacy of ritual performance, in this case a theatrical performance, to be determined by the transformative quality of the production. Drawing upon theatre theorists such as Peter Brook, Jerzy Grotowski, and Antonin Artaud, Schechner argues for the transformation of the performer as the evidence of an efficacious performance. Such a transformation occurs, according to Schechner, when a subconscious reality becomes manifest in the creation of a character (such as a shaman being possessed and channeling a deity). The performer's transformation becomes so powerful that the performance in fact becomes transformative for the audience.[16]

This perspective is helpful: an efficacious performance, either ritual or theatrical, is one that has a transformative effect. Actors tell the story by becoming the story. If they are able to transform themselves into their characters, and if a theatre ensemble is able to transform the theatre space into a place that is received as other than that space—if even for minutes or hours—then it is efficacious. If participants in a ritual tell the story by becoming the story, then transformation is likewise a sign of an efficacious performance. But ritual transformation is not short-term; it is for the long-term life beyond the ritual. In the terms introduced above,

---

15. Ibid., 112.

16. Schechner, *Performance Theory*, 186–97. It should be noted how much Schechner's work presupposes a Freudian anthropology.

through an encounter with the presentation of the narrative of God's story in Christian ritual, the participant's perspective on life beyond the ritual must be congruent with the perspective presented in the ritual. This is the response of individual faith to the Christian Faith.

Rethinking Performance

A common performative quality links theatre to ritual. It is the "doing" of the narrative that interests us in this exploration as well. A simple definition of a thing or person with a performative quality is "something that does something." An example of this would be in J. L. Austin's work where he defines some speech acts to be "performative utterances," where the speech act itself executes an action. For a Justice of the Peace to say, "I now pronounce you husband and wife," is to make them married. Performance does things, often because the action refers to a concept, returning us to the two qualities of theatre: imitation and action, signification and doing.[17]

There is, however, another perspective on performance. Talal Asad's work has challenged the notion that every action has a meaning behind it. Asad points out that the ritual practices of monks are not done for symbolic meaning, but as personal disciplines that establish virtues in their lives. They learn by doing, training their bodies, along with their minds, in the practices they will need to be monks.[18] These practices, called "technologies of the self," are akin to practicing a musical instrument. The practice time spent in learning to play the piano does not necessarily *mean* anything. However, it does rehearse certain skills one will need to perform musical pieces on the piano. Performances can be formative as well as informative to both those participating in the action and those merely observing the action.

Performing Roles

These performative concepts of ritual and theatre have resonance within the broader world of the social sciences. Peter Berger identifies three distinct types of approaches to sociology. Describing the works of Max Weber and Emile Durkheim, he portrays their two views of society as the

17. For a concise and helpful survey of performance theory see Macdonald, "Liturgy and Performance: Introduction," 1–5.

18. Asad, *Genealogies of Religion*, 62–65.

prison and the puppet theatre. In contrast to those two models, he offers a third model based on the works of Erving Goffman, which is "society as a stage populated by living actors."[19] Goffman understood all people to be performers; that is, each person plays a part or role in life and invites people to take their role seriously. This may seem a bit insincere, but Goffman insists that there are choices in the role or roles we play in life, and that we are free to step outside of our roles, change roles, or even maintain contradictory roles simultaneously. The point is we have been socialized into our roles, having had choices of behaviors and roles modeled for us and choosing our roles and how we perform them.[20]

Berger, using the works of Jean-Paul Sartre, develops this point about freedom even further. People are ultimately free to choose. People have the capability to chose one option or another. A person who claims they have no choice is acting in "bad faith." Bad faith is "to pretend that something is necessary when in fact it is voluntary."[21] An individual may claim that their role requires them to do certain things, but they are always free to step out of that role. Although the choice of stepping out of their role may have serious repercussions, it is a choice nonetheless. For example, a superior may order a soldier to burn a village down. The soldier is obligated to perform it, but he or she may step out of that role and refuse, which will of course invite disciplinary actions by the military. Still, this does not negate the choice.

To return to our concept of narrative, each person enacts their role or roles in life according to the narratives by which they make sense of their world. If these narratives come into conflict, or if one has been persuaded by the values of an alternative narrative to their *status quo*, they can change. In some ways, we are actors who are able to choose or even adjust our own scripts. We have choice, and our choices are in the context of our own life narrative as well as in the matrix of the larger narratives in which our lives participate.

Becoming Actors, Becoming Audience, Becoming Human

Philosopher Paul Woodruff will help us to bring these various strands of thought about theatre, performance, and society together. Woodruff

19. Berger, *Invitation to Sociology*, 138.

20. This very brief summary of Goffman's work is a distillation of major points found in Goffman, *The Presentation of Self in Everyday Life*.

21. Berger, *Invitation to Sociology*, 143.

maintains that theatre is not an option for a healthy human society and its individual members. Woodruff observes, "Theatre is everywhere in human culture, as widely practiced as religion. This should be no surprise: most expressions of religion belong to theatre. Like religion, theatre seems sometimes to be on the way out, but keeps coming back in unexpected disguises—some horrible, some wonderful."[22]

Woodruff maintains that central to the art of theatre is the art of storytelling. At the same time, there is the reciprocal art of listening that the art of telling requires. If we lose the art of telling, we will also lose the art of listening. But of course, as we have maintained in this essay, the story is told by being performed, by being done, so we would lose the art of watching as well as listening. Woodruff concludes this argument by stating:

> There is an art to watching and being watched, and that is one of the few arts on which all human living depends. If we are unwatched we diminish, and we cannot be entirely as we wish to be. If we never stop to watch, we will know only how it feels to be us, never how it might feel to be another. Watched too much, or in the wrong way, we become frightened. Watching too much we lose the capacity for action in our own lives. Watching well, together, and being watched well, with limits on both sides, we grow, and grow together.[23]

Theatre is an art form that can (and should) delight, as people perform actions that they believe are worth watching. But beyond pleasure, there are ethical reasons for theatre, as we practice the art of watching others because we need to learn to attend to and care for others.[24] Yet theatre is still an art and can be done either poorly or with excellence. So performances need to be done well to draw people's attention to the characters, their lives and questions, so we might watch well. All of this, as Woodruff maintains, is so we can become more human together. This is the art of empathy.[25] And this is an art that enables us to become more fully human.

Woodruff's definition of theatre is much broader than we have previously considered. For Woodruff, "Theatre is something we human beings do, when all of us who are involved are alive and present, and at

22. Woodruff, *The Necessity of Theater*, 11.
23. Ibid., 10.
24. Ibid., 20.
25. Ibid., 24, 184–85.

least some are paying attention to others, for a measured time and in a measured space. Some of us do things, while others watch."[26] Although it seeks to be an all-encompassing sort of definition, it does have limits; theatre is neither film nor literature. Theatre is a live human event, not a recording—either in text or video. Woodruff identifies five types of theatre: two (Mimetic and Art) describe what we traditionally think of as theatre, two others (Everyday and Extreme) speak of the observations of life as it unfolds, from the ordinary (a man proposing to a woman on a park bench) to the extraordinary (attending the wedding of the couple who have decided to get married).[27] The fifth category is Theatre of Presence, or a "theater of sacrament," which begins as mimesis, but ends "real." It invokes a presence from outside the realm of the ordinary and makes it manifest.[28]

Woodruff and his broad embrace (though I am about to narrow it) gives us a context for bringing together the various strands of performance we have been exploring in this section. First, his extension of theatre into the world of the everyday—however pedestrian, however dramatic—links to the social theory of Goffman and his understanding of human beings playing roles in this life: we make choices embodying the narratives that provide the context for our choices. Second, his elimination of the distinction between ritual and theatre is problematic. Although there is an overlap between the two, ritual and theatre are distinct at the point of intentionality. In everyday life, we play roles and we are watched as we do so, yet we are not operating in a context of intentional fiction. There is a distance that is created by the agreement of mimesis between the performers and the audience that does not exist in real life—even when you are being fleeced by someone who is not as they seem.

Third, Woodruff's definition of a theology of presence, which he equates with "theatre of sacrament," is an unhelpful overgeneralization. As I have written elsewhere, there is a distinction between theatre's incarnational and sacramental presences. An incarnational presence makes manifest that which is otherwise absent. A sacramental present is not simply making something present, but making something *present to*. It is a personal, directional presence. Just as in the classic understandings of Christian sacraments, they do not manifest an impersonal presence, but a presence that seeks a personal exchange. Theatre is a performance

26. Ibid., 38.
27. Ibid., 33–34.
28. Ibid., 34.

that assumes the actors are present to one another and that the actors and audience are also present to one another.[29] Even in the context of fiction, the sacramental quality of presence in theatre can be very real.

But these issues I have raised with Woodruff's work, both affirmations and adjustments, speak to the core issue of our exploration: the nature of becoming human together. Woodruff is correct that in watching and being watched we are learning of others, our world, and ourselves. This experience of shared watching is what helps create a cohesive community, a sense of caring for each other, even when we are more different than alike. Woodruff observes, "In communities, people approach this sort of closeness by sharing what they watch on special occasions. In traditional societies, entire communities share religious performance of various kinds, and these generally fall under my broad definition of theater. Modern communities, because they tend to blend different religions, are increasingly unable to share traditional religious events. Something must take their place."[30] Woodruff has articulated what I experienced in our very diverse neighborhood in Chicago, and described in some detail elsewhere.[31] In a multiethnic, multinational, multireligious elementary school, a yearly production of a standard work of musical theatre brought that community together, more than any school sporting event. In particular, I was struck by how the production of *The Wizard of Oz* spoke of my neighbors' immigrant experience in the strange and wonderful world of Chicago, and how watching that play with them—and watching them watch that play—helped me understand them in important ways.

In addition, Woodruff's insight that watching others provides us with models is essential for our exploration. In Woodruff's proposal, "[m]odeling takes an agent through mimesis to a new reality; . . . a new way of appearing becomes a new way of being."[32] Becoming human, we acknowledge our non-octopus nature. We observe, we imitate, and we have our imitation critiqued through positive and negative reinforcement. Being part of a community invites us to take responsibility for being people worthy of imitation. The mimetic quality of human development should not be overlooked. For spiritual formation to be efficacious, it requires a mimetic quality, and to this topic we now turn.

29. Johnson and Savidge, *Performing the Sacred*, 65–71.

30. Woodruff, *The Necessity of Theater*, 24.

31. Johnson and Savidge, *Performing the Sacred*, 64.

32. Woodruff, *The Necessity of Theater*, 127.

Becoming the Story: Perspective from the Rear View Mirror

Before moving on, let us take stock. We have defined theatre as an art form that uses human beings as their medium. We have presented human beings as creatures that are both symbol makers and meaning makers, communicating through signs, words, and gestures. Furthermore, we have argued that people are performers whose actions are at times symbolic, and at other times are rehearsals of behavior-forming patterns of activity, technologies of the self. Becoming fully human takes both of these elements seriously.

What is more, human beings are inherently faith-full creatures— that is, we are born with faith that we will be cared for, nurtured, and taught, that we might become fully human. A corollary to this is that humans are mimetic creatures, that we observe and imitate those around us as a primary means of human development. In the process, we choose both practices and beliefs from those available to us to assume the roles we play in our lives. Those choices are acts of faith essential to our becoming fully human.

This leads to theatre, where people intentionally focus on telling stories by mimesis, inviting observation, reflection, and even imitation. Theatre, like other art forms, extracts elements of life from their ordinary context and reframes them for closer examination. In doing so, it invites us to consider our life narratives, our values, the lives of others, and our own life choices. Though theatre and ritual are distinct, they share some essential qualities. The actors' stagecraft is in their ability to use signs, words, and gestures to create people other than themselves, to tell their story by becoming those people. Similarly, ritual's efficacy depends upon the participants allowing the signs, words, and gestures of a ritual to create a space to form human behavior. In both cases, the dynamics of execution engage our imagination, draw us in deeply to the narrative being performed, and can instigate our transformation.

All people are people of some faith, but this essay was undertaken to better understand how we might more fully form specifically Christian disciples and to create the possibility for a more truly human life, for both individuals and communities. Such a program requires that we take seriously both the performative and reflective qualities of the human person, as well as the communal nature of human life. So what does the birthing and development of people into the Christian faith look like from this perspective?

Initiation as a "Theatre of Faith"

There is no small amount of irony in linking Christian initiation with theatre, given the Christian ambivalence about theatre over the years, especially in the early centuries of the Christian church. For example, Tertullian represents the early African Christian rejection of worldly pursuits as a necessity for baptism, arguing that the theatre, coliseum, and all such spectacles were idolatrous and of the devil, and therefore against one's baptismal vows.[33]

So too, St. Augustine taught those preparing for baptism (a.k.a. catechizing the catechumens) not to be like the insincere or double-minded who will populate churches on feast days but fill the theatres on pagan festivals.[34] At the same time, Augustine himself recognized the similarities between the theatre and the rituals of the church. Christian worship is the performance of the biblical drama of salvation. As Augustine questioned his congregation with some frequency, "Do not think, brothers (*sic*), that the Lord our God has sent us away without theatrical extravaganzas; for if there are no extravaganzas, why have you come together today?"[35] In Augustine's church, Christian rituals have a dramatic quality; they tell the story of God's saving acts of history in ways that engage the imagination and convict the heart. And none were more dramatic in Augustine's day than the rituals of initiation.

For many Christians today, initiation into the faith is often a single rite, or a few rites at most. Most Christians are initiated by baptism with water. Some baptized as believers may have been dedicated as infants. Those baptized as infants may have a later rite of confirmation, and possibly a rite of first communion. But for many, these rites are loosely connected, if at all. The early practices of Christians until the fifth century were very different. There was an intentional process beginning with evangelism, followed by catechesis, purification, the rites of initiation themselves, and finally post-baptismal instruction. This process could

33. Harmless, *Augustine and the Catechumenate*, 46.
34. Ibid., 148.
35. Ibid., 164–65. See especially n. 36.

span years.[36] Although no period in Christian history has ever been perfect, the Christian West (Catholic and Protestant) has turned with great frequency to this early era of initiation as a model for what rites to use to initiate new Christians into the church and how to perform those rites. There was a performative quality to those rites that yielded transformation of people's lives that remains exemplary.[37]

Described in general terms, this process begins with someone interested in the Christian faith either because of the preaching they had heard or because of the lived witness of church members. After being taught and examined by the bishop, the individual would be enrolled into the catechumenate, the school for those preparing for baptism. This education was both informative and formative, as the catechumens would be instructed in the history of God's saving acts that culminate in Christ, while being required to practice disciplines such as prayer, fasting, care for the poor, visiting the sick, and so on. The season of Lent made these formative practices even more intense, demanding more of the catechumens, while requiring them to eat less and to have less interaction with the world overall.

The catechumens were required to attend church regularly and would often sit together. Frequently the preacher would turn to the catechumens in the middle of a sermon and explain something to them that they would not be expected to know. Their formation took place publicly; it was done both before the church and also within the context of the church's support. After the sermon, the catechumens were dismissed. No one who was not a full member of the church could be present for the prayers of the church or the celebration of the Lord's Supper. During Holy Week, the catechumens would attend the increased number of services commemorating Jesus' last week in Jerusalem. They would have even more special instruction and increased expectations of practices of both piety and service. And they would eat less and fast more. This would end at the Great Vigil, beginning at sunset before Easter Sunday.

36. For a description of the practices of initiation practiced in fourth-century churches, see Yarnold, *The Awe-Inspiring Rites of Initiation*, 3–49. For an exploration of this process as it is now practiced by the Roman Catholic Church, see Kavanagh, "Christian Initiation of Adults: The Rites," 118–37.

37. Beginning with the Rite of Christian Initiation of Adults (RCIA) in the Roman Catholic Church in 1972, many mainline Protestant denominations have developed some form of a process model of initiation similar to the RCIA, including the Episcopal, Lutheran and Methodist churches. More recently a model for evangelical churches has been proposed. See Webber, *Ancient-Future Evangelism*.

The Easter Vigil, still the centerpiece of the worship in many churches, was the service where this process of initiation came together. It is also the place where this essay converges. The Vigil was a service that began at sunset and ended around sunrise; it literally was an all-night vigil. It began then, as it does now, with a hymn of praise, the *Exultet*.[38] It continued with the systematic reading of Scripture beginning with the creation account in Genesis 1 and through the stories of the Old Testament. Recounted in the stories of Noah, Ruth, Abraham, Sarah, Moses, and Miriam is the God who is faithful. The reading then moved to the New Testament, which presents the full embodiment of God's faithfulness in Jesus, God's Christ. It is in the context of this full recounting of God's saving history that the Water Prayer mentioned earlier is found, drawing on strands from many of these stories and weaving them together into the tapestry of God's offer of salvation here and now in this church through these waters. That prayer literally draws the story of God and the story of the catechumen together, with their point of intersection being the waters of baptism.

When the time for baptism has come, not long before dawn, deaconesses take the women (and any infants being baptized) and deacons take the men to be baptized. Each person goes through the rites one at a time. The catechumens are asked if they renounce sin and Satan, and after saying yes they spit towards the west (where the sun sets) getting those distasteful words off of their lips. They are then given an anointing known as exorcism, sealing Satan out. They next remove their clothes, as baptism is in the nude, and enter a pool large enough to stand in. They are asked if they believe in God, and they respond with, "I believe in God the Father almighty, maker of heaven and earth." This is the first of three sections of what we now call the Apostle's Creed, which was originally a baptismal vow. After each section of the vow, they receive a washing with water.[39] Once washed three times, the baptizands leave the pool and receive a white robe, salt on their tongue, a candle in their hand, and an anointing with aromatic oil, sealing the Holy Spirit in. One can only imagine the sight, sound, and smell of the newly initiated women and men returning from the baptistery—entering a dim space wearing white, dripping wet, smelling sweet, and illumined by a candle. What a powerful image of

---

38. For the details of the Episcopal version of this service, see http://www.episcopal church.org/sites/default/files/downloads/book_of_common_prayer.pdf, pages 284–95.

39. Either by pouring or immersion.

transformation this must have been! And what a powerful reminder to those in attendance of their own initiation into the church!

Now reunited with the congregation as full members of the church, they received a cup of water, an internal cleansing echoing the external cleansing of their baptism, a cup of milk and honey—as they have crossed the river Jordan and have entered the Promised Land—and then the bread and cup of the Lord's Supper. These rites were seen for the first time as one participated in them. This was followed by a detailed explanation of the meanings of the rites, again received for the first time. It would begin with the first sermon after the Vigil.

In such a sermon by Augustine, the merging of personal and cosmic stories—the telling of God's story by becoming God's story—becomes obvious. In reflecting on Paul's teaching about the Lord's Supper, Augustine connects the collective nature of the body of Christ to the collective nature of bread.

> "One bread," he says. What is this one bread? Is it not the "one body," formed from many? Remember: bread doesn't come from a single grain, but from many. When you received exorcism, you were "ground." When you were baptized, you were "leavened." When you received the fire of the Holy Spirit, you were "baked." Be what you see; receive what you are. This is what Paul is saying about the bread.[40]

Augustine identifies that through these rites of initiation, the baptized have now become part of the body of Christ, and each time they receive the bread and cup they receive a sacrament of themselves in which they recommit themselves to their baptism, to the church, and to Christ. They have become the story of God's salvation in the world by virtue of their lives of faith.[41]

William Harmless, in his analysis of St. Augustine's ministry to the catechumens, identifies the theatrical quality of this process. Certainly, the dramatic effects of the initiation rites are heightened by their

---

40. Augustine, *Sermon 272*; http://www.earlychurchtexts.com/public/augustine_sermon_272_eucharist.htm.

41. "So now, if you want to understand the body of Christ, listen to the Apostle Paul speaking to the faithful: 'You are the body of Christ, member for member' [1 Cor 12:27]. If you, therefore, are Christ's body and members, it is your own mystery that is placed on the Lord's table! It is your own mystery that you are receiving! You are saying 'Amen' to what you are: your response is a personal signature, affirming your faith. When you hear 'The body of Christ,' you reply 'Amen.' Be a member of Christ's body, then, so that your 'Amen' may ring true!" Augustine, *Sermon 272*.

mysterious qualities,[42] being held at night, in secret, and an interweaving of symbol, story, and rite into a cohesive whole. This was accentuated by Augustine's own skill as a presider. As Harmless notes, "It was no accident that Augustine compared his efforts to the theatres he so often denounced. His catechesis was a theatre of the Word: its drama was salvation history, its script was the scriptures, and its actors included everyone."[43]

There are two comments to be made about this assessment. First, we understand that even though these rites have a "theatrical quality," they remain in the realm of ritual. Second, Augustine, whose journey of faith is so publicly chronicled in his *Confessions*, is exactly the sort of person Schechner describes who has undergone a significant transformation and inspires that sort of transformation in others. This is not acting like one who has been transformed; this is the honest living out of one's own transformation. Harmless is right in acknowledging that not everyone has Augustine's rhetorical or ritual skill, which came from training and practice, enhancing his innate abilities.[44]

But because this is a ritual—and everyone is an actor—then the performative quality of each person being initiated is crucial to the efficacy of the rite for that person. A social scientific analysis of an initiation process identifies some crucial elements for the success of the ritual. The ritual sequence must be "a gradual, developmental process by means of which a person is socialized into a community."[45] The sequence must also establish a context of trust for people to engage fully in the rituals. They must learn to feel comfortable with themselves as well as others in this process if they are truly to enact their own life with honesty and integrity.[46] This is not developed first and foremost through narrative and symbol, but through routinized practices of faith that create familiar and dependable patterns of behavior. The trust established in these formative, pragmatic practices provide that context of faith that invites the person into a reorientation of their life narrative according to the narrative of God's saving acts. When one compares the gestation of faith in this process of initiation to that of our friend the octopus, one can see that it is

42. "Sacraments," after all is the Latin translation of the Greek term "mysteries."

43. Harmless, *Augustine and the Catechumenate*, 349.

44. Ibid., 235, 349.

45. Duggan, "Reaction from an RCIA Perspective," 161.

46. Ibid., 161–62.

intentionally social and corporate, neither individual and interior, nor innate and natural. As Woodruff says, "We grow, and grow together."[47]

So What Does All This Have To Do with Theatre?

One of the early theatre games one learns when studying improvisation is the game of "Accept or Block." If you are partnered with another actor and they offer something, you have two choices: you can accept it or you can block it. For example, imagine Actor 1 says, "Is that a bird in your nose?" Actor 2 can accept, "Yes, I needed the money so I rent my nose out as a birdhouse"; or they can block, "Of course not." It is often more interesting to accept than block an offer. My improvisation instructor would say that the first thing to do in response to any offer is to say, "Why, thank you!" and then go on to accept the offer. We practiced this for weeks. Then we were permitted to accept without the verbal expression of thanks, but by that time we had developed an attitude of thanks and acceptance that was communicated in the way we responded, in our body posture and tone of voice.

It is interesting how long this exercise has stuck with me, and how it continues to shape my attitude. When I go into a meeting and I am asked to take on a project, I can accept or block the invitation. If it is obvious I have little choice in the matter, and if I respond with an attitude of gratitude, it actually changes the way I will approach the task. It has formed me into a more gracious and hospitable person, making me more a team player than I otherwise might have been.

Christian churches are struggling to attract and retain members. We have seen that the process of forming healthy human beings and creating lasting communities is rooted in a process of socialization in which individuals choose patterns of behavior and narratives of belief that hold them together. Historically churches have done this through an intentional process of formation. Although this process pertains to the realm of ritual, we have seen how closely connected this is to the qualities of theatre. The challenge of inviting people into the "doing" of God's story may well require the research and resources of theatre—something done intuitively in centuries gone by.[48]

---

47. Woodruff, *The Necessity of Theater*, 10.

48. In September 2013, Fuller Theological Seminary in Pasadena, California hosted an applied theatre conference to explore the potential of theatre in spiritual formation.

To do so we must establish patient, creative communities of faith, grounded in God's story and attentive to the stories of life in the twenty-first century, and execute both stories with imagination, excellence, and the passion of lives transformed. This may or may not look anything like what was done in the past. When done effectively, however, it will create a community of people transformed by God's story of salvation. Liturgical theologian Regis Duffy has observed the need for rituals that do not let people hide the hard realities of their life, but allow them to address these realities with confidence in God, buoyed by a caring and resourceful community of faith.[49] If this can be done, those people will become a living embodiment of God's story in the world, a light to the world, and a reflection of the glory of God—women and men fully alive.

Bibliography

Asad, Talal. *Genealogies of Religion*. Baltimore: Johns Hopkins University Press, 1993.

Augustine. *Sermon 272*. http://www.earlychurchtexts.com/public/augustine_sermon_272_eucharist.htm.

Berger, Peter L. *Invitation to Sociology*. Garden City, NY: Anchor, 1963.

Bradshaw, Paul. *Two Ways of Praying*. Nashville: Abingdon, 1995.

Chen, Karyn. "A Question of Presence: The Sacramental Theology of Regis Duffy, OFM." Unpublished Doctoral Seminar Paper, Fuller Theological Seminary, March 23, 2013.

Duffy, Regis. *Real Presence*. San Francisco: Harper and Row, 1982.

Duggan, Robert D. "Reaction from an RCIA Perspective." In *Alternative Futures for Worship*, vol. 2, *Baptism and Confirmation*, edited by Mark Searle, 157–69. Collegeville, MN: Liturgical, 1987.

Goffman, Erving. *The Presentation of Self in Everyday Life*. Garden City, NY: Anchor, 1959.

Harmless, William. *Augustine and the Catechumenate*. Collegeville, MN: Liturgical, 1995.

Irenaeus. *Adversus Haereses (Against the Heresies)*. http://www.ccel.org/ccel/schaff/anf01.ix.vi.xxi.html.

Johnson, Todd E. "Redeeming Performance." *Liturgy* 28 (2013) 17–24.

Johnson, Todd E., and Dale Savidge. *Performing the Sacred: Theology and Theatre in Dialogue*. Grand Rapids: Baker Academic, 2009.

Kavanagh, Aidan. "Christian Initiation of Adults: The Rites." *Worship* 48 (1974) 318–35.

Luhrmann, T. M. *When God Talks Back*. New York: Knopf, 2012.

Macdonald, Megan. "Liturgy and Performance: Introduction." *Liturgy* 28 (2013) 1–5.

Ruth, Lester. "A Rose by Any Other Name." In *The Conviction of Things Not Seen*, edited by Todd E. Johnson, 33–51. Grand Rapids: Brazos, 2002.

Schechner, Richard. *Performance Theory*. New York: Routledge, 2003.

49. Duffy, *Real Presences*, 92–95. For a very insightful analysis of Duffy's thought as it applies to a theological analysis of theatre, see Chen, "A Question of Presence."

Searle, Mark. "Infant Baptism Reconsidered." In *Alternative Futures for Worship*, vol. 2, *Baptism and Confirmation*, edited by Mark Searle, 15–54. Collegeville, MN: Liturgical, 1987.

States, Bert O. *Great Reckonings in Little Rooms*. Berkeley: University of California Press, 1985.

Turner, Victor. *From Ritual to Theatre*. New York: PAJ, 1982.

Webber, Robert. *Ancient-Future Evangelism*. Grand Rapids: Baker, 2003.

———. *Ancient-Future Worship*. Grand Rapids: Baker, 2008.

Woodruff, Paul. *The Necessity of Theater*. New York: Oxford University Press, 2008.

Yarnold, Edward. *The Awe-Inspiring Rites of Initiation*. Middlegreen, UK: St. Paul, 1971.

9

"And That's True Too"

Revelation, Drama, and the Shape of Christian Ethics

DAVID S. CUNNINGHAM

SOME TWENTY YEARS AGO, John Milbank used the title of an essay to ask the question, "Can Morality Be Christian?" The opening sentences of that essay answered the question as follows:

> Let me tell you the answer straightaway. It is no. Not "no" there cannot be a specifically Christian morality. But no, morality cannot be Christian. All those obscure men of Whitechapel and thereabouts, the Muggletonians and members of other forgotten sects and their heir, William Blake, were no doubt muddle-headed, culturally ill-fed and heretical, and yet in their central antinomianism they were essentially right. And had they known it, [they] were but struggling to say what Catholic tradition itself implies (but has never perhaps adequately articulated), that is, that Christian morality is a thing *so* strange, that it must be declared immoral or amoral according to all other human norms and codes of morality.[1]

---

1. Milbank, "Can Morality Be Christian?" 219.

Milbank's argument poses a stark challenge to the discipline of Christian ethics, one to which it has thus far responded with far too much timidity and evasion. And as he himself notes in his comment about what Catholic tradition implies, his claim is hardly an idiosyncratic one. From its beginnings until now, Christianity has repeatedly described itself as having engineered a decisive break with the law-based ethic of its Jewish forebears. Think of Jesus' reduction of the law to a twofold injunction to love, of Paul's declaration that Christ is the end of the law, of Augustine's "Love, and do what you will," and on through Luther and up to the present day. The claim keeps resurfacing: Christianity is not a book of rules, not a tablet of laws, not a series of commands. It is a way of life.

And then the ethicists enter the scene. After acknowledging all of the above, some statement is made to the effect that of course we couldn't possibly live without rules and laws and principles, and so these are promulgated, argued over, revised, and reissued with added vigor. And whenever it becomes obvious that no one is adhering to these rules, they are rescinded and revised again, or else their neglect is lamented with much wailing and gnashing of teeth. Very few Christian ethicists seem to wonder whether the rules and laws might not themselves be the problem—indeed, the very problem that Christianity had been attempting to solve.

The modern tendency to cling to rules and laws in the face of Christianity's own antinomian insights bears a marked similarity to the modern tendency to cling to violence in spite of Christianity's traditional embrace of pacifism. What is needed, in the face of this intransigence, is something analogous to John Howard Yoder's *The Politics of Jesus*. That book steadfastly refused to accept the idea that, in spite of the teachings of Jesus, people today just couldn't possibly live without resorting to violence. Yoder patiently and graciously exposed the fallacy of that claim and trumped it with the biblical and historical witness to nonviolence that lies at the very heart of the Christian gospel. The same kind of patient, graceful argument needs to be made against those who would turn Christian ethics into a new set of laws.

Unfortunately, "patient, graceful arguments" are not my *forte*, so I will not be playing the role of John Howard Yoder in a bold new production of *The Triumph of Christian Antinomianism*. Nevertheless, I have come to believe that the critique of a law-based and rule-based ethic may be advanced, at least in small measure, by attending to some of the ethical implications of Christian theology's growing interest in theatre, drama,

and dramatic theory. Not that a more theatrical theology *necessarily* warrants a less law-oriented approach to ethics, nor that my case cannot be
made within the more traditional territory of biblical hermeneutics and
ethical method.[2] Still, I believe that the conversation between theology
and theatre can, at a minimum, help us better to understand the antinomian character of Christian ethics, about which "those obscure men of
Whitechapel . . . were essentially right." And perhaps in the process of
better understanding it, we might also come to find it a bit less terrify-
ing—and perhaps even a cause for cheerfulness.[3]

In the three main sections of this paper, I will attempt to address
three of the claims most commonly advanced in defense of a rule- or
law-based Christian ethic. The first claim is that laws and rules are part of
the content of divine revelation, so we cannot simply ignore them; they
are not merely human inventions, but divine decrees, and so they warrant
our obedience. The second claim is that, even if these laws and rules were
not of divine origin, people would still need guidance and clarity. Faced
with an account of love, kindness, and justice as Christian virtues, for
example, they will misconstrue and misinterpret the meaning of these
terms, possibly in destructive or purely self-interested ways. Only rules
or laws, it is claimed, can provide specific enough guidance as to how
general claims about Christian virtue should be concretely instantiated.
The third worry is that any account of Christian ethics that avoids laws
and rules will make ethics into a wax nose, something that can be re-
shaped and twisted into any form, and therefore lacking any continuity
over time. In short, this view equates antinomianism with, if not all-out
moral relativism, then at least a kind of malleability and impermanence
that belies any claim that Christian teaching is *true*. Without rules or laws
to insure some moral continuity from one particular situation, location,
or era to another, so it is claimed, Christian ethics would become simply
a matter of justifying whatever we had been planning to do in the first
place.

2. This, in fact, is what I endeavor to accomplish in my ethics textbook (Cunningham, *Christian Ethics*).

3. I have always felt that Nietzsche's most potent critique of Christianity was his
claim that it was espoused by sour, dour individuals for whom cheerfulness was the enemy. I would like to think that a vision of Christianity charged by cheerfulness—a true
fröhliche Wissenschaft—might have had some appeal even to the Wanderer himself.
Some notes in this direction are offered in Hovey, *Nietzsche and Theology*; Hovey's perspective also seems to me to support the overall antinomian thrust of the present essay.

Revelation, guidance, permanence: these constitute three objections to Christian antinomianism, three oft-cited warrants for the ongoing relevance of law and rules, or at least of objective principles, which are given by God and provide a permanent form of moral guidance. The impetus for each of these concerns is understandable, as is their persuasive force. But when theatre and drama are brought into the conversation, each of these claims bends a little, and their light refracts in new and interesting ways. In the end, I will suggest, the ethical claims that are produced by an encounter with Christianity should look less like those produced by the study of law or logic, and more like those evoked by the experience of theatre.

This essay has three sections—one each on revelation, guidance, and permanence—each headed by a quotation from a play that will be discussed in that section. These are followed by a brief conclusion, headed by the quotation that appears in my title. Those readers who find themselves annoyed, incredulous, or merely bored by this essay can find distraction in figuring out the source of the quote for each section before I begin discussing the play. In the case of the first section, such readers will have to act fast.

"Who's there?"

In the late 1990s, Peter Brook offered a new production of a very famous play. First performed in his trademark laboratory space at the *Bouffes du Nord* in Paris, the production later came to the Chicago Shakespeare Theater. Brook's minimalist interpretation employed a company of just eight actors and a percussionist; it used no sets or props other than a few pillows and candles (and one skull), and it halved the play's typical running time to just over two hours, with no intermission. Certain lines and scenes were rearranged in ways that brought some peripheral elements of the play's texture to the forefront, while some of its better known (or even hackneyed) elements were submerged or omitted.

One of the more radical alterations was the repositioning of the play's very first line to become its very last line. As written, its first line is spoken by a guard, who has apparently heard a noise and demands, "Who's there?";[4] the text ends with the arrival of a foreign emissary, who

---

4. Shakespeare, *Hamlet*, I.i.1. Further quotations will be cited parenthetically by line number.

appears just after the final act's notorious bloodbath that has left most of the principal characters dead. But in Brook's production, the play stops short of Fortinbras's arrival. Instead, it ends with the few surviving characters looking out toward the front of the stage, where new light is streaming in from an unknown source. A look of uncertainty fills their faces, and Horatio asks the question with which Shakespeare's text begins: "Who's there?"—followed by a blackout.

This rearrangement of lines highlights certain elements of drama's revelatory nature. The play's original ending suggests that a new course for Denmark's future is about to be unveiled; but as typically staged, this element is easily lost, since the curtain usually comes down upon a static stage filled with dead bodies. (Parodies of the play make much of this, of course: "Fortinbras here, I just want to—geez, what a mess!"[5]) By keeping the new arrival off stage, and by allowing Horatio to ask the obvious question, Brook's staging underscores the uncertainty and curiosity that would naturally accompany the arrival of an unknown "other." Like the characters in the play, we would like to know more about this new visitor and about the future of the kingdom. But—also like them—we don't yet have that knowledge.

The original text of *Hamlet* begins on the battlements of Elsinore castle, where the night watchman seems nervous about who might be approaching from beyond his range of vision. From these same battlements, Hamlet will pursue someone whose identity he does not yet know—one of the play's many "visitors from beyond." Transposing the play's opening line to the end once again draws our attention to the future arrival of someone new, evoking a sense of anticipation and expectation. Like Barnardo on the watch, like Hamlet following the ghostly visitor, and like Horatio looking out into the light at the end of Brook's production, we too want to know "who's there." Will this newly entering character make a difference in the drama? How will the new arrival affect the other characters, the relationships among them, and the overall plot? What if this new person turns out to be the most important character of all?

These questions are particularly salient for the audience of a play, but one reason that they are felt with such force is that they are also part of our ordinary experience. Whenever we sense the impending arrival of someone into our lives, we are naturally interested to know something about this person. Our desire for such knowledge may be fulfilled or it

---

5. This particular line appears in Garrison Keillor's hilarious "Six-Minute Hamlet."

may be frustrated, but in either case, our sense of anticipation and interest is sure to come alive again the very next time we are faced with an unknown "other" arriving in our midst.

If such questions arise in everyday encounters with the arrival of every new person into our lives, how much more will this be the case when the new arrival happens to be the creator of the universe, the savior of the world, and the ground of our very being? Even those who have grave doubts about the existence of God may still recognize that, within our world—"this wide and universal theater"[6]—the character named "God" has played a very significant role. Admittedly, anyone to whom we are willing to grant this name will necessarily defy easy characterization. Yet the longstanding significance of God as a "character" on the world stage makes us eager to learn something—anything—that might enlighten us.

But on the stage as in life, no one will learn much about this new arrival until that person actually lets herself or himself *be known*—which almost always requires an appearance on stage. Of course, the other characters may ask one another for information or offer information that they have gleaned from others, but these sources may prove spectacularly unreliable. Some may make inferences based on past experience, but each newly arriving personage is different from every other, so such knowledge is rarely decisive. Some characters may even leave the stage and venture forth to meet the new arrival in an effort to find out more information; but the space beyond the stage is dark and inaccessible to everyone else (including us), so these "character-scouts" shouldn't be surprised if their testimony is greeted with skepticism, both by the other members of the cast and by the audience. No one will really begin to learn anything reliable about a newly arriving character until that person *reveals* herself or himself to the other members of the cast. Until then, all they can do—all *we* can do—is wait. And we have to *keep* waiting—even if (as, notoriously, in Beckett's *Waiting for Godot*), the much-anticipated new arrival never actually shows up.

These musings help to illustrate three points that I want to make about the idea of revelation—not only in this paper, but in a larger project I am completing on this topic. First, *revelation is an event*. It is not merely a body of knowledge that is generated at a particular time and place. Rather, the word *revelation* describes an activity in which an unknown

---

6. Shakespeare, *As You Like It*, II.vii.144.

(or imperfectly known) "other" makes herself known. Second, revelation takes place within a *network of mutual participation*. It certainly implies a relationship—a connection between the one who reveals and the one who receives this revelation—but, as our theatrical analogy demonstrates, "relationship" may be too weak a term. Revelation takes place within an interconnected network of meaning, in which the revealer, the revealed, and the receiver of revelation are all involved in one another's worlds. Each of their identities is deeply determined by others within the network. And third, this example illustrates that, ultimately, revelation is about the knowledge of *persons*, rather than objects or abstract ideas. We may of course be interested in the new knowledge that comes from the unveiling of a work of art or the announcement of a scientific breakthrough, but what interests us most profoundly is the human source behind it all. Our most pressing question, like Shakespeare's, is not, "what's there?" but "who's there?"

All of this suggests that theatre has significant potential to illuminate the questions and issues surrounding the theological idea of revelation. It prompts an investigation of script, actor, and acting company as the textual, physical, and corporate body of Christ through which revelation occurs, and of the active role of the audience as its recipient. Although I have written on these matters,[7] they are well beyond the reach of the present paper. My purpose here is to take note of the implications of a dramatic account of revelation for Christian ethics, and in particular, for the possibility of a Christian ethics without laws, rules, or principles.

The three points that I have just outlined—call them the eventful, participative, and personal aspects of revelation—are hardly original claims on my part; nor are they unique to an account of the doctrine that calls upon theatre as its chief conversation partner. But theatre does illustrate, perhaps better than does any other analogy, that these elements are not merely supplements to an account of revelation; they are of its essence. Accepting them as such raises serious questions about the use of the term *revelation* in ways that ignore its eventful, participative, and personal elements. And this, I think, is exactly what a rule-based approach to Christian ethics always does; it focuses almost entirely on the *content* of revelation, not on its character as an event.

7. In various conference papers delivered and essays published over the last several years, all of which are related to the larger work that I am (slowly) completing, tentatively titled *Theatre to the World: The Drama of Divine Revelation*, under contract with Eerdmans.

Laws and other concrete injunctions regarding human behavior are sometimes understood to be inscribed in revelation because they are inscribed in the text of Scripture, as its content. On this view, the tablets of the Decalogue are valuable because of the words written on them, which tell us how to behave. The alternative is to understand this moment of revelation as an encounter between God and Israel—an account that specifies and solidifies that relationship, and in the process tells us something about the identity both of the revealer and of the recipients of revelation. Here, the Decalogue's value is as testimony to that encounter, not as a mere artifact that can be detached from its moment of production and treated as a self-authorizing object. It gives us some clues about the character of God, but these will need to be sifted and weighed together with whatever additional clues we gain from an encounter with Scripture. The move that we often try to make so quickly—from a few lines of biblical text to a more general claim about its content—is rendered highly suspect by the eventful, participative, and personal character of revelation.

Consider again the opening line of *Hamlet*, this time in a more traditional production of the play. What is being revealed? We might answer, "Francisco" (that's the other guard, the one whom Barnardo actually hears, I.i.2), or "the ghost of Hamlet's father," who will eventually arrive (I.i.47). But these answers require a bit of cheating, because they depend on a previous viewing of the play or reading of the text. The characters themselves do not yet know "who's there," and even when they find out, much remains unknown. Moreover, to provide an answer to this question with our previous knowledge of the play would obscure the complexity of the first scene, treating it as a mere dispensary of information rather than as a work of art. The revelation that takes place in I.1 concerns more than the identity of the visitor, and even more than the information that he provides, essential though it may be for us to learn the backstory. This moment of revelation is an *encounter*: an event in which we learn a great deal about the character of those who are involved and of the network of their relationships. Of course, it is only one small piece of the puzzle; after all, if we were to evaluate Hamlet's character based on this encounter alone, we'd imagine him determined, decisive, and resolute. In every revelation, there remains still more to be revealed.

If we take these musings back into the realm of Christian ethics and the role of revelation in helping us to understand its nature, we will find ourselves asking a different set of questions. Instead of focusing on the distilled and rather uninteresting "content" of revelation, we will be more interested in the parties involved in the encounter. Who received this revelation, and how did their physical and psychological state shape their understanding of the event? How did the differing perspectives of the participants alter their experiences of the encounter? And, of particular importance in the case of divine revelation, how is the character of God to be understood in light of the event? Asking these questions makes it much more difficult to make the simplistic claim that "revelation warrants a rule-oriented approach to Christian ethics." In fact, it discourages us from basing theological claims of any sort on revelation's "content," without giving attention to its eventful, participative, and personal character.

"Where love and justice finally meet"

Even under a significantly revised understanding of revelation, the antinomian undercurrent in Christian ethics meets a second form of resistance. This second objection is more practical in nature; it has to do with the human ability—and inability—to make decisions and to shape the moral life in the absence of principles, rules, or laws. Even if the revelation of the law is understood as a dynamic event that is fulfilled in Christ, ethicists have found it difficult to part with the idea of principles or rules as providing much-needed moral guidance. Explanations for this phenomenon vary. One is that human beings lack the discipline necessary to do the kind of moral evaluation that leads to the right response in any given situation. Another is that humans are too easily distracted or too self-interested to see the whole field of moral action clearly. These concerns are legitimate, and they are sometimes given specifically theological warrants, based, for example, on an account of the fall. Nevertheless, these claims are not sufficient to explain why Jesus himself offered so few principles, rules, or laws, but instead told stories, called disciples, and repeatedly observed how adherence to principles could still lead to moral failure. At the very heart of much modern Christian ethics is an essential contradiction between the very practical need to provide guidance through principles and rules, and the nearly complete absence of such guidance in the teachings of Jesus.

But here too, theatre has something to teach us. By enacting the human predicament on stage, theatre addresses the strongly felt need for practical guidance in matters of the moral life, yet does so without the promulgation of rules or laws. As the curtain falls, the playgoer has typically seen characters address a wide variety of moral circumstances and respond in ways that encouraged the audience to render judgments as to the goodness of those responses. By its very nature, theatre is highly nuanced in this regard. Even a short and simple ten-minute one-act can encourage a whole series of judgments about the moral viability of the characters' actions. How much more is this true in the plots and subplots of a five-act spectacle with a wide range of *dramatis personae* whose lives are interwoven with one another in complex and sometimes surprising ways. Throughout the play, the attentive spectator will ask: why did that person make that choice? What are her motivations? Why can't he see the problems? And, most significantly: what would I do?[8]

Of course, all of this creates a certain degree of moral ambiguity, and this is why many modern ethicists avoid drama and narrative, preferring principles and rules as the basis of the Christian moral life. Various members of the audience may make very different judgments about the moral worth of particular characters and of their specific choices; Falstaff is a foolish drunken oaf to some and an insightful and jovial patron to others, so how does his character offer any real moral guidance? And even this ambiguity seems small in comparison with the radically different judgments rendered on particular plays or playwrights at different times in history. Today we regularly praise Shakespeare's moral insight, but in his day neither he nor his fellow playwrights could escape the oft-repeated refrain that the plays incited people to moral degradation. Today we may smirk at such censoriousness, but the question that prompts it still remains: can plays possibly make us better people? My own sense is that scholars have spent far too little time trying to provide a serious answer to that question, and it is not my purpose to answer it here. But I can offer an example of how theatre can provide genuine, practical guidance for moral behavior—not only satisfying our felt need for that guidance, but also avoiding the complex casuistry demanded by an ethic based on rules and principles.

Take, for example, one of the least complicated of the prohibitions in the Decalogue: "You shall not steal" (Exod 20:15). Like many rules and principles, its application seems obvious enough; but before long we will come up against cases where this is no longer true. For example, in the encounter of two civilizations, each having very different understandings of property, the selfsame act may be interpreted as theft by one side

---

8. Theatre allows us to "try on" these character properties, a point made by Kierkegaard and noted in George Pattison's essay in this volume (chapter 6).

but not by the other. The excess food I'll never eat, and will eventually throw out, may still be "mine" in some sense, but is the hungry child, who feeds on what I would otherwise waste, really guilty of stealing? Like the other commandments, the injunction against theft presupposes a broad level of agreement about property, equity, and the availability of the most basic necessities of life—all matters that vary across cultures and circumstances. This is why the discipline of ethics cannot simply announce "you shall not steal" and be done with it; this is why ethics employs definition, explanation, and casuistry, so that the rule might actually provide practical guidance. And perhaps this is also why Jesus was so reticent to make use of principles and laws as the basis of an ethic. Can we not imagine him saying, "You have heard that it was said, you shall not steal. But I say to you: if you think about the property of another, and wish it were your own, you are already guilty of theft in your heart" (cf. Matt 5:21–48). On this account, we all steal, practically all the time, and in violation of the Decalogue.[9] The only way to avoid this conclusion is to redefine theft in such a way as to exclude most of our everyday activities from its scope— to create a series of definitions, exceptions, and caveats that allow us to go about our daily business free from the thought that we are engaged in a relatively constant process of theft. This is what much of modern ethics has done, and it is, I would like to think, precisely what Jesus would have told us not to do.

Theatre operates differently. Consider, briefly, the stage version of *Les Misérables*. (And no, that's not the source of my title for this section—readers will have to keep working on it.) Jean Valjean may have stolen a loaf of bread, but by the end of the stage version of the novel, few members of the audience would consider him morally blameworthy for that act. Indeed, the audience usually comes to see the futility of trying to do so, particularly as the moral universe of his pursuer collapses in upon itself. Moreover, the audience is presented with a concrete alternative to moral condemnation: when Valjean steals the Bishop's silver, he is not only allowed to keep it; he is given more. There is no law to cover these cases: we cannot universalize the principle "do not steal" or "do steal" or "let people steal" or "give more when people steal from you." In a sense, the play itself, and the novel upon which it is based, both point out the insufficiency of any principle or rule to cover the various cases. What

9. Indeed, this point is made by the Decalogue itself, in its injunction against coveting; this, in turn, was the source of one of Luther's clearest examples of how we fail to follow the law, and therefore of how the law fails us.

they offer instead is attention to character: we see this man across a significant span of his life, and we are thereby able to evaluate his character in ways that transcend individual acts of theft. He is a good man, in spite of his crimes and misdemeanors. Our moral universe expands, beyond questions about theft and truth-telling and resisting arrest, to take the picture of an entire life.

But only on stage can we witness the broad arc of a human life in a three-hour span, so the moral power of theatre does not translate directly into the rest of our lives. Instead, it builds up in us the power of moral reasoning—a kind of practical wisdom—that will allow us to make judgments without the benefit of seeing the entire story played out on stage. It is precisely this kind of practical wisdom that allows the bishop to see into the character of Jean Valjean and to encourage him to imagine that it might be a good idea to supplement an act of theft with additional gifts. The bishop might have been wrong; Valjean might well have run off with the silver and continued a life of crime. But even if that had happened, the bishop would only have lost a few pieces of silver tableware. Instead, as it happened, he gained a saint.

Consider a different, harder example. In Tony Kushner's play *Perestroika*,[10] the second half of *Angels in America*, a significant act of theft is contemplated and then carried out. Roy Cohn, the notorious henchman of Joseph McCarthy, and also the man most responsible for the execution of Julius and Ethel Rosenberg, is hospitalized, dying of AIDS. He has steadfastly refused to acknowledge his own homosexuality and has reconstrued his disease as something more befitting his own sense of himself. He has, however, used his corrupt connections to obtain his own private supply of AZT, at that time a highly experimental drug for the treatment of AIDS. One of the nurses on his floor, Belize, knows plenty of people who are dying of the disease and who would gladly take the risk of receiving the drug if they could only have access to it. Belize manages to talk Roy into giving him one bottle and to take a few more by stealth. But when Roy dies, leaving a refrigerator full of AZT that will otherwise be returned to the lab, Belize contemplates a more serious act of theft.

Of course, no rule or principle can cover this case. What would it be? "Do not steal, except when the owner is an evil, corrupt, and dead lawyer, who has come by the property through immoral means"? And

10. Kushner, *Angels in America*.

yet, I'd wager that most members of the audience actually want Belize to get those pills—and, from the perspective of Christian ethics, I think this is exactly what we *should* want him to do. Prohibitions against theft notwithstanding, we have come to know enough about the lives of people living with AIDS, and especially about Prior Walter, the protagonist of the play, that we want him to be able to take AZT. We want Belize to have the practical wisdom to reason through the moral implications of this potential act of theft, and to carry it out. We want this because part of the play's moral force is its call for compassion on those who suffer with this disease, its claim that they should be granted the blessing of "more life." This doesn't automatically lead us to want to break a lot of laws. But it does lead us to approve the breaking of this law, if it is one, in this particular circumstance.

In the end, Belize not only takes the AZT; he confirms our approval of this violation of the law by giving the owner of the medicine something in return. Belize is already one of the most likeable characters in the play; he is the voice of conscience for Louis, who has abandoned his lover and partner, Prior, who is dying of AIDS. Moreover, Belize is a nurse; he embodies in his work the kind of compassion that we feel for victims of this disease.[11] But in spite of this highly positive assessment of his character, we may still be a little amazed when he says that, in exchange for the AZT, he wants to give Roy something in return. Roy certainly doesn't strike us as deserving anything good; indeed, as much as we may dislike Louis for his act of abandonment, we are probably tempted to agree with his assessment of Roy Cohn: "He's like the polestar of human evil, he's like the worst human being who ever lived, he isn't *human* even."[12] Thus, Belize's willingness to give Roy Cohn a posthumous gift, perhaps as a kind of payment for the medicine in his fridge, seems like a real act of supererogation. And so is the act performed in this scene by Ethel Rosenberg, whose ghost has haunted Roy throughout the play. Having suffered the death penalty at Roy's insistence, Ethel understandably finds forgiveness to be difficult. Just before his death, she tells him that she has made her hatred for him into a sharp little star in the sky, a star that burns acid green. She says to him, "I came to forgive but all I can do is take pleasure in your misery. Hoping I'd get to see you die more terrible than I did. . . .

11. We first meet him in I.v. of *Millennium Approaches*, where he arrives at Prior's hospital room with a jar of ointment (Ibid., 65). The echoes of Mark 14:3–9 ring fairly loudly for anyone who knows the story.

12. Ibid., 227.

And when you die all anyone will say is: Better he had never lived at all."[13] But her hatred cannot last forever; and at his death, she cannot follow through on her desire to see the memory of his life obliterated.

In the final scene in the hospital room,[14] Roy's body is lying on the bed and Ethel's ghost is sitting in a chair. Belize enters, bringing with him Louis, to whom he begins explaining why he has brought him here—namely, to steal the remaining AZT from the refrigerator. "I needed a pack mule," he says, "so I called you."

Louis responds, "Why me? You hate me."

Belize explains, "I needed a Jew. You were the first to come to mind. . . . We're going to thank him. For the pills."

Louis can't imagine thanking a dead person, least of all Roy Cohn; and he is even more incredulous when he learns that Belize wants him to say the Kaddish, the Jewish prayer for the dead. Louis objects vehemently: "My New Deal Pinko Parents in Schenectady would never forgive me, they're already so disappointed, 'He's a fag, he's an office temp, and *now look*, he's saying Kaddish for Roy Cohn.'"

Belize tries to help Louis understand: "He was a terrible person. He died a hard death. So maybe . . . a queen can forgive her vanquished foe. It isn't easy, it doesn't count if it's easy, it's the hardest thing. Forgiveness. Which is maybe where love and justice finally meet. Peace, at last. Isn't that what the Kaddish asks for?"

Louis complains, Moses-like, that he isn't equipped for the task, but Belize won't let him go: "Do the best you can." Louis looks around and spots a tissue box, so he puts a tissue on his head as a yarmulke and begins to say the Kaddish. He makes several mistakes, starts over again, and then seems ready to give up, saying, "This is silly, Belize, I can't . . ." But at this point the ghost of Ethel Rosenberg stands up and says the next line of the Kaddish for him. Louis repeats what she says, line by line, and eventually they start saying it together. Louis's voice is choked with emotion.

13. Ibid., 246.

14. Ibid., 254–57. When this essay was presented as a conference paper, I showed a clip from the HBO film version of the play. I encourage readers to watch the scene in that version, which is not quite like seeing it on stage, but is much better than reading my summary of the scene. It helps, I think, that the set of this scene is small, easily imagined onto the stage, and also that all four of the actors that readers will see there are also very fine stage actors: Jeffrey Wright as Belize, Ben Shenkman as Louis, Meryl Streep as the ghost of Ethel Rosenberg, and, although you don't get to see his brilliant acting in this particular scene, Al Pacino as Roy Cohn. Those without access to the film version might consider simply reading the scene (aloud if possible) from the book.

The scene ends with them each saying the final line of the Kaddish, and an extra line to boot ("You sonofabitch"), at which point Ethel vanishes.

I am tempted to allow the scene to speak for itself, but I will make one further comment. In addition to providing nuance and clarity to our moral evaluation of theft, this scene (and the play as a whole) goes well beyond anything that law can do to form the moral character of its audience. The play enjoins us to compassion and forgiveness; it fosters in us a hope that people can change for the good; and it offers a trenchant critique of forcing people to closet their sexuality and the often dire consequences to which such actions lead. It is a brilliant instantiation of the superiority of theatre as a means of moral formation and of the shaping of moral judgment.

In fact, it seems to me that a simple reading of the Gospels can reveal one of the obvious reasons why theatre is so easily aligned with Christian ethics. One of Jesus' favorite forms of teaching is the parable, a short vignette containing dramatic action. The characters are not as fully formed as those in a play, and narration is often more important than dialogue; nevertheless, these vignettes are often structured in ways that emphasize their dramatic arc. They are easily made into skits, and children sometimes learn them by performing them as plays in miniature. However, as many biblical scholars have noted, parables are not usually reducible to a simple "moral of the story," like Aesop's *Fables*, and in any case, the narrative tends to overflow any straightforward ethical dictum one might use to contain it.

My goal in this section has been fairly modest: I have simply wanted to show that concrete moral guidance does not necessarily require the promulgation of rules and laws, but can also be offered by theatrical performance. While most of us are unlikely to face the exact circumstances that Belize faced, we may sometimes have to think through the issues surrounding theft. Moreover, experiencing this play may help us to develop the practical wisdom necessary for our moral reflection and decisions.

"Wouldn't it be funny if that was true?"

Permanence is the third concern which is sometimes thought to warrant a rule-based ethic and makes antinomianism impossible. Without rules, or at least clearly stated principles of some kind, Christian ethics is a mere will-o'-the-wisp: it moves in whatever direction the wind is blowing. If a particular act is morally culpable, then it must always have been so; but an antinomian account provides no way of insuring this continuity.

In addressing this objection, a good place to start is with Sam Wells's book *Improvisation: The Drama of Christian Ethics*. This book begins with a genealogical account that helps us understand why Christian ethics began to focus on discrete acts rather than on the shape of the Christian life. Wells points out that this move is a modern anomaly; for most of its history, Christian moral reasoning relied on an account of the virtues as describing the excellences of character that should be formed and habituated in the Christian life. The continuity that is built into Christian ethics, its "permanence" if you will, is the ongoing conversation about which virtues are properly Christian and how they should be defined. This means that discrete moral acts cannot be prescribed in advance, but need to be improvised by the actor who is well trained in Christian living. Wells then goes on to employ, as illustrative of this work, the analogy of theatrical improvisation, which requires a group of people who spend a great deal of time together and come to understand one another (the improv troupe, analogous to the worshiping community). It requires a great deal of training and practice; its results cannot be predicted in advance.

I do not plan to enlist Wells's argument as an ally to my cause. I suspect that, based on some aspects of this book and on his other work, he might be uncomfortable with the degree of antinomianism that I am advocating here.[15] I mention the book primarily as a way of clearing the ground with respect to the concern about "permanence." For Wells, demanding that discrete acts receive the same moral evaluation in every circumstance is akin to evaluating discrete acts in improvisational theatre without any attention to their context. Obviously, an exchange that works well in one moment of an improv skit may fall completely flat in another. Any account of Christian ethics that treats discrete acts as its primary point of reference is not sufficiently attentive to ethics as an account of character (*ēthos*).

But Wells may simply add fuel to the fire by focusing only on improvisation, and not on scripted drama, as a possible analogue for ethical reflection. Those who worry about permanence, or at least continuity, in ethical reflection may be particularly cautious about an account that dispenses with a text altogether. Although Wells sometimes speaks of "improvisation on the basis of a text" or "with a text in the background,"

---

15. See, for example, Wells, *God's Companions*.

he seems to oppose the notion that text-based drama can provide an analogy for Christian ethics. He is concerned that the "script" that lies behind theatrical performance will be misconstrued as too comprehensive, or that its performance will become a nostalgic quest for a golden era or will ignore contemporary realities.[16] But I think this is a significant underestimation of what occurs in a theatrical performance. Perhaps the worry about permanence and continuity in ethics can be assuaged by emphasizing that the script provides a certain degree of continuity, in spite of variations among performances.

Consider, for example, moral reflection on truth-telling and mendacity. Many theologians and ethicists have suggested that principles such as "one should always tell the truth" or "one must never lie" should be a feature of the Christian moral landscape. And yet, "Do not lie" is just as deceptively complex as the prohibition against theft described in the previous section. Moreover, recent claims to the contrary notwithstanding, I do not think a case can be made that the prohibition against lying can function as a straightforward moral rule. This seems to me to be underscored by the "script" with which Christian ethics most frequently operates, namely the Bible. While we can cite plenty of stories in which a lie is told with bad consequences, or in which lying seems to be condemned, we can also cite cases in which lies are told for good reasons and even receive some degree of moral approbation. It is, at best, a decidedly mixed message.

What would it mean to "enact" this mixed message in the moral realm? What does it mean to enact any dramatic text that deals with truth telling and mendacity? In some sense, theatrical performance is a particularly powerful space for this analysis. Lies are more easily illustrated on the stage than they are in other forms of fictional mimesis, since the audience can often hear one thing being said while seeing a contrary thing being done, without anyone having to point out the difference. We've seen how Iago obtains Desdemona's handkerchief, so we can immediately identify his lie in a way that Othello cannot. Richard III announces his own mendacity to the audience from the very outset, in a series of asides. George exposes the "pleasant lie" in which he and Martha have indulged, concerning their fictional son, by the announcement of his fictional death.[17]

---

16. Wells, *Improvisation*, 62–63.

17. In Albee, *Who's Afraid of Virginia Woolf?*

But theatrical performance also presents us with a problem: because its characters and plots are specific, we sometimes find ourselves attaching its moral implications to particular people or circumstances, while exempting ourselves because we are "not like them." Iago and Richard are sometimes thought to be so villainous, so morally intolerable, that every act of villainy gets quickly subsumed under the banner of the character; these are just evil people. We are not like them at all; we don't come to understand our own temptations through them, because they are so wholly different from us. They provide us with an opportunity for moral reflection only if they become sympathetic enough characters that we can imagine ourselves in their places.

But does this make the texts of *Othello* and *Richard III* less than useful for moral reflection? Or is the question less about the text itself and more about the way it is performed? For it is possible to present these characters in such a way that they do win our sympathy at first, that they draw us into their worlds from the outset. Some of the most successful performances of these plays, I think, are those that avoid the immediate melodramatic casting of these roles as villains, and give them time to win us over before we realize just how troubling their moral faults really are.

In order to examine this problem more closely, I want to consider a play in which mendacity is an important theme, a play in which characters tell lies to entire groups, to various individuals, and to themselves. Some of the lies may strike us as necessary, at least in the moment; others seem destructive of relationships or even of a character's own identity. As members of the audience, we are unlikely to take away any universal principle about telling lies; still, the moral force of the play may depend on our ability to imagine ourselves into various roles.

But if that play has a very specific setting—the American South in the 1950s—and if its characters seem too deeply embedded in that world, then it can be all too easy for an audience to attribute the characters' flaws to their region, their era, or the social structures in which they lived. I'm thinking of Tennessee Williams's *Cat on a Hot Tin Roof*, which is often better remembered for the larger-than-life personalities who played the various characters than for the story it tells or its moral impact. But the reason for that has much less to do with the author or the actors than it does with its first director, who felt it could not succeed on Broadway as Williams wrote it, and urged him to make some significant changes to the text.[18]

18. Not that Elia Kazan was a timid director; a decade later he managed to get

The play is set on a southern plantation, where the family has gathered for a birthday party for its patriarch, who bears the highly descriptive name of Big Daddy. His younger son, Gooper, is married to a Memphis socialite named Mae, and they have already produced five children with a sixth on the way. But the much-favored older son, Brick—although married to the seductive and tenacious Margaret—has yet to produce an heir. Tormented by questions about his sexual identity, he spends most of his time drowning himself in drink.

Margaret, or Maggie, is the eponymous "cat" of the play's title: both a sex kitten and an alley fighter. With more strength of character than almost anyone else in the play, she consistently points out the disguises and masks worn by everyone else, from Brick's closeted sexuality to her in-laws' efforts to take over the plantation. But she is also the source of the play's most complicated lie. In the final act, as the family becomes increasingly aware of the true state of Big Daddy's health—he has inoperable cancer—she announces that she is pregnant and will bear the heir that her father-in-law has so deeply desired. Her husband, who is present at the announcement, doesn't call her out; later, alone with him, she thanks him for that gesture, thus confirming for the audience that she has in fact lied about her condition. But then, in the play's closing lines, she observes that it need not remain a lie.

In the play's closing dialogue (in the final version as Williams rewrote it[19]), Brick and Maggie are back in the bedroom, after Mae has called Maggie a "liar" and slammed the door. After a short interlude during which Brick throws down three shots of liquor in quick succession, Maggie gathers the bottles out of the liquor cabinet and runs out of the room with them. When she returns, she makes it clear that they should go to bed together for the purpose of conceiving a child. She even throws his crutch out the window to prevent him from going back to the liquor to avoid her. She then says, "And so tonight we're going to make the lie true." When it becomes clear that Brick won't resist her, she says, "Oh, you weak people, you weak, beautiful people!—who give up with such

---

Who's Afraid of Virginia Woolf onto the Broadway stage in relatively unexpurgated form. But *Cat* arrived in the 1950s, not the 1960s, and Kazan undoubtedly did the best he could. Still, those who have only seen the 1958 film version have not seen the play that Williams wrote.

19. At the conference, some brave delegates staged the scene for the attendees. I am only sorry that their efforts were not recorded for posterity! I can't recommend a film in this case, though there is an HBO version that uses Williams's rewrite. Readers may want to read the final two pages of the book edition.

grace. What you want is someone to . . . take hold of you.—Gently, gently with love hand your life back to you, like somethin' gold you let go of. I *do* love you, Brick, I *do!*"

And then Brick, "smiling with charming sadness," offers the final line of the play: "Wouldn't it be funny if that was true?"

Brick can't believe in his wife's love for a man who isn't really attracted to women, and an alcoholic to boot; yet he's willing to imagine the possibility, in all its ludicrousness. The ending does not announce a reconciliation between Maggie and Brick, nor suggest that they will indeed act to "make the lie true," as did the radically altered ending of the original Broadway production and the film version. But neither does it definitively pronounce against this possibility. It leaves the audience in a state of uncertainty: perhaps the greatest uncertainty that they have felt during the whole experience of watching the play.

And that uncertainty is precisely where the audience should be: asking questions about the various lies that are told throughout the play, asking about their moral validity, and particularly wondering about this final lie-that-could-become-truth. But the entire enterprise would lose its effectiveness if it were possible to write off the characters as a gang of backwater rednecks, mere instantiations of the stereotypical nastiness that is hidden behind America's famous "Southern hospitality." And there is some evidence that this is precisely what happened during one of the play's early runs, in which critics referred to the boys and girls who careen out-of-control through the play as "the South's most horrifying children" and its protagonist as "scorchingly Southern."

Given all these circumstances, it may be difficult for audiences to grasp the full moral force of the play. Is the text simply too regional, too dated, incapable of drawing us in and allowing us to identify with its characters and with the lies that they tell? Is the text of this play additional evidence for Wells's claim that the script actually becomes an impediment to recognizing the moral force of theatre, thereby justifying his preference for the analogy of improvisation?

Most of the play's history of performance would seem to suggest an affirmative answer to these questions. Until 2008 it had seen only one Broadway revival, and a few other scattered productions at major theatres. The casting was often very strong, and individual actors often received very positive reviews; but the play as a whole continued to be seen as deficient. In particular, few reviewers surmised that audiences would be moved to think very deeply about the moral implications of mendacity, nor to consider whether it might propose certain legitimate exceptions to the general ethical injunction against lying. The specificity of the play's time and place made its moral implications difficult to grasp.

In 2008, director Debbie Allen hit upon an improbable solution: to cast *Cat on a Hot Tin Roof* entirely with African-American actors. This obviously required an updated setting, but interestingly enough it required almost no changes in the play's language. The casting was phenomenal, with Anika Noni Rose as Maggie, Terrence Howard as Brick, and Phylicia Rashad as Big Mama, almost all of whom received very positive reviews. Most impressive of all, the character of Big Daddy came to life more fully than in any of the previous productions in the extraordinary stage presence of James Earl Jones. But then again, the actors had not usually been the problem with this play, and this is where the director's achievement was most marked: audiences understood it. They couldn't attribute the characters' idiosyncrasies to the redneck South; they were instead faced with a genuine black middle-class family in crisis, and yet without any particular reference to race. Oddly enough, by casting the play within the world of an ethnic minority, the director took away the audience's tendency to stereotype. (Few playgoers would allow themselves to think, let alone say, something like "well, black people are like that"—though many would have no difficulty making similarly stereotypical claims about white southerners.)

Nor was this production's appeal limited to American audiences. It came to London soon after, bringing along the African-American actors for the two older roles but casting two young British actors in the younger ones: Sanaa Lathan as Maggie and Adrian Lester as Brick. The production also found a very positive reception in the UK and certainly was seen by more people than the original production in 1958, when it had to be produced privately because the Lord Chamberlain refused to approve it for public theatres.

Note, again, how little the director altered the play. No major changes in the text, no change in the locale, no technical fireworks to distract the audience—just a change in casting, along with the modernization of the period setting which such a change required. This is a clear reminder, if one is needed, that the script of a good play does not need to become an impediment to the creative director. The best directors can, with very minor changes, bring out the text's most salient implications, and probably find others that had never been noticed.

What are the implications of this for the shape of Christian ethics? First, it raises serious questions about the charges leveled by Wells and others about the limitations of the script in the analogy of "ethics as performance." Far from pushing us into mundane reiterations or nostalgic glances back to a golden age, the script can become the vehicle for artful reinterpretation in ways that we may be unable to imagine at the present moment. If the texts of Christian ethics, which would include at a minimum the Bible and certain traditions of the ecumenical church, are read neither as epic narratives nor as lyric poetry but as dramatic scripts, and if skilled readers and "performers" are given the freedom to offer their own creative interpretations, then the texts can acquire a degree of moral force that far outstrips that of an individual's encounter with the printed page.

Second, this performance demonstrates how a text that is decidedly lacking in clear and concise "rules and principles" about a certain set of ethical questions can, nevertheless, become a vehicle for significant moral reflection. Like the text of the Bible, Williams's play helps us recognize that mendacity is a moral problem without resorting to didactic prohibitions or the casuistic interpretation of rules. The script sets up the problems and raises the questions, but it does not bring them to a neat and tidy conclusion. In this respect, one of Williams's extended stage directions is particularly *à propos*. During the conversation between Brick and Big Daddy, when performers and directors might be tempted to resolve Brick's inner conflict in one way or another, Williams offers an alternative plan:

> The bird that I hope to catch in the net of this play is not the solution of one man's psychological problem. I'm trying to catch the true quality of experience in a group of people, that cloudy, flickering, evanescent—fiercely charged!—interplay of live human beings in the thundercloud of common crisis. Some mystery should be left in the revelation of character in a play, just as a great deal of mystery is always left in the revelation of character in life, even of one's own character to himself.[20]

Rather than faulting the text—whether that of the Bible or the play—for failing to provide us with definitive moral judgments, we should embrace the opportunity that it gives us to work through the moral questions for ourselves.

---

20. Williams, *Cat on a Hot Tin Roof*, 77.

Third, and closely related to this last point: this performance shifts the balance of moral judgment away from discrete acts and toward an ethics of practical wisdom. Just as the text does not contain definitive moral judgments, neither does the performance itself. It does not tell us what we should think about lying, whether it is ever morally justifiable, and if so, in what circumstances. Instead, it offers us a kind of training, a habituation in moral judgment that encourages us to become persons of practical wisdom and to think about the complexities involved in a decision to tell a lie in a particular situation. Instead of evaluating discrete acts as to their moral character, we are asked to inhabit the roles that these characters represent, and to think about the kind of moral training that is required in order to judge rightly. This, I think, is the kind of work Christian ethics needs to do, rather than promulgating rules and principles and then arguing over their application in any particular case.

Conclusion: "And that's true, too"

Despite the length of this essay, it has barely scratched the surface of the topic at hand. Even if it may have made some headway in raising questions about the tendency of Christian ethics to resort to laws and rules, it has not made a positive case for the antinomianism endorsed in my introduction. At the outset, I made it clear that this would not be a Yoder-like reclamation of a long-lost Christian truth. Nevertheless, I would like to conclude by offering a brief glimpse into my own vision for a radically different approach to Christian ethics, by way of one last work of theatre.

One aspect of the contemporary practice of Christian ethics that I personally find most annoying—and sometimes even a bit painful—is its tendency to make immodest pronouncements about moral truth. In addition to being at odds with the essential antinomianism that I believe is at the heart of the Christian witness, this absolutism has led a great many Christians, and sometimes the church as a whole, into some of its most notorious errors—matters about which they would later come to express deep regret. For readers of this volume, I need not elaborate the great crimes of Christianity; they are well known. Of course, I also believe that individual Christians and the church as a whole have done great good in this world. But in seeking to do more good and less evil, the church might take a cue from theatre. I doubt that theatre has done more *good* than the church, but I suspect that theatre has done considerably less evil—and not because theatre is less effective or less persuasive. I have a different theory altogether.

What theatre offers, and what the church too often does not, is the simultaneous presentation of multiple voices. A typical play offers a great variety of perspectives on a host of questions. It stands to reason that, in the theatre as in life, some of these perspectives will participate more fully in the true, the good, and the beautiful than will others. But good theatre refuses to mark, grade, or evaluate these various perspectives; it refuses to tell us which ones are the right ones. Those decisions we must make for ourselves. Not that theatre doesn't provide us with plenty of clues: if you walk out of a production of the "Scottish play"[21] and say to yourself, "Boy, I'd sure love to be *that* title character," then something, somewhere, has gone terribly wrong. Still, the best plays are populated with characters with some good traits and other not-so-good ones, and usually both of these reside in the same character. Even more significantly, a single character can recognize the truth that can be found, simultaneously, in two opposing points of view. And there are no neon signs that light up to tell the members of the audience which ones to choose.

The title of this essay is the final line spoken by a character in *King Lear*—one of Shakespeare's plays that is often assumed to challenge most radically the Christian worldview,[22] but ultimately, I think, most radically affirms it.[23] The Earl of Gloucester, having already been saved from his own attempt at suicide, finds himself again at the end of all hope, and once again calls on death to take him away: "No more, sir. A man may rot even here." But his son, not yet revealed to be his son, provides a different point of view. Edgar replies:

> What, in ill thoughts again? Men must endure
> their going hence, even as their coming hither;
> Ripeness is all: come on.

And Gloucester replies: "And that's true too."[24]

---

21. I'm not superstitious, but at the conference where this paper was presented, the tea failed to arrive during our break only once, and it was shortly after two of the presenters spoke the name of the play aloud!

22. One of the standard-bearers of this claim is William R. Elton, *King Lear and the Gods*.

23. For my defense of this claim, see chapter 3 of David S. Cunningham, *Friday, Saturday, Sunday*.

24. Shakespeare, *King Lear*, V.ii.12–16.

And that is what I would wish for Christian ethics, for the church, and for Christianity as a whole: to listen to the wisdom of others and not always to say that the other is wrong, nor to say that oneself is wrong and the other is right, but to receive whatever truth might be present in each. Such a perspective is only possible in the realm of Christian ethics, I propose, if we are willing to set aside the misplaced search for rules and laws and begin searching for a different way forward. On this score, I think Christianity has much to learn from the theatre, a claim that has been affirmed over and over again throughout this book. May Christian theology's embrace of theatre continue and prosper; and "may we cram, within this wooden O," not merely "the very casques that did affright the air at Agincourt," but also the collective wisdom of theologians past, present and future, so that we might learn to speak our speeches plainly, and that our audiences might say, "Let them roar again."

Bibliography

Albee, Edward. *Who's Afraid of Virginia Woolf?* New York: Scribner Classics, 2003.

Cunningham, David S. *Christian Ethics: The End of the Law.* London: Routledge, 2008.

―――. *Friday, Saturday, Sunday: Literary Meditations on Suffering, Death, and New Life.* Louisville, KY: Westminster John Knox, 2007.

Hovey, Craig. *Nietzsche and Theology.* London: T. & T. Clark, 2008.

Keillor, Garrison. "Six-Minute Hamlet." In *The English Majors' CD.* Minneapolis: HighBridge, 2008.

Kushner, Tony. *Angels in America: A Gay Fantasia on National Themes.* Including *Part One: Millennium Approaches* and *Part Two: Perestroika.* New York: Theatre Communications Group, 1995.

Milbank, John. "Can Morality Be Christian?" In *The Word Made Strange: Theology, Language, Culture,* 219–32. Oxford: Wiley-Blackwell, 1997.

Schönberg, Claude-Michel, Herbert Kretzmer, Charles Hart, and Andrew Lloyd Webber. *Les Misérables.* Based on the novel by Victor Hugo. MMO Music Group, 1986.

Shakespeare, William. *The Tragedy of Hamlet, Prince of Denmark.* New York: Simon and Schuster, 1992.

―――. *The Tragedy of King Lear.* New York: Simon and Schuster, 1993.

―――. *As You Like It.* New York: Simon and Schuster, 1994.

Wells, Samuel. *God's Companions: Reimagining Christian Ethics.* Oxford: Wiley-Blackwell, 2006.

―――. *Improvisation: The Drama of Christian Ethics.* Grand Rapids: Brazos, 2004.

Williams, Tennessee. *Cat on a Hot Tin Roof.* London: Methuen, 2010.

Yoder, John Howard. *The Politics of Jesus: Vicit Agus Noster.* Grand Rapids: Eerdmans, 1972.

10

Eucharistic Drama

Rehearsal for a Revolution[1]

Marilyn McCord Adams

Cultic Drama, Sacramental Effects

CULT IS SACRED DRAMA. Whether high church or low, it is played out on a stage, with liturgical hardware and costumes, scripts and plots, choreography and gestures, lead roles that call for careful casting, and a host of others in the surround. Torah will tell you that many such details are dictated, the whole drama produced and directed by God.[2]

Cult condenses cosmos. Cosmic problems are symbolically enacted and resolved on the cultic stage. Sacramental theology forwards the idea that participating in these problems and their resolution in the cultic world somehow "carries over," participates in, and empowers cosmic resolution. Yet, "carries over" is a metaphor that demands to be cashed out better in order to avoid Reformation charges of magic-mongering and superstition. How *does* cultic drama produce cosmic effects?

Happily, help is at hand from a source both natural and surprising: theatre theory! Coming from different angles, a number of brilliant

---

1. I am grateful to Professors Shannon Craigo-Snell, Christine Helmer, Wendy Boring, and to the Reverend Dr. Terri Bays for helpful objections, challenges, and guidance.

2. Exod 23–31; Lev (entire); Num 3:5–10; 7–9; 28–29. See also Ezek 40–47.

twentieth-century directors, producers, and writers—most of them thoroughly alienated from conventional religion—came to see the vocation of theatre to mediate life's meaning, to recognize acting as a sacrificial offering of the whole self that aims to confront people with themselves, social realities, and the sacred in fresh and transformative ways. Because they in effect assign theatre a sacramental function, their reflections promise to shed light on what the church has been doing all along.[3]

In what follows, I will open up this line of inquiry by focusing on eucharistic drama. Whether or not one argues—with some Roman Catholics—that Holy Eucharist is the *principal* Christian sacrament,[4] it is undeniably one of the two *dominical* sacraments.[5] In contrast with baptism, Holy Eucharist is the oft-repeatable sacrament, a drama into which Christians insert themselves regularly, expose themselves to its effects over and over again.[6] For that reason, it seems an apt place to begin.

Beginning with Tragedy

The Christian gospel is arguably comic, but it affords no cheap and easy laughs. The Christian gospel is not about Pollyannaish denial or quick fixes that pretend there isn't much of a problem. The Christian gospel calls us first to be grimly realistic about ourselves, about the human condition, and about divine-human relations. At its most cheerful, the Christian gospel is tragi-comic. Unsurprisingly, Holy Eucharist begins with tragedy. The tradition handed on by St. Paul identifies its purpose: to show forth the Lord's death (1 Cor 11:26). How does cultic tragedy transform and propel participants into cosmic plot resolution?

3. See Schumacher and Singleton, *Artaud on Theatre*; Boal, *Theatre of the Oppressed*; Willet, *Brecht on Theatre: The Development of an Aesthetic*; Brook, *The Empty Space*; Grotowski, *Towards a Poor Theatre*; Stanislavski, *An Actor Prepares*. See also Schechner, *Performance Theory*.

4. Aquinas, *Summa Theologica* I, q.65, a.3.c.

5. That is, Christ explicitly commanded baptism (Matt 28:19) and Eucharist (Matt 26:26–29; Mark 14:22–25; Luke 22:19–20). In the middle ages, sacramental theology finally settled on five others: confirmation, ordination, marriage, confession, and unction.

6. Baptism is not repeatable; see Aquinas, *Summa Theologica* III, q.66, a.9c.

"Aristotelian" Dynamics

In his provocative manifesto, *Theatre of the Oppressed,* Augusto Boal arrives at a theory of what ought to be through a history of pernicious mistakes. Perhaps predictably, Boal takes Aristotle as his foil. On Boal's reconstruction, the paradigm of Aristotle's tragic hero/heroine is one who is thoroughly virtuous except for a single weakness or flaw. She is always, or at least for the most part, someone the spectator would be glad to be. Even the weakness or flaw is at first presented sympathetically, sometimes as a source of the heroine's initial good fortune, wealth, or well-being. Dramatic tension builds to a turning point in which the heroine suffers a catastrophic reversal of fortune, one that is also traceable to the character's flaw. At tragedy's end, the heroine admits her fault and—along with the chorus and the play's author—acknowledges the disastrous turn as its natural and appropriate outcome. On Boal's reading, *Oedipus Rex* is a paradigm case.

On Boal's analysis, "Aristotelian" tragedy works on the spectator through the psychological mechanism of *sympathetic identification.*[7] Because the hero is like us, or someone we can admire or would like to be, Aristotle says, we feel *pity* that someone so good should suffer something that bad. Sympathetic identification with the hero also allows our own flaws to be psychologically aroused and somehow activated as we vicariously live through the stage character's experiences. This is why the hero's fall fills us with *fear,* which in turn triggers *catharsis,* a purging of the spectator's own flawed tendencies.

Boal emphasizes that the play will not set this process in motion unless the heroine is sympathetically presented. If the main character is an utterly detestable scoundrel, spectators will most likely rejoice in her ruin, enjoy the fact that she gets what she deserves. No identification means no activation of the spectator's flaws. The result is that ruin on the stage does not produce fear in the spectator or real-life purgation. Likewise, when good guys finish first, there are no flaws with which to identify and no catastrophes to fear. Boal also stresses the importance of the heroine's admission of fault, which the sympathetically identified

7. Boal, *Theatre of the Oppressed,* 28–32, 36–37, 40, 50. Boal is offering us a distinctive reading of Aristotle's *Poetics,* chs. 6–18, 1449b20–1456a32. The interpretation of these passages is highly controversial, and it is not my purpose to enter the debate about the right reading of Aristotle. I indicate this caution by speaking of "Aristotelian" poetics. Instead, I want to show how the distinctive dynamic outlined in Boal's analysis helps us understand how eucharistic participation transforms the worshipper.

spectator experiences as his or her own. The conviction that the flaw is the root of the catastrophe and not just its accidental occasion is key to catharsis.

Revolutionary Critique

Marxist that he is, Boal identifies "Aristotelian" tragedy as an instrument of conservative propaganda and social control. Boal concedes that the highest goal at which humans can aim is the common good, a flourishing body politic.[8] Societies are organized by division of labor and role differentiation. Virtues are character traits that enable an occupant to perform well in the role to which she is assigned and so contribute to the preservation of the social *status quo*.[9] Faults are anti-social or counter-cultural tendencies. Boal argues that the establishment uses state-funded drama as a tool of oppression to purge the populace of any and all revolutionary tendencies.[10]

Moreover, Boal contends, "Aristotelian" drama keeps the spectator in a passive posture. It juxtaposes two people (one fictitious and one real) and two worlds (the spectacle and the real world) and, through the seduction of sympathetic identification, makes the real person surrender the power of decision-making and action to the stage character. Without acting, the real person feels as if she is acting, as if she is experiencing what is happening to fictional others. The real person gives herself over to loving and hating what the stage character loves and hates. In short, the real person surrenders herself to manipulation, to being formed and reformed according to the whims of those who produce the play![11]

Overall, Boal has no doubt that "Aristotelian" drama (as he analyzes it) *works* to produce effects that "carry-over" from the theatre to real society. His quarrel is that it is an apt tool for the wrong political agenda. Its functioning to reinforce virtue and purge counter-cultural tendencies presupposes a clearly defined social ethos relative to which personal characteristics can be evaluated as good or bad. Hence, he proves the utility of "Aristotelian" tragedy for conservative projects of *status quo* maintenance. In periods of revolution, however, social institutions turn fluid. The old is passing away, and it does not yet appear what should or

8. Boal, *Theatre of the Oppressed*, 21.
9. See Adkins, *Merit and Responsibility*, 31–48.
10. Boal, *Theatre of the Oppressed*, 33–34.
11. Ibid., 34–35, 40, 113.

shall be. To motivate theatergoers to change and transform society, Boal concludes, a different sort of poetics is required.[12]

By contrast, Boal's own experiments banish spectator passivity and thrust theatergoers into an active role. Ordinary people are given some elementary training, and then "facilitated" by professionals in brainstorming, producing, acting, and critiquing their own dramas. Boal's theatre is a workshop for social change; its productions are rehearsals for real-life revolution.[13]

Resourceful Complications

Surely eucharistic drama is not meant to coerce congregations into passivity, but to send them out into the world, to empower them as agents of the kingdom of God. Personally, I am happy to promote eucharistic participation as rehearsal for a revolution. Weren't political charges of sedition among the reasons why Jesus was crucified?[14] Nevertheless, Boal's dismissal of "Aristotelian" poetics seems hasty, because his version of "Aristotelian" poetics enables us to explain how eucharistic drama can produce revolutionary effects.

Double Framing

On Boal's analysis, "Aristotelian" tragedy uses a stable social frame to generate dramatic conflict. But Boal himself recognizes variations on this theme. Dramas can play off of the clash between two well-articulated social systems. Thus, in Cervantes' *Don Quixote,* the hero's character is perfectly conformed to the ideals of an anachronistic society. Plot tension arises when the embodied but bygone past confronts the present.[15]

Certainly, Boal is right: past and present social realities have a textured complexity and concreteness lacked by evolving revolutionary ideas. Sometimes rebels against oppressive governments have no idea where they are going or what would make things better; they just cannot tolerate the present reality any more. But other times, revolutionaries do have a platform, even leaders and cell groups who embody and live

12. Ibid., 47.
13. Ibid., 122–41, 155.
14. Mark 15:2–20; Matt 27:11–31, 37; Luke 23:1–5, 38; John 18:33—19:22.
15. Boal, *Theatre of the Oppressed,* 45.

out the lifestyle "ahead of its time." Think of Mahatma Gandhi and his ashrams, or Martin Luther King Jr., the Southern Leadership Conference, and its associated congregations of nonviolent protestors. These movements worked by creating a crisis that both activated and exposed the conflicts within the majority population's double allegiance. Gandhi recognized how much the powerful in England were attached to the empire. But he also knew how deeply identified they were with their own sense of human decency. His nonviolent resistance campaigns provoked British troops to "act out" the brutality of colonialism.[16] King imitated this strategy, since cherished ways of life for white Americans were embedded in patterns of racial segregation. Moreover, white Americans also defined themselves in terms of the American dream of equal opportunity. Nonviolent protests brought out how racism violated these ideals.[17]

Eucharistic drama divides into two acts: the Liturgy of the Word—with its Gospel lessons and other Bible readings—and Holy Communion with its eucharistic prayer over the bread and wine, and eucharistic reception by the faithful. Both parts present a conflict between competing world orders and norms, between any and every merely human social organization and the "higher righteousness" (Matt 5:20) enjoined by Matthew's Jesus, whose definitive messianic interpretation of Torah lays out the governing principles for the coming reign of God (Matt 5–7). We eucharistic participants come with socially constructed identities that bind us to this present age, that define who we are in terms of social orders rife with virulent systemic evils—tribalism, racism, classism, sexism, and homophobia, to name a few. Far from being purely passive, we come to Holy Eucharist to affirm our allegiance to Jesus and to reassert and strengthen our alignment with kingdom-coming. (Even Zwingli would agree![18]) We take the initiative to enter the cultic drama where we know in advance (whether or not we consciously think of it every time) that we will be confronted with Jesus' embodiment of social aims that contradict the deep structures of our everyday world. We eucharistic participants thus set ourselves up to have our contradictory allegiances exposed, to

16. See Gandhi, *Autobiography*, 284–303, 363–81. See also Richards, *The Philosophy of Gandhi*; Borman, *Gandhi and Non-Violence*.

17. This analysis is articulated by Cone, *Martin and Malcolm and America*.

18. Ulrich Zwingli does not believe that the body and blood of Christ are located on altars where the eucharistic rite is performed. Rather, sacraments are signs, and to participate in them is to take an oath of allegiance and to bear public witness to one's faith. See Zwingli, "An Exposition of the Faith," 259, 265; "On the Lord's Supper," 198.

be confronted with the choice between our conventional selves and who Jesus says we are and who we should become. Voluntarily entering the cultic drama, we accept the risk of divine judgment, Gethsemane-struggles, and the hour of decision!

Double Feature

Boal notes how some tragedies have not one but two heroes whose complementary flaws destroy each other. Boal instances Antigone and Creon, whose drama pits an excessive love of family against an excessive love of state.[19] If we try to step back from the polemical nature of the Gospels and listen through the lens of "Aristotelian" poetics, we can hear them telling more than one tragic tale, and so—once again—offering us a choice. On the one hand, Jesus is a wonderful person, who speaks amazing words of wisdom, who performs many signs and wonders, and who shows great compassion to the shepherdless crowds. From the point of view of the religious establishment, Jesus' "flaw" is his sense of his own authority, which disregards the tradition of the elders, even going so far as to count himself equal with God! Taking authority to teach without footnotes (John 8:12–20), to forgive sins (Mark 2:1–12), and to command scurrying demons (Mark 1:21–34) is at first a source of astonishment and a recipe for popularity. But it is also what precipitates Jesus' downfall and what motivates his enemies to plot his catastrophic death by crucifixion, something his enemies are sure will falsify his messianic pretensions by cutting him off from God and from the people of God.[20]

On the other hand, the Pharisees are religiously zealous. They hunger and thirst for Messiah's reign. They prepare the Lord's way with meticulous Torah observance, set high hedges around the law, engage in fasting and many ritual washings, and even tithe dill, mint, and cumin to wall out any neglect. They sit on Moses' seat and are knowledgeable interpreters of Scripture and arbiters of orthopraxy.[21] From the evangelists' point of view, the Pharisees' flaw is overweening zeal that spawns hypocrisy, self-righteous contempt towards the masses, and still worse, an idolatrous identification with their religious projects (Matt 6:1–8;

19. Boal, *Theatre of the Oppressed*, 42.

20. See Deut 21:23 and Gal 3:13, which make clear that according to Jewish law, anyone who dies by hanging from a tree is ritually cursed.

21. These features of the Pharisees are satirized in Jesus' woes on them in Matthew 23.

7:1–5). They have invested so much in trying to be perfect as their heavenly Father is perfect (Matt 5:48), that they feel entitled to demand that God redeem Israel their way. Their flaw is tragic because it drives them to liquidate Jesus, ritually to curse the Messiah whose way they meant to prepare, and so to betray their deepest purposes.

Thus, the Gospels run a double-feature of how religious ardor and claims to authority lead to disaster. But contrary to "Aristotelian" tragic form, neither side acknowledges that its zeal was misplaced. As Boal predicts, this omission destabilizes the reader/hearer. Luke's Gospel intensifies this teeter-totter effect with its echo of accusation and counter-accusation: "Jerusalem was destroyed because Jesus was a false prophet that led Israel astray!" "No, Jerusalem was destroyed because she failed to realize the hour of her visitation!" (Luke 19:48).

Within "Aristotelian" dynamics, the spectator will be purged of the flaw of the character with which he identifies. But here it is a question of double identification: with which character should we identify? Will we eucharistic participants recognize ourselves in Jesus' enemies, with the religious establishment who try to nail God down? Will we choose to strengthen kingdom loyalties by acknowledging the idolatry of our socially constructed identities? Or, will we see that following Jesus leads to crucifixion and—like the rich young ruler—feel that we have too much to lose, turn away sadly, and settle back into conventional ways (Mark 10:17–31; Matt 19:16–30; Luke 18:18–30)? Once again, most eucharistic participants already know the old, old stories. Joining the service, we sign the consent form and agree to be put on the spot, to be confronted with a Kierkegaardian either/or.

Subordinate Plot

From the evangelists' point of view, Jesus is the hero and his enemies the anti-heroes of the Gospels. By contrast, the disciples are neither. Rather, they are heroes-in-training but, and in advance of Pentecost, they fall tragically short of the mark. Here "Aristotelian" poetics have a more straightforward application. With the exception of Judas, the disciples are sympathetically presented as having many good points: they love Jesus and they have left everything to follow where he goes, listen to what he says, watch what he does, and obey his commands. Their story activates our kingdom-loyalties and stimulates our desire—in these respects—to be like them. In Mark, the disciples' flaw is deficient understanding; in

Matthew, lack of faith.[22] These have disastrous consequences, as when Peter denies and deserts Jesus when his hour comes. They live to admit their mistake. Sympathetic identification with them and vicariously living through their story of good intentions gone to hell is supposed to produce "Aristotelian" catharsis, to purge us of our own faithless obtuseness about who Jesus is and what that means.

The function of the story of Judas bears pondering. Traitors are worse than enemies, because they have been woven into the social fabric and because they have been insiders, who give and take and share in the most intimate ways. When they turn on us to hurt and destroy, they do violence to the core of who we are and what life means. Precisely because treason is so damaging, social groups want to make it unthinkable by presenting the traitor's behavior as unintelligible. So far from portraying Judas as an "Aristotelian" tragic hero—a sympathetic character whose many good points come to naught because of his tragic flaw—Gospel pictures of Judas are worse than one-dimensional. Not only are no merits cited, but John's Gospel declares that he is not among the elect (the Father hasn't drawn him), that he was predestined to play this role, and that the devil entered him and made him do it.[23] From the viewpoint of Gospel poetics, to identify with Judas is itself tantamount to treason, because it means counting oneself out by numbering oneself among those whom God has reproved. Traitorous impulses are not to be activated and purged, but to be denied and repressed!

Nevertheless, down through the ages, Gospel poetics have not altogether succeeded. The dramatic reversal of fortune—to be so close to, to taste and see, to participate in so great a good, and yet to turn, to use that intimacy as an occasion to destroy the good one prized—is sufficient to lend Judas' story an aspect of the tragic. If the story does not invite identification by portraying Judas as an otherwise or previously wonderful person, it remains open to us to recognize that as human beings we are like him in two respects. We are like him in longing to be intimately and specially related to great goodness. And we may fear that we are like him in fragility: there may not be enough to us to hold on to great goods brought near (like the other disciples who forsook Jesus and fled). Furthermore, how can we be sure that there does not likewise lurk in our hearts the impulse, in losing such goods, to destroy them?

22. For detailed coverage of this contrast, see Luz, "The Disciples in the Gospel according to Matthew," 99–105.

23. John 6:64–65, 70–71; 10:29; 13:1, 11, 18–19, 21, 27; 17:12.

Manifold Manipulation

Taking Down Defenses

For theatre to transform in any of these ways, it is necessary for the defenses of spectators to be lowered. However manipulative, traditional theatre and cultic drama succeed at this by working—in many and various ways—to make us feel safe. First, Aristotle mapped out a precise form for tragedy, so that plays both old and new would be *structurally familiar,* representing and analyzing a rise to wealth, power, and privilege, followed by disastrous descent. This is similar to how liturgy—especially pre-Vatican II rites and the 1662 Book of Common Prayer—fostered a sense of security by frequent repetition within ordered patterns of familiar words, rhythms, and gestures. Likewise, Bible stories read over and over in the same translation were absorbed into memory by osmosis, forming and informing worshippers' conscious and unconscious selves, until the very texts and tales made the faithful feel at home.

Second, traditional theatre and pre-Vatican II liturgies gave spectators space by *distancing* them from dramatic action, which was confined to a clearly demarcated stage, chancel, or altar accessible only to theatre and religious professionals. Narratives themselves ostensibly add to the distance, portraying events that happened to *others,* often fictional, mythological, or at least long ago and/or far away. Such distancing is permissive. Like Jesus' parables, it allows the spectator or hearer to relax into inattentiveness, to remain too preoccupied to catch the connections, and to back off from engagement. *Pace* Boal, traditional theatre puts lack of coercion in service of seduction. By leaving the spectator-hearer with the flexibility to enter in or not, traditional theatre and cultic stage create confidence, reassuring that the playhouse is not a perilous place, that it will not be dangerous to give oneself over to the drama. Implicitly, such literary, theatrical, and ritual conventions promise to contain the confusion, to house the chaos occasioned by any challenges the drama might present.

Close Encounters

Lulled and lowered defenses open up spectators and worshippers to more than sympathetic identification with one or more characters on stage. Each person brings a wealth of experience and associations to the dramatic presentation. Depth psychology tries to systematize the many and various ways symbols and similarities stir up conscious and unconscious connections, creating psycho-spiritual energy within the individual. Fifties furniture and hairstyles; sixties bell bottoms, beads, and blenders; liturgical smells and bells, hymns or graduals—all of these are fishhooks for the soul. Showing forth the Lord's death, playing and replaying the holy week tale of treachery, betrayal, desertion, cruelty, and torture stands a good chance, sooner or later, of evoking the pain and the shame of our own individual abuse and abusiveness. Participation in theatre or cultic drama is apt to confront us, not only with our own perverse twists of character, but also with our wounds.

Public pageants create group experience. Taking down defenses willy-nilly makes participants more present to one another and more affected by the psycho-spiritual state of those around them. Effective performances—such as Hitler's speeches to mass rallies[24] and Martin Luther King's "I Have a Dream" at the March on Washington for Jobs and Freedom—constellate an *ésprit de corps* that, whether momentarily or over the long haul, galvanizes the community for effective action.

Cultic drama was invented to create safe space for trafficking with the Divine. Its presupposition is that contact with the Holy is both necessary for life and dangerous to our health. Its ritual structures aim to domesticate just enough to keep close encounters beneficial, without flattening the force of their transforming power. Eucharistic participants know this. We come because some core part of us hungers and thirsts for intimate connection. We enter the household of God and have the chutzpah to trespass on Divine turf in hope and fear of bumping into its Master. Christians from different traditions will agree that eucharistic drama exposes us to real presence in more than one kind. On the one hand, there is the utterly reliable discrete presence, robed in ritual costume: Christ's body and blood hidden under forms of bread and wine. Like other distancing devices of theatre, this courtesy allows us room to equivocate, to decide on any given occasion just how intimate we are prepared to be. On the other hand, there is what we might call "naked" presence, or—as with Isaiah in the temple (Isa 6:1–5)—Holiness *sans* disguise, utterly compelling, even if incomprehensible and uncomprehended, so big and so real as to call into question our whole way of being

---

24. The liturgy of the 1934 Nazi Party Congress in Nüremberg—complete with several speeches by Hitler—is vividly documented in Leni Riefenstahl's film *The Triumph of the Will.*

in the world and our most cherished conceptions of who we and others are. We eucharistic participants know this: we barge onto the stage, belly up to the table, put ourselves in the way of Holiness, and trespass at our own risk![25]

Moreover, eucharistic participation is corporate. People who worship together regularly get used to each other—in a good sense—and become for one another part of the stability-creating dramatic frame. Even where worship styles are formal, the ritual repetition of coming together helps to lower defenses, so that each of us is individually more in touch with indwelling Holy Spirit in our hearts, laboring and groaning with sighs too deep for words (Rom 8:26). Dropping defenses together allows members to experience and to be influenced by Holy Spirit at work in others. This also removes obstacles to Holy Spirit's moving back and forth through the assembled company to organize us into Christ's body. In eucharistic drama, Christ is really present, and Holy Spirit is our constellated *ésprit de corps* (1 Cor 12).

Energizing Transformation

Boal calls "Aristotelian" tragedy coercive. Well-executed theatre is arguably manipulative. In any event, its aims are pedagogical: skillful theatre "works on us," uses the spectacle to inform, and "sets us up" to re-form our sense of ourselves. Nevertheless, theatrical rites are not merely magical. Except where the Holy has "broken out" on us (Exod 19:22; 2 Sam 6:6–8), there are no wand-waving, incantation-muttering, "twinkling of an eye" transformations. "Carry over" into the real world is more complicated and requires a context and perseverance. Dramatic confrontations—conscious and unconscious—have to be digested if they are going to re-birth us into new life.

Even if Boal is right that "Aristotelian" tragedy aims to enforce conventional values by purging us of anti-social tendencies, theatre attendance could be at most a contributing factor in catharsis. Theatre focuses and makes explicit values and judgments that the wider society daily asserts and enforces in countless obvious and subtle ways. Greek tragedies themselves represent flaws as deeply rooted in our characters and personalities. Even Chairman Mao would tell you, you can't turn an effete intellectual or aristocratic playboy into a socially useful citizen

---

25. For the dangers of unauthorized approach to the altar, see Lev 10:1–3.

simply by making her or him watch morality plays. Weekly correction groups were deployed to back up the message and to bring it to bear on the concrete particulars, on thoughts, feelings, and actions of the individual's daily life.[26]

This is truer with the disclosures of cultic drama. Like the "ah-ha" insights of creative problem solving, they create crises and release energy. But for transformation to occur, that energy has to be used. Remember how Archimedes was wracking his brain to discover how to calculate the volume of an irregularly shaped crown, the better to measure its density and discover the percentage of gold it contained? During this process, he took a break, went to the public baths, noticed how the water in the pool rose when he submerged his irregularly shaped body in it, shouted "Eureka!," and ran naked through the streets all the way home to work out his "Archimedes Principle" for how solid bodies displace fluids. Remember the story in Luke 24, how the disciples on the Emmaus Road were telling and retelling the pieces of their shattered world, searching Scripture with the stranger to find a way for "all that had happened" to make sense? Their hearts are burning within them and they are on the verge of discovery when they arrive at Emmaus. So they urge the stranger to stay with them to finish the lesson. Remember how their worlds—their sense of who they are, of who Jesus is and his relation to Israel, of what Jesus and the disciples mean to each other—figure-ground shift when they recognize the stranger as Jesus, breaking bread with crucified and resurrected hands! Remember how the energy of that disclosure sends them running all the way back to Jerusalem in the dark, to begin to put their insight into practice with confession and counter-confession: "The Lord has risen and has appeared to Simon!" "The Lord was known to us in the breaking of the bread!" (Luke 24:34–35).[27] Likewise, when the behind-closed-doors Pentecost novena is interrupted by an invasion of Holy Spirit, the disciples are propelled into preaching and healing in the marketplace. Their transformation from cowering immaturity to bold leadership required them to use the energy, to allow it to work on the inside and to empower them for gospel proclamation: to Judea, Samaria, and the ends of the earth (Acts 1:8).

26. These facts are dramatically portrayed in *The Last Emperor* (1987), a film that tells the story of Puyi, the last emperor of China.

27. These examples are favorites of James E. Loder, who works out the psycho-spiritual dynamics of transformation in Loder, *The Transforming Moment* and *The Logic of the Spirit.*

Eucharistic participation courts confrontation with our own divided loyalties, with repressed memories, denied feelings, and hidden wounds. It risks conscious and unconscious exposure to these deeper realities in others. And it risks a rendezvous with the really present Christ, seeking and finding a meeting with our Maker. When the materials of our individual and collective lives are *experienced* in the presence of Christ crucified and risen, and are up against the reality of outclassing Divine Goodness—i.e., when we experience the problem in the face of its solution—we are figure-ground shifted into a high energy situation. To make the most of it, we have to take courage, roll up our sleeves, and get to work kneading light into clay! Ninety-nine percent of the time this does not happen "all at once" and is surely not brought to completion before the dismissal from the service. Deep-structure individual changes need the help of therapists, spiritual friends or directors, and a wider community of faith that bear witness to kingdom values in word and deed. Likewise, social change is a collective effort of which the church should be the harbinger, an instrument and icon. This too is a process that calls for continual discernment and much common prayer.

High energy left to idle and not used to transform the worshippers, their community, and the wider world is the root of common liturgical neuroses. We come to Holy Eucharist because we long to be God's people, conformed to Christ in the fullest sense of the Word. We risk exposure because part of us—our deepest selves—really want it. We come because we somehow know that—in the Augustinian manner—our hearts will be restless until we taste and see the Goodness of God! But when intimate contact is made, we shrink back like the children of Israel at Sinai (Exod 20:18–20), like the rich young ruler who turned away sadly (Mark 10:17–31; Matt 19:16–30; Luke 18:18–30). We act out our ambivalence by continuing to participate in liturgy while refusing transformation. Freud will tell you that all that high energy has to go somewhere. How unsurprising if it gets displaced onto the rite, if it fuels fixation on liturgical details. Our need for God gets transposed into the demand that the ceremony be performed often and with precision, perhaps with increasingly dramatic epicycles, scripted words, and gestures. Like Synoptic Pharisees with the tradition of the elders, our refusal of transformation energizes a vicious circle of seeking and refusing the very thing that would make us whole. Like the manna in the wilderness not taken and used according to God's purposes (Exod 16:19–20), participating in eucharistic drama while refusing its potential for revolution is sure to make us sick (1 Cor 11:27–32)!

Comic Violence?

So far, my treatment of eucharistic drama has been lopsided in several dimensions. The time has come to make adjustments to get a more accurate picture.

Comic Relief

Theologically, the most important yet neglected point is that Christianity is *neither finally tragic* (offering us a world in which fatal flaws take even the good guys down), *nor merely Stoic* (making the cosmos the scene where a self-transcending spiritual elite wins the victory and rises above degradation by praising their Maker for the cosmos whose natural processes are destroying them). Christianity is *tragi-comic*: grim realism that wins through to a happy ending. Ordinarily, comic plot complications offer us near misses. Comedy presupposes that its spectators have background knowledge that the world is full of tragedy—a fact at which comedy then winks, offering a shred of hope. Sometimes the worst is averted. Yes, the world is tragic, but it isn't *always* tragic. Sometimes, despite everything, good outcomes zoom in from left field to surprise![28] Christian tragi-comedy heightens the dramatic tension: the Bible's God does not usually step in to *prevent* the worst, but waits until it is *already too late*—until the worst has already happened—before acting to turn the plot around. As the honor code assures us, such Divine policy makes perfect sense as a glory-maximizer. YHWH, God of armies, is mighty to save, and not only against light infantry and artillery. Even when the enemy deploys its most powerful weapons, even when it uses all of its ammunition and unleashes its full destructive force, YHWH can restore, recreate, and reverse the damage! Thus, Abraham and Sarah are over ninety years old when God starts to fulfill the Divine promise of star-numerous offspring (Gen 17:1, 21). Israel descends into slavery in Egypt and hears nothing from YHWH for four hundred years (Gen 16:13). Jesus waits until Lazarus has been dead four days, after the rot had set in, to raise him up (John 11:17). Emmanuel calls down no angelic rescue

28. Thanks to Shannon Craigo-Snell for this characterization of comedy.

from crucifixion! To be God-with-us, Jesus has to die the ritually cursed death and descend into hell before rising from the dead.[29]

Violent Disclosure

Psycho-dynamically notable is the fact that there is more than one way for defenses to come down. Theatrical distancing devices take an indirect approach, creating space for drama to coax or seduce us into relaxing our defenses. Such indirection has the vices of its virtues, risking failure because it leaves our lived world sufficiently intact and so allows us to ignore, dismiss, or even sleep through the drama. Twentieth-century theatre of cruelty, advocated by Antonin Artaud,[30] does the opposite, mounting a frontal assault by using intense, vivid, and explicit perfor-mances and highly condensed symbolic staging, gestures, and move-ments to crash through our defenses. Aggressive confrontation does not "soften us up" for conversion: it aims to shatter our psyches, to destroy our lived worlds, and to give us no choice but to deconstruct. We don't need Freud to tell us that the direct approach risks failure a different way by provoking rage that kills the messenger and heightens defensiveness to rebuild worse worlds than before.[31]

In the Synoptic Gospels, Jesus strides into ministry with the direct approach—taking authority to forgive sins, touching lepers and bleeding women, healing on the Sabbath day, eating with tax collectors and sin-ners, and violating every taboo in sight. We don't need Freud to tell us how predictable it was that Jesus would make enemies behaving that way. In the middle of his ministry, Jesus "backs off," withdraws geographi-cally, and teaches in parables to give the religious establishment a chance to savor their evidence and reconsider. When that doesn't happen, Jesus returns to attack their defenses with messianic demonstrations, with Palm Sunday parade and temple cleansing, with rabbinic disputations, outright rebukes, and eschatological woes on scribes and Pharisees and Jerusalem itself. We don't need Jesus' passion predictions to recognize how he was really "asking for it" in the end. Within the frame of the Syn-optics themselves, the disciples are initially reluctant to let their whole

29. I elaborate this point at greater length in Adams, *Christ and Horrors*.

30. See Artaud, "The Theatre and Its Double," 97–156.

31. In Freud's theory, unmasking another's defenses is experienced by that other as a hostile act. For an articulate explanation of Freudian ego-defense mechanisms and how they work, see Freud, *The Ego and the Mechanisms of Defense*.

reality be figure-ground shifted by the apocalyptic breakthrough of Jesus' resurrection. Lucan men are "slow to believe" (Luke 24:25), while Marcan women flee from the tomb terrified, at first saying nothing to anyone (Mark 16:8)!

Eucharistic drama can be experienced both ways—as gentle coaxing and subtle seduction *and* as the apocalyptic invasion of the one who comes in the name of the Lord. Either way, eucharistic participants are given evidence about ourselves by "acting out" who we are.

The Marriage Feast of the Lamb

Boal charges "Aristotelian" tragedy with coercing theatergoers into passivity that delegates powers of choice and action to fictional or mythological characters on stage. Holy Eucharist does not do this. Even seen as a drama about the life and times of Jesus, it functions to activate and expose the participants' divided allegiance, to bring them to the hour of decision, and to confront them with the demand for choice. Because worshippers know this in advance, attendance constitutes tacit informed consent, voluntarily setting oneself up for an existential crisis.

At a further level of analysis, the demand for active participation is even clearer. Holy Eucharist is a communal meal, where real people meet, embodied-person-to-embodied-person, to celebrate life together by sharing real (if ritually minimalist) food. Indeed, Holy Eucharist is not just any dinner. It is a wedding banquet where really-present God and the people of God feast their covenanted household and toast their common life. Eucharistic participants exchange greetings, address requests, make apologies, express appreciation, listen to God and others, and, of course, eat and drink!

Holy Eucharist is a supper eaten in the present, but Holy Eucharist is not only about the present. Boal is right: cultic drama plays with time. Holy Eucharist makes essential reference to the past. Moreover, Holy Eucharist is not only a dress rehearsal; it participates here and now in the coming reign of God. Like annual family holidays, Holy Eucharist is a feast with precedents, which are explicitly remembered. The meal Jesus had with his friends on the night before he suffered and that exodus-eve Passover in Egypt are, even for Jesus, long ago and far away. Synoptic chronology identifies the former as a re-presentation of the latter, so that Holy Eucharist recalls a play within a play. According to Joachim

Jeremias's speculations, it was customary for the *pater familias* who presided at Passover to give theologically significant, special interpretations of the ritual foods.[32] On the night before his passion, Jesus turned the Passover celebration into a shocking exposé, theatre-of-cruelty style. Jesus took bread, blessed, and broke it, saying, "This is my body." He took the wine, blessed it, and declared, "This is my blood of the new covenant." Jesus was saying that the society that they were celebrating would be bound together by the sacrifice of his life. In John's Gospel, Jesus goes further to insist that Christian conviviality is at least symbolically *cannibalistic*: in a society where the consumption of blood was taboo, Jesus delivers the hard saying: "Unless you eat the flesh of the Son of Man and drink his blood, you have no life in you" (John 6:53).

The truth that Jesus was exposing is absolutely fundamental: *human community and its celebration always involves the substitution of a life for a life.* Israel's liberation from Egypt was won by YHWH's slaughtering the firstborn in each Egyptian family. Hebrew households were passed over if and only if their doorframes were smeared with the blood of the Passover lamb, which they had roasted and eaten (Exod 12:7–13). In the days of King Ahab, Hiel of Bethel laid the foundations of Jericho at the cost of his firstborn and set up its gates at the cost of his youngest son (1 Kgs 16:34). A life for a life! Freedom for some requires others to be slain and/ or degraded into food, so that winners are cannibals and vampires who live by (literally or figuratively) devouring the life of others. The ancient story captures a truth at once general and mythological, real and true. Human community—material well-being, good personal relationships, high cultural accomplishments—often depends on the willingness to deprive, degrade, and destroy. In hierarchical societies, higher-ups depend on the lower-downs who make their luxurious living possible. But etiquette co-opts everyone into a conspiracy of pretending that higher-ups are self-sufficient by treating the lower-downs as only partial persons, as those who see and hear all but say nothing, invisible providers whose service is scarcely acknowledged. Between the sixteenth and twentieth centuries, colonies existed to feed imperial powers. In our present global economy, sweatshop labor works night and day for slave wages to provide developed countries with cheap food and clothing. African oil workers go without necessities to make North American three-car families a reality. We Europeans and North Americans live to an unprecedented

---

32. Jeremias, *The Eucharistic Words of Jesus.*

high standard by consuming their fair share, by eating their flesh and drinking their blood, and by devouring their life! What is more, by acting out our sense of entitlement—to life and the necessities of life, to defend ourselves at any and all costs—we behave as if we own the universe and signal our underlying desire to get God out of the way.

Jesus' editorial comment on Passover bread and wine turns eucharistic drama into an exposé of the bestiality and blasphemy of the human social project. By eating the flesh and drinking the blood of God—whether literally, as some Anglicans and Roman Catholics believe, or figuratively, as Zwinglians maintain[33]—we become actors who eat and drink our own condemnation by (at least symbolically) re-enacting the primal crime. We give ourselves away as cannibalizers of the lives of others, determined to keep our social fabric going even if it means killing and cannibalizing God!

Moreover, this eucharistic drama conforms to the pattern of "Aristotelian" tragedy as Boal analyzes it. The tragic flaw is our animal nature. On the one hand, the fact that animal life is not self-sustaining makes sharing food an expression of our life together. When I offer someone food that might have sustained me, it signifies that our lives are so bound together that I have nothing to gain by depriving you. When I eat food that someone offers me, it shows that I trust this person not to be offering me poison, asserting my willingness to be related, and—when otherwise appropriate—reciprocating in kind. On the other hand, the fact that animal life is not self-sustaining keeps us from being universally altruistic, making our social project parasitic on devouring others' lives! Because our tragic flaw is not accidental and contingent but *essential* to us, both as individuals and societies, catharsis is humanly and naturally impossible. Fear and recognition of abhorrent consequences are by themselves insufficient to uproot such dynamics from human beings.

How, then, can eucharistic drama turn comic? Jesus himself gave the answer. It all depends on our eating his flesh and drinking his blood. Jesus extends the cup of the blood of the covenant. Our self-incriminating (literal or figurative) acts of eating and drinking are at once a re-enactment of the primal crime *and* our covenant-sealing and covenant-renewing consent to live by God's life. We eat God's flesh and drink God's blood, degrading God into food that will nourish by becoming part of us. But Holy Eucharist turns this inside out. Eating God's flesh and

---

33. See footnote 18.

drinking God's blood converts us into Christ's body, members through which Christ puts his purposes into action and lives out his life. This could seem like one more magic trick: we meant to consume God's life for our own sustenance, but God turns out to be mouth-of-hell Molech who gobbles us up instead![34]

Happily, this is metaphysically impossible, because *divine life is essentially self-sustaining; divine being and well-being do not depend on the existence or destruction of anything else!* Comic potential in creation depends on nothing less and nothing more than what and who God is! For us to live by God's life is to live as if our being and well-being do not finally depend on the destruction of anything else either. To live by God's life is to live in the confidence that even though we are destroyed, we will be held in life eternally by God. Aided and abetted by the Spirit of Christ, our constant coach and live-in teacher, we can gradually learn to let go of our sense of entitlement. We can come instead to receive our lives and well-being as gifts from a God who intends to keep on giving them forever. We can work with God in the context of covenant community to subvert our Darwinian tendencies, eventually to domesticate our animal nature into patterns of courteous consumption that honor God's other creatures.

To live by the power of God's indestructible life is how we enter the kingdom and how our very selves become heralds of kingdom-coming. Eucharistic participants know this and are forewarned: come to Holy Eucharist, and comes the revolution! Eucharistic participants long to desire this unequivocally. We are actors more than rehearsing, and the kingdom is coming even now.

Bibliography

Adams, Marilyn McCord. *Christ and Horrors: The Coherence of Christology.* Cambridge: Cambridge University Press, 2006.

Adkins, Arthur W. H. *Merit and Moral Responsibility: A Study in Greek Values.* Chicago: Chicago University Press, 1975.

Aquinas, Thomas. *Summa Theologica.* New York: Benziger Brothers, 1947–48.

Aristotle. *Poetics.* Translated by S. H. Butcher. New York: Hill and Wang, 1961.

Artaud, Antonin. "The Theatre and Its Double." In *Artaud on Theatre,* edited by Claude Schumacher with Brian Singleton, 97–156. Chicago: Dee, 2004.

34. According to the Hebrew Bible, Molech was a pagan god who was believed to demand child sacrifice (Lev 18:21; 20:1–5; 2 Kgs 23:10; Jer 32:35).

Boal, Augusto. *Theatre of the Oppressed*. Translated by Charles A. McBride, Maria-Odilia Leal McBride, and Emily Fryer. London: Pluto, 1979.

Borman, William. *Gandhi and Non-Violence*. Albany, NY: State University of New York Press, 1986.

Brook, Peter. *The Empty Space*. New York: Simon and Schuster, 1968.

Cone, James H. *Martin and Malcolm and America: A Dream or a Nightmare?* Maryknoll, NY: Orbis, 1991.

Freud, Anna. *The Ego and the Mechanisms of Defense*. Translated by Cecil Baines. New York: International Universities Press, 1946.

Gandhi, Mohandas K. *Autobiography: The Story of My Experiments with Truth*. Translated by Mahadev Desai. New York: Dover, 1983.

Grotowski, Jerzy. *Towards a Poor Theatre*. London: Methuen, 1968.

Jeremias, Joachim. *The Eucharistic Words of Jesus*. Translated by Norman Perrin. New York: Scribner, 1966.

King, Martin Luther. "I Have a Dream." In *A Testament of Hope: The Essential Writings and Speeches of Martin Luther King, Jr.*, edited by James M. Washington, 217–20. San Francisco: Harper and Row, 1986.

The Last Emperor. Directed by Bernardo Bertolucci. Hollywood: Columbia Pictures, 1987.

Loder, James E. *The Logic of the Spirit*. San Francisco: Jossey-Bass, 1998.

———. *The Transforming Moment: Understanding Convictional Experiences*. San Francisco: Harper and Row, 1981.

Luz, Ulrich. "The Disciples in the Gospel according to Matthew." In *The Interpretation of Matthew*, edited by Graham M. Stanton, 98–128. Philadelphia: Fortress, 1983.

Richards, Glyn. *The Philosophy of Gandhi: A Study of His Basic Ideas*. London: Curzon, 1982.

Schechner, Richard. *Performance Theory*. New York: Routledge, 1988.

Schumacher, Claude, and Brian Singleton, eds. *Artaud on Theatre*. Chicago: Dee, 2004.

Stanislavski, Constantin. *An Actor Prepares*. London: Methuen, 1986.

The Triumph of the Will. Directed by Leni Riefenstahl. Universal Film AG, 1935.

Willett, John. *Brecht on Theatre: The Development of an Aesthetic*. Translated by John Willett. London: Methuen, 2001.

Zwingli, Ulrich. "An Exposition of the Faith." In *Zwingli and Bullinger*, edited by G. W. Bromiley, 239–87. Philadelphia: Westminster, 1953.

———. "On the Lord's Supper." In *Zwingli and Bullinger*, edited by G. W. Bromiley, 176–238. Philadelphia: Westminster, 1953.

11

Holy Theatre

Enfleshing the Word

RICHARD CARTER *and* SAMUEL WELLS

Argument

THE BIBLE IS A book. More accurately, perhaps, the Bible is a collection of sixty-six books, many of which are collections or anthologies of disparate material. Thus, intertextual frissons, synergies, resonances, and echoes are inherent to the Bible as a whole and the individual books it contains. But the Bible is undoubtedly a book. That much seems obvious.

But actually, this may not even be true. In fact, before the Bible became a book, it was a collection of scrolls. It was not a vehicle for private devotions, encased in leather and cocooned by a zip. It was a script for performance, a rallying cry for mission, a tirade seeking repentance, and a chorus of comfort. It was a community-forming sacrament, and reading it aloud was a church-creating event. It did not have a static meaning; it was not reduced to easily memorized fundamentals. Every time it was read aloud in a congregation its truth became new in the context of its hearers, and every time those hearers returned to listen again they were a new and different community to the one that had heard it before. When Jesus laid down the book in the synagogue in Nazareth and said, "Today this Scripture has been fulfilled in your hearing" (Luke 4:21), he set a template for every reading of Scripture ever since. Rather than the familiar "This is the word of the Lord" or the somewhat tame "Here ends the reading," the announcement after the reading might better be, "Lord, fulfill this Scripture today." Furthermore, and in the same spirit, the response might be, "And make our lives and our deeds a scripture for the blessing of your people in days to come."

In other words, the Bible is always a drama—often the record of dramatic words and actions that took place on the stage of salvation history centuries ago, but always the dynamic interaction of word and world today. That drama is not a book that can be closed and put back on a shelf: once the news is out, it cannot be controlled, but is living and active. This is the spirit of Hans Urs von Balthasar's call to let the Bible speak as a drama and in its context, rather than regarding it as a fact or object:

> We must allow the encountering reality to speak its own tongue or, rather, let ourselves be drawn into the dramatic arena. For God's revelation is not an object to be looked at: it is an action in and upon the world, and the world can only respond, and hence understand through action on its part.[1]

The work of Bob Ekblad offers a helpful way to introduce the case we are making in this essay.[2] Ekblad locates himself in the tradition of participatory reading at the margins, or *lectura popular de la biblia*, as practiced and recorded by Carlos Mesters and Ernesto Cardenal, and inspired by Paulo Freire.[3] Ekblad provides a succinct summary of Freire's project.

> Monologuing educators who effectively deposit information alien to people's daily lives into passive-recipient students keep people dependent, passive, and uncritical of the authorities. . . . In contrast, the liberating educator must seek to empower people through engaging them in careful analysis and discussion of their own contexts . . . beginning with context rather than text. . . . Facilitators are urged to constantly create an environment of trust that draws out voices and perspectives of people on the margins that are usually squelched by the powers (that is, those

1. Balthasar, *Theo-Drama*, 1:15.
2. Ekblad, *Reading the Bible with the Damned*.
3. See Mesters, *Defenseless Flower and God, Where Are You?*; Cardenal, *The Gospel in Solentiname*; Freire, *Pedagogy of the Oppressed* and *Education for Critical Consciousness* and (with Faundez) *Learning to Question*.

who have a voice). Educators are encouraged to facilitate group analysis and to help people express their opinions through a variety of means that do not depend on literacy (such as, socio-dramas, art, music, street theater, poetry, cartoons).[4]

Ekblad's book offers a series of gripping descriptions of such encounters, not as closely recorded and exactly reported as those of Cardenal, but with the same intensity of dialogue and discovery. At one point he is with a group of Chicano prisoners in a county jail, discussing how Moses went out to his people and saw their forced labor. Ekblad asks what a contemporary Moses would see if he "went out" today.

> "A lot of poverty," says Vicente. "In Mexico one makes in one day what one makes in an hour here."
>
> "Discrimination," says Chris. "Last week in court there were five of us Mexicans and twelve *gabachos* [white people]. Every one of the white guys was released. All of us Mexicans are still here."
>
> . . . "So in what sorts of ways do we react to injustices or hardships in our lives?" I ask the men.
>
> "We use violence. We take out our frustration on someone," says someone.
>
> "Some of us use drugs to blow it all away, to escape the pain," says someone else.

Ekblad then draws to the group's attention that Moses "looked this way and that, and seeing no one he killed the Egyptian and hid him in the sand" (Exod 2:12). The prisoners aren't impressed. Ekblad asks if Moses gained respect in the Hebrews' eyes by using violence. The prisoners say no. Ekblad transfers the focus to the prisoners' own upbringing, and whether being beaten by their parents earned respect or not. Again, the prisoners say no. "Punishment didn't work," says one; "It just made me more angry," says another. The same is true, they say, for harsh sentencing in the courts, and for George W. Bush invading Iraq. So what would Moses have had to do to gain respect? "He'd have to show respect, and be more humble," comes the answer.[5]

Here we see the Bible provoking, revealing, illustrating, stirring, unveiling, and transforming in the tradition of Freire, Mesters, and Cardenal. Ekblad's book is teeming with such stimulating examples. This is one sense in which Scripture can be "fulfilled in our hearing." Ekblad is

4. Ekblad, *Reading the Bible with the Damned*, 4.

5. Ibid., 104–6.

engineering—midwifing, to use his apt word—a new exodus. This is the dynamic of encounter the Bible presupposes, unleashed from its Western, bourgeois, and pious chains.

And yet we still seek something more. What Ekblad presents is dynamic encounter. But it is not yet the fully-fledged drama of the Bible. The Bible here remains a text—a text to be introduced by being soaked in the context, a text that ignites tension, conflict, discernment, and revelation—but still a text. And, as we stated at the outset, the Bible is not fundamentally a text. It was originally and should have always remained a drama: a drama with a script, for sure, but a drama that is rehearsed and improvised anew in each setting, in each telling. Ekblad's account gives us the electricity of the encounter but only whets the appetite for what might be possible. The goal is not for the Bible to become a means of liberation through study, conscientization,[6] and renewed praxis; the goal is for the drama of the Bible itself to enact and create a new reality, that all might be drawn into its action and become participants in the world it creates and makes possible.[7]

Thus we are searching for a form of drama that opens eyes to a new way of seeing, a drama like a seed that grows within, a drama where the audience is not divided from the performers but all are drawn into an action that can transform. We need a drama that is not a tract or a message, but which forces us to drop the subjective "I" and see the world through different eyes: a drama that communicates the multivalence of life and allows us to carry the story away with us and let it grow in our lives and continue its work as memory. We are looking to rediscover the drama of our faith not as a watered-down retelling or as a superficial presentation, but in a way that connects us with the origin of that faith—a dynamic equivalent.

The purpose is to be instruments that transmit truths that otherwise remain out of sight. As Peter Brook asks: "Can the invisible be made visible? We know the world of appearance is a crust, under the crust is the boiling matter as we peer into a volcano. How can we tap that energy?"[8]

---

6. Conscientization is a concept at the center of Friere's project, and it means the process of developing a critical awareness of one's social reality through reflection and action.

7. For further reflection on the issues Ekblad raises, see Saunders and Campbell, *The Word on the Streets*; West, *The Academy of the Poor*; de Wit et al., *Through the Eyes of Another*.

8. Brook, *The Empty Space*, 58.

Drama means action. The event itself stands in the place of text or teaching. Richard remembers the lesson of Pak Bismoko, the Head of the English Department at the University of Sanata Dharma where Richard taught drama in Yogyakata, Indonesia. Every week Richard saw him carrying all his family on one Vespa motorbike back to the village where he came from. Richard still remembers his words:

> My children are from the city. They do not even know the drama of the natural world. When they think of rice, they think of a plastic packet. When they are in need, they think of the money in my pocket. You see, they don't know where things come from. When I was small I followed my father as he prepared the land, channelled the water, and planted the rice. I watched the rice grow, helped in the harvest, and touched the warm grain drying in the sun. When we ate I knew where it had come from. But my children do not know these things. At night, their safety comes from living behind locked doors. When I was young I could find my way home even when there was no moon. Truly, I knew every stone on the path. I had felt them with my feet, for I was part of the action of creation.

If faith is to live, it is not simply a truth distilled and then passed on. Instead, faith requires self-involvement: we too are asked to become part of the drama. There is no other way of entering into the mystery of Christ than to allow oneself to be grasped by it. "To be initiated is not to have learned truths to believe but to have received a tradition, in a way, through the pores of one's skin."[9]

Testimony (Richard Carter)

In Solomon Islands in the South Pacific, I was a member of a community where drama—real drama—became our means of learning, teaching, and living the Christian faith.[10] I was the chaplain and later a brother myself in the Melanesian Brotherhood, a community of more than 400 Brothers living vows of poverty, chastity, and obedience.

Like a group of medieval players, part of our ministry and mission work consisted of traveling from village to village witnessing to the gospel in word but most of all in action. In islands where there are so many

9. Chauvet, *Liturgy and the Body*, 31.

10. This section is a first-person account of Richard Carter's experience of gospel drama. For further reference and reflection, see Carter, *In Search of the Lost*.

different languages spoken, where there is no television, and in most cases no access to books and a high level of illiteracy, the use of drama was often the best and certainly the most popular method of conveying the gospel. It was a time of great social unrest and animosity between two of the island groups on the brink of breaking into violent conflict. We developed a form of drama based on New Testament parables and stories. The word for "drama" in pidgin English is "action." Our method was to tell a story through action: a story that would transform lives. Let me describe the process.

The Wedding at Cana

In John's Gospel the drama of Christ's ministry begins with a wedding (John 2:1–11). This wedding is in many ways the overture for everything that is going to happen in the Gospel, so it's a good drama with which to begin.

I have decided that this story will be the theme for a drama I am preparing with the Melanesian Brothers and Novices to celebrate our feast day. We begin discussing this scene by asking what, for Melanesia, is the major dilemma this story poses: not *how* does Christ turn water into wine, but *why*? In Melanesia, alcohol is a major social problem. Most people have direct experience of seeing alcohol lead to serious domestic abuse, drunkenness, the squandering of money, and violence. These are social issues the church has addressed, and alcohol carries with it the taint of scandal and sinfulness. Yet at Cana we see Christ not just making wine, but gallons of it.

The discussion leads to the idea that wine is a symbol. From our knowledge of the Bible, we discuss what it might mean within a Jewish and then a Christian cultural context, and how this might relate to a marriage. If wine in this context is a symbol of *covenant* or relationship, then we must look for a culturally powerful equivalent within a Melanesian context. "Pigs!" one brother volunteers, "and strings of shells to pay the bride price!"

"How essential are these things to a wedding ceremony?" I ask.

"Too important. Shell money and pigs are both part of paying for the bride. A marriage for the people of Malaita without the boy's family presenting pigs and shell money would be impossible."

Several people offer reasons why: "It is a sign of the marriage contract between the two families."

"It binds them together . . . shows that they have become one."

"It is a sign of honor . . . generosity . . . reciprocity . . . relationship."

"The gift is essential as an outward sign of respectability."

"What would happen," I ask, "if the pigs did not arrive and the shell money was not enough?"

"Impossible! A family must give more not less!"

"It would bring great shame, shame to the boy and the bride in the eyes of everyone."

"The marriage would be considered worthless, cheap!"

"What if in the middle of the ceremony we tell the bride's family that the shell money has run out and that we have brought no pigs—only a few chickens and coconuts?"

"Impossible! They couldn't do it. It's too shameful. There will be no marriage. It is an insult. There would be a feud . . . fighting between the families!"

"What happens if that shell money is a sign of your relationship with God?"

"The relationship is betrayed."

Our drama has begun here and now.

"What happens if the girl's family is from Malaita and the boy's family from Guadalcanal [two key islands in the Solomon archipelago] and there was this insult?"

"Someone would die!"

First of all, we need to develop the dramatic and cultural context in which the Christ's miracle will be set. Our wedding at Cana becomes a wedding between these two different tribal groups. There is already hostility between these two tribes. When a young boy from Guadalcanal falls in love with a girl from Malaita, our drama has an instant sense of conflict and danger. We begin with improvisation, an improvisation that will later be written down, sharpened, and later prepared for performance. We see the boy trying to tell his parents that he has fallen in love with a Malaitan; then we witness the girl trying to tell her family that she wants to marry a boy from Guadalcanal. There is shock, then prejudice, then growing hostility. But the boy is persuasive, and finally, when things have gone too far to escape a scandal, a bride price is arranged between the two sets of parents, much to the disapproval of the extended family who predict the worst.

The day of the wedding arrives but the bride price fails to materialize. The boy's extended family have all promised to bring pigs and shell money. Instead they arrive empty-handed making excuses or worse, still bringing even more insultingly inappropriate gifts: a pile of coconuts, a skinny chicken, and two possums on a stick. The audience roars with laughter as the groom becomes increasingly desperate. In the other village, the extended family is preparing the bride for marriage: dressing her, decorating her according to *kastom*, and offering her advice and warnings. But as the bride's family wait, they grow increasingly impatient and angry. Then gossip reaches the bride's family that the bride price cannot be met. They are insulted and incensed; it seems to confirm their suspicions and all their prejudices about the other tribe. Some of the uncles talk of taking revenge.

In the Guadalcanal village, the groom is in total despair, torn between love for his bride and the humiliation he knows the wedding will bring. The groom's aunt turns to her son and says, "Do something! You must do something!"

"Mother, this is not our business. It's not the time or place," the cousin replies.

"Whatever he tells you to do, do it!" his mother implores some of the villagers.

Now the son does give instructions: "Take those six empty wooden drums for pounding yam," the young man tells them. "Go to the beach and fill them with sand." To another group he says: "Go to the chicken coop and bring back all that you see inside."

The first group do what they have been told.

"Now take the drums and pour them out in front of the groom's father."

As they pour them out center-stage the crowd gasps in amazement. Beneath the sand emerge strings and strings of shell money, the most valued and respected possession in Melanesia. Actually, as the signs of covenant and social binding going back to their earliest ancestors, they are beyond the value of money and treasured beyond any other possession, holding an indescribable cultural power. These are beautiful polished shells shining in the firelight, held up in trembling hands by the astonished groom.

"Why?! Why?!" he says to his equally astonished family. "You have saved this greatest gift until last!" But now there is whooping and shouting because the second group has arrived back. In the chicken pen they have found seven pigs. These are now strung screaming on poles between them. The audience is cheering now, and they cannot believe their eyes; a miracle of huge cultural proportions is emerging in front of them.

"Get the panpipers . . . music!" the father calls. The village panpipers and dancers stream in, dancing and swaying with the vibrant music, and begin a huge procession. They are carrying the strings of shell money, swinging pigs, and pallets of food hoisted on their shoulders, and thus they lead the Malaitan boy and his parents to meet his bride. The Malaitan village hear them coming and stand dumbfounded, dropping the bush knives and sticks they had taken up in fury. They rush for woven mats instead, which they lay out in front of the bride. And so the bride price is paid, far more than is expected. It is an astonishing act of generosity and the bride's parents are overwhelmed by the beauty and quantity of these shining strings of polished shells and all that they symbolize.

The bride and groom step onto the mats, bound together by a miraculous gift that has transformed anger into dancing, conflict into community. The audience is roaring their approval, whistling and encouraging the couple for their wedding night. The whole crowd is dancing now. No one is quite sure where this bride price has come from, no one, that is, except a very proud, aging aunt, some stupefied servants, and the aunt's son: a young man of great authority, standing humbly and slightly apart from the crowd, smiling as the couple make their vows to the cheers of the audience.

We performed this drama on the night before our Community's Feast Day of St. Simon and Jude. About a thousand people had gathered to watch—villagers from all tribes, many of them from Malaita and many from Guadalcanal. It combined elements essential to powerful dramas: simplicity, conflict, a sense of danger, and powerful symbols. And there was also a sense of wonder, that somehow a divided people—as divided as the audience who watched—had been transformed by a miracle in their midst: a gift, a free and overwhelming act of grace. No one would forget the Wedding at Cana. The same audience shared the Eucharist together the following day, and some of us glimpsed a little more of the wonder of the miracle of this wedding too. Perhaps others, who tasted the bread and wine, experienced the joy and unity of the celebration, and later enjoyed the pigs of the feast, felt divisions dissolving like guests at Cana, and similarly did not realize the origin of this wine. It was of course only the beginning. The wine would become blood. It would take several years of bloodshed and ethnic conflict and the death of seven Melanesian Brothers before some of those who watched that night would be able to learn its meaning and the islands could feast together in peace again. But those of us who performed this "action" knew who the Savior was and believed in him, and when the conflict came we remained bound together by his same grace.

The Good Samaritan

Violence had erupted and began to develop a momentum of its own. Prejudice had hardened into hatred on the Island of Guadalcanal and once there were atrocities and death, the island became caught in cycles of payback and revenge. The headquarters of the Melanesian Brotherhood, where we were living, was the only sanctuary in the middle of the conflict. The drama we were now called to live was to be those in between this frightening and destructive ethnic divide. We were living on the road to Jericho.

What would be our drama? We performed *The Good Samaritan*. We played the parable in all the surrounding Guadalcanal villages, with the militants standing around with guns. The parable confronted them with a Malaitan—their enemy—beaten up by their own militants and left dying on the road. They witnessed the priest walking by and refusing to get involved and then the government military in hot pursuit of the militants but refusing to stop to save the victim. And then they saw an old man from their own tribe, speaking the home language of the audience, hearing cries in a different language—the language of his enemy—stopping, bending down, gently cleaning away the blood, binding the wounds, and then picking up the Malaitan and carrying him to safety. There was a dangerous silence, a tension so great that one feared the audience may suddenly attack the actors and one no longer knew whether they saw the Good Samaritan as savior or traitor. "Which of these was a true neighbor?" Some of the women in the audience began to sob. The militants who were watching stayed until the end and then quietly disappeared into the night, perhaps carrying this parable with them. It touched the wound of ethnic hatred and cried out for a similar healing. And it was only the audience who could make that possible. It was a time when moralistic teaching would never have been heard; but the parable, as drama, slipped past their defenses and demanded response.

The Parable of the Talents

We wanted to work on one of the parables to address civil conflict and to perform in all the villages around Guadalcanal. We chose *The Parable of the Talents*, and we wanted it to be like a mirror held up so all could see what was happening in the conflict. But more than that, we desired the cast and audience to become part of a drama in which we could somehow discover God's promise of a future beyond the conflict. We longed for it to be as hard-hitting as Christ's original parables: a parable about both potential and waste.

To begin, we determined the context. A father, who is the chief of his village, calls the village together for a feast. There is joy and celebration and it is obvious that this chief is greatly loved and respected, but then unexpectedly in the midst of the celebration he announces to the villagers that he has decided to leave the village and go away. He chooses three of his sons and divides his shell money between them: five for the first, three to the second, and one to the third. He hands over his authority to these three. He points to the sea, to the plantation, and to the village, charging these sons to use their talents wisely for the good of the community. And then, quite simply, he walks out on them. In the village there is a sense of upheaval. The chief and chiefly tradition have provided everyone with a sense of order and authority. But now no one is sure who is in charge or what will happen. Traditions and old structures of authority are being swept away, but no one is sure what will take their place.

What is left behind? There is all the youth, raw talent, possibility and expectation of Melanesia at this time. There is a feeling of liberation and excitement and yet, coupled with this, there is also a sense of bewilderment and betrayal; the old order and securities have vanished, leaving a vacuum in which anything seems possible. There are tremendous resources, and yet very little experience in leadership. There is memory of the old order, but few rules for the new. There are opportunities never dreamed of before but all the temptations and deceptions of a new world.

The three sons make their way to Honiara, the capital city. The first son, John Paul, much to the anger of the village, seems to waste his talent by buying empty oil drums. The villagers are disappointed when he returns because he has not bought any of their desired consumables. The second son, Dicka, likewise is a disappointment, buying a massive, empty fiberglass icebox, bigger than himself, which he carries on his head. But how will we portray the third son: the one who wastes his talents, the one who seeks to defend what he has rather than invest in the future? Examples of the paranoia of possession and defensiveness of "my land" are pervasive. The third son, Kaibo, follows this path. He makes friends with the militants and politicians. Their money flows, as do the women; he stays in the Honiara clubs and hotels and returns to the village dressed in military fatigues and dark glasses with a new status as a "Commander," derived from the high-powered guns he is carrying. He tells the village that he will not spend but defend his inheritance, and he will use the guns to protect their property from intruders and migrants.

The first son, John Paul, initially scoffed at by the village, builds a hot air drier with the oil drums for drying coconut and slowly encourages the community to get this *copra* business running. The second son, Dicka, starts fishing; at first people laugh at him, but he catches a huge fish (the size of a man) which he drags ashore flapping and inspires others to come with him to fill the ice box to feed the village. The third son, Kaibo, creates nothing but builds up a cult-like militia, stealing, destroying and extorting money and alcohol. The parody of present life in Solomon Islands is both comic and uncomfortable.

We plough on to the final scene of the drama, which I thought would be so hard to direct, but now it begins to flow naturally and powerfully. Kaibo, drunk with his men, attacks the village store to get their hands on more alcohol. The storekeeper, his firstborn brother John Paul, confronts them, and Kaibo and his men start to shoot. In the ensuing pandemonium, their father, the village chief, returns. The father now calls his sons to account for the gifts he has given his sons, but Kaibo turns his gun on his father, shooting the beloved chief in front of all his people. The father crumples, reaching out toward his sons. The firstborn son John Paul runs forward to hold his dying father in his arms, and his father tells him that he is the one fit to look after the village, calling on him to use the gifts of creation for the good of all his people. John Paul now turns towards his youngest brother, suddenly empowered, wise, and brave. He rips the gun from his younger brother's hands, telling him that he has created his own hell and ordering him out of the village. Then as the music changes and the Brothers begin to sing the beautiful *Let All the Islands Rise and Sing*, John Paul, backed by the whole village, looks up to the sky and calls out in love, grief, and gratitude to his father for all the gifts of his inheritance. Lighting a fire, he smashes and burns the guns that have murdered his father and caused havoc in the village. And above the mourning villagers, the transfigured spirit of the father rises, calling on the people of

Solomon Islands to use the gifts of creation to build up their nation in peace, and promising that he will return. There are times when there is no mistaking the power of drama; in the context of violence and turmoil, we know that somehow this "action" has been able to articulate the cry of a nation.

When we perform *The Parable of the Talents* we know that many of those who watch have been directly involved in the ethnic violence. Even the Prime Minister comes to watch. "If you have ears to hear then hear!" In the villages where we perform, many of those in the audience are militants. They carry their SR88s and strings of bullets across their shoulders, as if they are posing. In one performance an old man at the end of the drama started shouting at them "You see now! Do you understand now? That's what happens. That's what your guns are doing! That's the destruction you are causing! That's *you* in the drama!"

But can a drama really change lives? In the final village in which we were staying, one of the warlord's militants escaped from them and, as a deserter, came to join us. Frightened and ashamed, he followed us, keeping out of sight for fear he would be suspected. In the final performance of our parable, there was a new actor in the drama. It was this former militant. He had asked the Brothers if he could join them, and of course they accepted him. For him it was a moment of catharsis, because as the play reached its conclusion he was among those stripping off the army uniforms, stamping them into the mud, and smashing the guns against the rocks. When we left the Weather Coast he came with us.

The Lost Son

The action of drama can work in the Solomon Islands; but what about performing in the United Kingdom? Can these "actions" of Christ still challenge those who have become dismissive or cynical of religion?

I am with a group of Melanesian Brothers. We are performing the Prodigal Son in schools, prisons, churches, cathedrals, and day centers around England. Our Prodigal has become a black Melanesian asylum-seeker who has come to London to seek his fortune. He has lost everything and is on the streets. He has been stitched up by the middlemen who have trafficked him, and now he is destitute, forced to eat the remnants of a sweet and sour pork Chinese take-away in a polystyrene carton he finds thrown on the pavement.

We make this drama into a workshop in which school students can join. They become the crowds in the town scenes and at one point they are instructed to walk past the lost son who has been beaten up and left homeless in the street. "Imagine he is one of those homeless people you walk past quickly without looking, like someone selling the *Big Issue*," I instruct them. Everyone follows my instructions and walks past our lost son laughing, everyone except one ten-year-old boy, who comes up to me and asks,

"I don't want to walk past him. Can I help him?"

"That's not part of the story," I reply. "It's not in the script."

"But I want to help him."

"It's not in the story."

"Let's make a new story."

"You try," I tell him.

He knelt down beside the lost son, and put his hand on his shoulder, and said, "Look, if you're hungry, I can get you something to eat. You can come to my Mum's: she'll cook for us."

The lost son had crossed the barriers. A Solomon Islander from the other side of the world had become this young boy's neighbor. A young ten-year-old had stood out against group conformity and had the courage of his compassion. This story of Jesus, 2000 years after it was first told, was still doing its work.

The Catch of Fish

How do you portray the Risen Christ? What does he wear? How does he look? How has he changed, and how does he change us?

We were in Solomon Islands, preparing the last scene for a production of *The Passion of Our Lord*. We had decided to perform this passion for the nation after seven Brothers in our community had been taken hostage and brutally murdered in the Guadalcanal conflict. Only Christ's own passion could somehow give shape to or make any sense of the horror of this tragedy. We would perform this Passion play to thousands in the Solomon Islands, both on Guadalcanal and Malaita, and in many different countries. But like those disciples in the upper room after the crucifixion, it was as though the action had died. We could enact death, but then what? We had wanted a final scene of resurrection, but we did not know how we could ever express it, especially when our hearts felt broken. Those playing the disciples went down to the beach. We talked about how the disciples must have felt after Christ's death. We knew, from our own recent experiences, something of the grief and loss they had known, their feelings of guilt, and the trauma of the brutality. And then we saw someone in the distance coming toward us, coming out of the morning light. And so I asked: "Imagine he is one of the Brothers who had been taken hostage and we were told had been tortured and killed. Imagine it is Francis! What would we do?"

"Run!" Run as the two disciples had run towards the empty tomb. I would run fast for fear the one we loved would be lost again, run to catch the vision. And so we ran through the sea, ran with the spray flying, ran with all of ourselves to touch the one we loved and thought we had lost for ever, ran to reach him and know that salvation was real. And in the waves he opened his arms: "Courage, do not be afraid!" This would be our action of resurrection.

I have a dream of an early morning resurrection scene down by the sea where the disciples will cast their nets on the other side of their fishing boat and there will be a huge catch of fish that will swamp the boat, with more than enough for all the audience and actors to sit down and have breakfast together and with fish left over for those who did not come. We will never be able to create dramas as timeless and as powerful as Christ's own, but each time we enter into their mystery there is always the potential to make all things new and to discover again the revelation that has forever changed our lives. And each time one group of actors puts this drama down, Christ waits for another group to take it up to make his story live again through the action of their lives.

Reflection

The testimony of drama in Solomon Islands demands a label. Is it performance? Exegesis? Improvisation? Conscientization? *Lectura popular de la biblia*? Of course it is all of these. It fulfils the dramatic criterion of Scripture: "Today this Scripture has been fulfilled in your hearing." It is fundamentally an invocation of the Holy Spirit, a declaration that "the Spirit of the Lord is upon us," and a true calling on the Spirit to enflesh the Word.

It is truly dramatic, in a number of senses. It fulfils Hegel's prescription, in that it synthesizes the epic—the detached, objective, universal perspective—with the lyric—the intense, subjective, personal, and emotional engagement—to attain a character that is truly dramatic, as Balthasar would describe it.[11] It is embodied and almost liturgical, in the sense that many parties have assigned roles and there are elements of confession, praise, intercession, and thanksgiving sprinkled across the narratives. It is profoundly visual and tangible, much more so than, for example, Ekblad's otherwise stirring discourses. It is unambiguously political, a genuine component in both the "liberal" notion of politics as the just distribution of limited goods and the more Aristotelian notion of politics as the living tradition of debate about the good. And it is open-ended: this is no safe and circumspect message distilled into bite-size digestible elements, but rather an explosive cocktail of inflammable themes and echoes that can only resonate deeply with its audiences and absorb responses into the texture of the drama itself.

But it is also exegesis. Ekblad's inmates and Cardenal's peasants discovered liberation in analyzing, reading, discerning, and re-reading; they entered a hermeneutical spiral of empowerment and transformation. But these dramas have genuine movement. The warlord's militant joins the Brothers when they leave the Weather Coast: is that drama or life, gospel or history? Does it not challenge the difference we customarily draw between the two? Parable creates a new reality; reality is transformed into parable. The wedding at Cana isn't turned into a contemporary, culturally appropriate scene for more seamless communication. Rather, it changes the reality around it and changes the way everyone involved will read the parable for the rest of their lives.

It is undoubtedly improvisation, not just in the sense that the old stories are put in new wineskins, but much more in the sense that responses bounce back into the drama. When a critic of the government says in the prime minister's hearing, "If you have ears to hear then hear!" then this becomes a different kind of drama, one in which the actors' role is not simply to replicate the script as polished in rehearsal and let the audience do the rest, but now to work with the audience's response and absorb that into the drama.

In every one of these ways, this form of theatre and this form of exegesis is pushing at a vital but often-suppressed or overlooked question: is the Bible a closed book? It certainly is if by this we mean that God's nature and purpose have been fully disclosed and that God has been fully revealed fully revealed in Jesus. But the Bible may be open in other ways.

---

11. Hegel, *Hegel on the Arts*, 142–200.

Have we yet witnessed the full range of human responses to that story? Are there responses—faithful and foolish—to that full revelation that will induce God to demonstrate and manifest yet more wonders in an effort to draw all creation back into the fold of grace? Are we, right now, in the middle of the drama as participants as well as hearers and spectators as it unfolds? Solomon Islands was going through its own passion—civil war—while these performances were taking place. It is difficult not to believe that such dramas altered the destiny of Solomon Islands, the character of audience and performers alike, and even, dare we say it, the nature of the story itself.

Bibliography

Balthasar, Hans Urs von. *Theo-Drama: Theological Dramatic Theory*. Vol. 1, *Prolegomena*. Translated by Graham Harrison. San Francisco: Ignatius, 1988.

Brook, Peter. *The Empty Space*. London: Penguin, 1968.

Campbell, Charles L. *The Word on the Streets: Performing the Scriptures in the Urban Context*. Grand Rapids: Eerdmans, 2000.

Cardenal, Ernesto. *The Gospel in Solentiname*. 4 vols. Maryknoll, NY: Orbis, 1976–84.

Carter, Richard. *In Search of the Lost: The Death and Life of Seven Peacemakers of the Melanesian Brotherhood*. London: Canterbury, 2006.

Chauvet, Louis-Marie. *Liturgy and the Body*. London: SCM, 1995.

Ekblad, Bob. *Reading the Bible with the Damned*. Louisville, KY: Westminster John Knox, 2005.

Freire, Paulo. *Education for Critical Consciousness*. Translated by Myra Bergman Ramos. New York: Continuum, 1974.

———. *Pedagogy of the Oppressed*. Translated by Myra Bergman Ramos. New York: Seabury, 1970.

Freire, Paulo, with Antonio Faundez. *Learning to Question: A Pedagogy of Liberation*. Translated by Tony Coates. Geneva: WCC, 1989.

Hegel, Georg Wilhelm Friedrich. *Hegel on the Arts: Selections from G. W. F. Hegel's Aesthetics, or The Philosophy of Fine Art*. Abridged and translated by Henry Paolucci. New York: Ungar, 1979.

Mesters, Carlos. *Defenseless Flower: A New Reading of the Bible*. Translated by Francis McDonagh. Maryknoll, NY: Orbis, 1989.

———. *God, Where Are You? Rediscovering the Bible*. Translated by John Drury and Francis McDonagh. Maryknoll, NY: Orbis, 1995.

West, Gerald. *The Academy of the Poor: Towards a Dialogical Reading of the Bible*. Sheffield, UK: Sheffield Academic, 1999.

Wit, Hans de, et al. *Through the Eyes of Another: Intercultural Reading of the Bible*. Elkhart, IN: Institute of Mennonite Studies, 2004.

12

The Church as a Theatre
of the Oppressed

*The Promise of Transformational Theatre
for a Youth-Led Urban Revolution*

PETER GOODWIN HELTZEL

"The theater is not revolutionary in itself,
but it is surely a rehearsal for the revolution."[1]

Introduction

SHORTLY AFTER OCCUPY WALL Street began on September 17, 2011, in
Zuccotti Park, a group of ministers gathered to work alongside the occupiers. This faith-rooted protest movement called themselves *Occupy
Faith*. When the occupiers were thrown out of Zuccotti Park, several
congregations took them into their fellowship halls, including Judson
Memorial Church and The Riverside Church. The church—the prophetic church—was opening itself up to the revolutionary spirit of the
occupation.

1. Boal, *Theatre of the Oppressed*, 122.

241

The Occupy protest movement was a wake-up call for many clergy in the city. Older clergy, who had been working for justice for several decades, were joined by many younger clergy who experienced the Occupy movement as a baptism by fire into the movement for justice. Together, this intergenerational clergy network became interested in developing creative ways to organize for economic justice in a city dominated by billionaires and led by a billionaire, Mayor Michael Bloomberg. Given the brute economic strength and persuasive political influence of New York City's permanent government—Wall Street, Real Estate Developers, and the Insurance Industry—any confrontation with these ruling powers would need to be well coordinated and dramatic.

During New York State's budget season in the Spring of 2012, Occupy Faith saw an opportune time to intervene. On Wednesday, March 7, 2012, as political leaders in Albany finalized the details of the New York State budget, a group of clergy from Occupy Faith met for an enactment of Parables of an Immoral Budget in front of Governor Andrew Cuomo's Manhattan Office. Nearly fifty faith leaders from across New York engaged in a theatrical intervention to expose the immorality of the proposed budget that harmed poor and working class New Yorkers. Faith leaders demanded the restoration of human services budget cuts. In their prayers, they highlighted the unjust tax loopholes that permit corporations—like Goldman Sachs, Verizon, and News Corporation—to earn billions in New York State but pay less in taxes than a working class family of four. The act of prophetic, public theatre unveiled that it is sinful to balance the budget on the backs of "the least of these" while we permit wealthy corporations to evade their responsibilities to our communities.

Faith leaders deployed a strategy of creative activism to dramatize the injustice. Clergy set beds out in front of Governor Cuomo's office and climbed in them, covering themselves up with sheets, as if they were homeless people themselves. This prophetic act of resistance blocked the entrance to the 633 3rd Avenue office building in lower Manhattan. The beds represented all of the homeless and hungry who would be affected by New York State budget cuts, blocking the entrance to a New York State office building and dumbfounding the staff as they quickly grew into a large crowd, including a battalion of New York City police officers.

Through these prophetic theatrics, business as normal was interrupted in the city. Though the ministers were arrested, Governor Cuomo received a direct, disruptive message through this street theatre. The homeless people of New York were not "trash that could be cleaned up," but flesh and blood humans like the rest of us, who have the right to food, shelter, and respect. Sometimes drama is necessary to capture the imagination of the ruling powers of our cities and nations.

Theatrical theology is integral to Judaism and Christianity. The Jewish prophets often used art installations to dramatize the state of Israel. Jesus of Nazareth would engage in performance art, like his cleansing of the Temple, to awaken the religious and political rulers of his day. The Spirit of disruption on behalf of justice was also witnessed in the founding moment of the early Christian movement. According to Acts 2, the Holy Spirit descended on this early Christian community in a disruptive way that included flames of fires and folks speaking in different languages. This movement not only disrupted business as usual in the Roman marketplace and Jewish Temple, but also embodied a new economy. The early Christians sold everything they had and gave to those as they had need (Acts 2). In this way, the early Jesus movement imagined and creatively achieved a more just political economy.

Drawing inspiration from the theodrama of Scripture, we need to imagine new ways to express our prophetic theology *dramatically.* Occupy Wall Street was a dramatic intervention questioning the economic inequity caused by neo-liberal capitalism. It also presented an opportunity for the church to reimagine its vocation in more colorful, concrete, and dramatic terms.

My own prophetic ecclesiology was birthed in this Occupy protest movement. Since losing my job at Fidelity Investments on September 11, 2001 and volunteering on Ground Zero, I was in search of a prophetic church in the city: a Spirit-empowered Christ-community that was courageous in confronting the "powers and principalities," while working for healing and hope. I have come to envision the church as a theater of the oppressed that seeks to reimagine space and time through the liturgy, baptizing the community into festival time and creating spaces of hope. Occupy protesters often chanted "take it to the streets." I think it is time for the church to take liturgy to the streets. By taking liturgy to the streets we can disrupt business as usual and embody creative forms of the new economy. As we reimagine the church today through this dramatic disruption and work toward a new economy, theology has lessons to learn from theatre, especially Augusto Boal's vision of a theatre of the oppressed.

Augusto Boal's Theatre of the Oppressed

Theatre director Augusto Boal (1931–2009) developed the theatre of the oppressed to speak to the people of his beloved Brazil. Boal was concerned that the bourgeoisie used the classical theatre of the West to quell the revolutionary impulses of the people. Consequently, he started writing and staging theatrical productions that sought to unmask the power and privilege of the elite, while empowering writers from the Brazilian underground to claim their own distinctive, artistic voice.

In his manifesto, *Theatre of the Oppressed,* Boal critiques the ways in which the ruling class had taken possession of the theatre.[2] He called Brazil to reimagine theatre *by* and *for* the people. Reclaiming theatre as a space of freedom could unleash the creative power of the audience. Prophetic theatre had the power to inspire audience members to become subversive moral agents in the struggle for liberation. The oppressed themselves would have to take the lead, liberating themselves, creating their own theatre, celebrating festivals, and transforming the world.

Theatre began as festivals celebrated by free artists in the streets of the city. For Boal, the essence of these festivals, carnivals, or feasts was the frenzied and impassioned songs that "free people" sang in "the open air." Later, however, these free spaces became commodified by the ruling class. And it was after this commodification that "dividing walls" were built. "First, they divided the people," writes Boal, "separating actors from spectators: people who act and people who watch—the party was over! Secondly, among the actors, they separated the protagonists from the mass."[3] In order to emancipate the audience, Boal's prophetic task was to destroy these dividing walls and unveil the strategies of indoctrination deployed by the ruling class, ushering in a theatrical festival where spectators are transformed into revolutionary political actors.

Boal develops a "poetic of the oppressed" to critique conventional theatre, while creating the conditions for the emergence of a new revolutionary theatre. Analyzing classical theatre from the position of the oppressed unveils the strategies that classical theatre uses to *sedate* the populace into utter passivity, including a strict divide between the audience and the actors. Inspired by Aristotle's writings on tragedy, classical theatre aspires to instill virtue in the citizenry, but in most instances these theatrical productions are deployed as normalizing systems that

2. This work was originally published in Spanish as *Teatro de Oprimido* in 1974.

3. Boal, *Theatre of the Oppressed*, 119.

legitimate the status quo. Boal writes, "The coercive system of tragedy can be used before or after the revolution . . . but never during it."[4] The audience member "lives *vicariously*" through the experiences of the protagonist, while remaining a passive spectator.[5] Through their empathetic identification with the protagonists, the audience has a collective, cathartic experience of the transfiguration of tragedy. However, they are neither inspired nor energized to join the struggle for the liberation of the oppressed in the *polis* today, but are subtly coerced into complicity with the elite ruling power. In this way, classical theatre is sentimental theatre.

In contrast to the sedative inebriation of classical theatre, Boal advocates the radical transformation fostered by the Theatre of the Oppressed. Giving the audience the power of interpretation creates the conditions for a deeper social transformation. Karl Marx was one of Boal's muses, writing "The philosophers have only *interpreted* the world, in various ways; the point, however, is to *change* it."[6] It was Marx's desire to *change* the world that inspired Boal's dramaturgy. Theatre should add a log to the fire of the revolution for radical social change. Boal was interested in theatre that did not merely *interpret* the human experience through theatrical performance, but inspired the audience to *change* the world to be more just and equitable through concrete, collective action.

Boal was concerned about the way that the ruling class was economically exploiting the oppressed, while the theatre made them feel good about it. Classical theatre had to be disrupted, reimagined, and reconstructed. Boal saw the transformation of theatrical arts as integral to the transformation of the socio-economic system. In solidarity with the freedom dreams of the oppressed, Boal believed that the Theatre of the Oppressed offers an important pathway toward liberation today through the formation of emancipated spectators—spect-actors who can become protagonists in their own struggle for justice in their local communities.

4. Ibid., 46.

5. Ibid., 34.

6. Marx, "Theses on Feuerbach," in *The Marx-Engels Reader*, 145. Boal was influenced by the German playwright Bertolt Brecht (1898–1956) in appropriating Marx's ideas for his dramaturgy. For Boal's discussion of Brecht, see "Hegel and Brecht," in *Theatre of the Oppressed*, 83–115.

Transformation is the Struggle for Justice

Boal's dramaturgy was influenced by his friend Paulo Freire's classic work, *Pedagogy of the Oppressed.*[7] The material circumstances of the poor and oppressed are the starting point for Freire's educational philosophy. He developed a pedagogy that raises consciousness in the oppressed of their plight, and provides a pathway to their empowerment and liberation. Freire posits an educational paradigm through which the "teacher-student contradiction" is overcome, as teachers and students worked together in the struggle for liberation.

For Freire, the *telos* of the liberation struggle is *transformation.* Freire writes, "Liberation is praxis: the action and reflection of men upon their world in order to transform it."[8] Faith-rooted activists seek transformation as a pathway to the liberation of their community through which they find their own liberation.

What is transformation? Manfred Halpern has described transformation as seeking the social embodiment of the fundamentally new and better.[9] I would like to deepen Halpern's definition theologically by giving it the moral content of the prophetic imperative in Holy Scripture— social justice (*mishphat*) and steadfast love (*hesed*).

As we see in Micah 6:8, the call of the Hebrew prophets is "to do justice" (*mishpat*). The justice of God is the basis of the law and the prophets. The prophetic call is always a call back to God, fulfilling a just and right relationship with God *and* the whole community of creation. *Mishpat* calls Israel to be in right relations in every dimension of its life together— in relationship with God, in its internal life as a tribe, in its relationship with other nations, in its treatment of the widow, orphan, and stranger, and in its care for the whole community of creation.

As Cornel West argues, "Justice is what love looks like in public."[10] Love is the animating force of the Hebrew and Christian Scriptures. It is the heart and soul of the Christian theological vision. In Hebrew, the word *hesed* means steadfast love. The ancient Near Eastern practice of covenant making is the context through which this notion of steadfast

---

7. Freire, *Pedagogy of the Oppressed,* 82. This book is translated from the original Portuguese manuscript, which was published in 1968.

8. Ibid.

9. Halpern, *Transforming the Personal, Political, Historical and Sacred in Theory and Practice.*

10. West, "Justice is What Love Looks Like in Public."

love is forged. YHWH will remain lovingly loyal to Israel. God is faithful and longsuffering, the One who will never leave us nor forsake us. Israel's destiny depends on being able to be completely open to receiving the steadfast and gracious love of the Lord. No matter how difficult times get, or how far Israel has wandered in the wilderness, the Living God is there guiding and caring for the people of God.

The steadfast love of the Lord is the font of the never-ending stream of love that flows through God's people into the world. The *hesed* love of God anticipates the double love commandment of Jesus—the call to love God and love neighbor. Micah's challenge, "To do justice (*mishphat*) and to love kindness (*hesed*)," brings justice and love into close proximity (Mic 6:8). To love God and our neighbor entails embodying God's shalom justice in our communities. While the people of God join with others in the struggle for justice, all of our work must be marked by love.

Jesus the Jewish prophet proclaims and embodies the Hebrew prophet's message of shalom justice. He understood his identity and mission as a continuation of the prophets of Israel (Mark 8:27–28; Luke 13:33–34; 24:19). While the song of Israel anticipated God's coming reign of righteousness, Jesus announces that God's reign is here and now. "The *basileia* of God has come near to you," proclaimed Jesus of Nazareth (Luke 10:9, 11). In the Greek, *basileia* was the word for kingdom. In empire-critical studies of the New Testament there is a growing consensus that Jesus used "kingdom of God" as a critique of the imperial pretensions of the Roman monarchical kingdom. The prophetic vision of Christianity imagines an alternative world that is governed by justice, equity, and love. Since the empires of the world are often marked by violence, oppression, and injustice, a liberative vision of transformation must entail a commitment to mobilizing people to work for structural changes in society.

Transformation is personal *and* political. It is more than a personal process, but is simultaneously a social one. Socially embodied transformation is fundamentally just and loving. However, achieving genuine and lasting transformation demands an honest engagement with the antagonism that animates history. Given the church's complicity in the Western civilization project, especially through the missionary enterprise, churches in Europe and North America must resist Eurocentrism and work for deep solidarity with the poor and oppressed, who have been hurt and harmed by the neo-colonizing and neo-liberal powers of the West. Engaging this deep antagonism—the colonial logic of violence in what Foucault called the Western *episteme*—was made possible by its encounter with the rest of the world in the project of colonization. Thus, the *anti-racist*, transformational, theatrical theology offered here is committed to a prophetic post-colonial ethic that is expressed in working toward the flourishing of communities of color among the communities of the dispossessed. Thus, a post-colonial vision of transformation creatively exercised by the prophetic church can deepen the socio-political impact of the Theatre of the Oppressed.

Revolutionary Activists Move the Work of Transformation

Boal's Theatre of the Oppressed offers important resources for the construction of a Christian theology of transformation. I draw on Boal's theatrical vision because we share a strong commitment to the preferential option for the poor, a belief in the transformative power of theatre, and the need for revolutionary change—actively mobilizing people to dismantle unjust social structures and collaboratively build ones that are more just and equitable. Boal writes, "The poetics of the oppressed focuses on the action itself: the spectator delegates no power to the character (or actor) either to act or to think in his place; on the contrary, he himself assumes the protagonic roles, changes the dramatic action, tries out solutions, discusses plans for change—in short, trains himself for real action. In this case, perhaps the theater is not revolutionary in itself, but it is surely a rehearsal for the revolution."[11] Theatre by and for the people is a "rehearsal for the revolution." It helps people claim their identity as subversive moral agents in the political lives of their cities. There needs to be structural change in our cities, and theatre has an important role to play. Boal's Theatre of the Oppressed inspires the church to make revolutionary disciples, followers of Christ whose activist faith makes a concrete difference in the cities that they live in.

Boal suggests that the primary way in which theatre can change the world involves transforming spectators into "spect-actors." In theatre, the audience is never completely passive, but has an ever-present role to play in the drama. While one strategy is to activate the audience to be more attentive and emancipated spectators *qua* spectators, Boal's vision pushes toward the formation of revolutionary actor-activists.

11. Boal, *Theatre of the Oppressed*, 122.

After living in political exile in Argentina for fifteen years, Boal returned to Rio de Janeiro in 1986 and founded the Center for Theatre of the Oppressed. Wanting to have a broader political impact on Brazil, he was also successfully elected as a councilor in Rio de Janeiro in 1993. In that position he was able to begin to legislate policies that worked toward a more just and equitable Rio de Janeiro. Yet he longed for a larger impact, wanting to incite revolutionary fervor among the masses. To awaken the Brazilian citizenry, he developed forum theatre to explore political ideas in the form of drama. This provided citizens with a transitional space to discuss and act out different political problems in order to find creative solutions. Acting out alternatives to community problems left the participants with a restless heart for change that could culminate in revolutionary action for social transformation.[12]

This unleashing of the audience's creative power has multiple political implications. Transformational theatre offers spect-actors tools that enable them to take action in artistic performance, personal life, community organizing, economic activities, and political advocacy. As spectators become actors, the conditions become ripe for a lasting cultural revolution. The threat of transformational theatre lies in its unveiling of the oppressive logic of the ruling class and the prevailing economic order. It inspires and equips freedom fighters for coordinated action and advocacy for a more just and equitable world.

While Theatre of the Oppressed blurs the line between actors and spectators, forum theatre blurs the line between the arts and politics. The goal is not just to disrupt business as usual, but also to create the conditions, structures, and policies that inaugurate a new way of doing business, and a socioeconomic order that is fundamentally new and better, more just and loving.

Boal's pushing the theatre to be more politically engaged is a great inspiration to Christian leaders today who are seeking to lead their churches in transforming the institutions of urban life through prophetic activism and the creative arts. Theatrical theology is the heart of Holy Scripture and has erupted with ferocity throughout the history of the world Christian movement. The medieval mystery plays were one example where the dividing wall between the actors and audience was dissolved. During these dramatizations of the Scriptural narratives, everyone participated in the collective mystical experience of the

12. Ibid., 141ff.

Christian faith in festival time. In order to deepen our understanding of transformational theatre and its relevance for the church, we need to understand that it is oriented by festival time. In this next section I develop a notion of festival time in dialogue with Hans-Georg Gadamer. Gadamer's notion of festive time is weighted in the past, while my notion of festival time is anchored in the future—the horizon of the coming of God.

Festival Time: The Cadence of the Church as a Theatre of the Oppressed

Festival or festive time is a pregnant pause within our daily routine when we experience "community in its most perfect form." Gadamer writes, "If there is one thing that pertains to all festive experiences, then it is surely the fact that they allow no separation between one person and another. A festival is an experience of community and represents community in its most perfect form. A festival is meant for everyone."[13] Within festive time there is a collective sense of unity among all participants in the festival. In these moments there is the cathartic, collective realization that each belongs not to time and a pressing work schedule, but to a deep experience of the collective Other, a form of communal catharsis through self-transcendence.

Gadamer qualifies festive time as "autonomous time," meaning that it operates free of chronological time and its restrictive regimentation. Gadamer's festive time is similar to *kairos* in the New Testament literature. *Kairos* is one of two Greek words used to describe time. *Chronos*, the other word for time, refers to chronological or sequential time. In the New Testament, *kairos* refers to God's time, a sort of time that is independent of *chronos* time, a moment in history when God decisively intervenes and change occurs. The transcendent also erupts in festive time, but the weight is often on the way the wisdom of the past breaks into the present, while Christian eschatology is oriented toward the future.

Gadamer does not develop a sense of an eschatological future in his conception of festive time. For Gadamer, festive time is a moment of collective pause in the present to join with the past, commemorate some event or story, and bring it alive in the present. Within eschatological time there is always an equal eye on the past, present, and future. Festive time, when conceived eschatologically, is grounded in the Living God

13. Gadamer, *The Relevance of the Beautiful and Other Essays*, 39.

who has promised to come again. We are to live today in light of the coming of God from the future to resurrect the body and restore shalom in the community of creation.

When Jesus inspired the people of Israel to imagine the reign of heaven, he described it as a banquet to which many would come, from East and West (Matt 8:11). The great and future feast was always in Jesus' field of vision. Since heaven is conceived as a great feast, it is wise for us to reimagine time as a place for celebrating the process of this growing union between the kingdom of God and the world, which is to be fully realized at the eschaton, the end of time. Recovering this eschatological destination of all time—the great feast—explains why I prefer to speak about *festival* time instead of Gadamer's "festive time." A lasting festival in resurrection city is our great hope. Our job in the interim is to host anticipatory feasts that capture the spirit of the great feast to come.

We can see the rhythm of festival time in our weekly celebration of Holy Eucharist. When "we proclaim the mystery of the faith," it is always "Christ *has* died, Christ *is* risen and Christ *will* come again." Liturgical time is thus a festive sharing in the call and response of the eschaton, joining the great cloud of witnesses in a collective celebration that transcends chronological time. When we gather for weekly worship of the living God as a community of singing selves, we join our voices with angels and archangels, with the whole company of heaven—a cosmic communion.

As social celebrations, festivals tap into the depths of our humanity, our grief and surprise, mourning and wonder. They are full of color—the bright yellow of the sun, the verdant green of the meadow, and the blood red of sacrifice. They tap into the walled-up child that is waiting to break out of each of our hearts, as we seek to play joyfully together, releasing the God-given creativity that reveals the image of God.

Festivals invoke and inspire our playful precocious self in the context of a larger, communal celebration of life. Festivals are richly poised to perform two transformational acts. First, they invoke communion, whether through sharing food, stories, or even the same table, and they facilitate a culture of camaraderie and sharing, even charitable giving. Second, through the lure of festival time, they usher the community to the threshold of *kairos*, for they bring into a single moment the legacy of the festival, as well as a newness of its contemporary expression. Each time the community keeps a feast, "each repetition is as original as the work itself."[14] Every time a community celebrates a festival, it is repeating a ritual of the past, but in a new and unique way.

When festival time is viewed eschatologically, it orients us to the Christian hope that is to come, and motivates us to reimagine the spaces we inhabit in light of the city of God. Neo-liberal capitalism has imagined space as discrete plots of personal property for the rich, which is demonstrated in the rapidly expanding gentrification of New York City. Rich and affluent individuals, mostly white, are moving into Brooklyn, Harlem, and Queens, buying brownstones and condos, thereby raising the overall market value of the neighborhood. Subsequently, poor people of all colors are forced to relocate to the Bronx or New Jersey. As New Yorkers search for home, the opportunity to buy or rent a home is increasingly out of poor people's reach.

Space is a site of theo-political-economic contestation. Just as the church reimagines chronological time as festival time, it must also reimagine space, embodying alternative forms of community. The Christian community must engage the contestations of geography through a concrete activism that transforms places of despair into spaces of hope.

Spaces of Hope: The *Telos* of Transformational Theatre

Jesus' resurrection inaugurates a space for hope. When Jesus bursts forth from the tomb, he breaks open the place of ultimate oppression—the place of death. Suddenly, as never achieved in cosmic history, the laws of nature, the wages of sin, and the inevitable fate of us all were opened like the drawing of a curtain between stage and house. The tomb was now, of all places in the universe, a space of hope; its reputation as the place for the end of being had been transformed into a space where one could rise and walk again. A place of death was transformed into a space of life, a place of despair into a space of hope.

Michel de Certeau approaches the dichotomy of place and space using the rubrics of spatial philosophy. He conceives of place as part of "the order (of whatever kind) in accord with which elements are distributed in relationship of coexistence."[15] In other words, everything has

14. I am following Hans-Georg Gadamer here. In *Truth and Method*, he discusses the logic of non-identical repetition with reference to the reading or performance of an archaic literary text, writing, "Each repetition is as original as the work itself." Gadamer, *Truth and Method*, 122.

15. On the movement from place to space, see de Certeau, *The Practice of Everyday Life*, 117–18.

its place, and that place is known in relation to others. Consider a holy sanctuary, and how, from high church to low, everything has its place. The altar goes here, the pulpit there, the organ here, the Paschal candle there, and so forth. Place is also commensurate with rest, a trajectory ended. This may apply to a stone tossed along the shore, or the span of a life drawn to a close.

Space, however, as articulated by de Certeau, is the "consideration of vectors of direction, velocities, and timelines."[16] Space is dynamic and open, providing room to roam. The minister, moving, confronts the congregation. The moment the relocation of the pulpit is considered, the holy place is acknowledged to have space. When the pews are taken out of the church, there is new space for grace—for yoga, dance, strength conditioning, lunches for homeless, recovery ministries, and jazz concerts. For de Certeau, place signifies closure and co-existence, while space signifies openness and dynamic, transformative interactions.

The moment the stone is lifted from the ground, there is hope in where it might land. When a person dies, and their life seems to have come to its place of rest, the community gathers to celebrate the person's life. The grieving community hopes against despair that though the cadaver is placed in a grave, the body is a symbol of a hope in coming resurrection, transforming the place of death into a space of everlasting life.

According to de Certeau, while place is seen as a relationship between static members, space is a vector, a relationship of and in motion. Releasing this dynamic transformational force is vital today in our urban vectors and ecclesial spaces. We need to reimagine these places so they can become spaces of hope. When Jesus is raised from the dead and the stone is moved from the entrance of the tomb, we see the conditions of change realized. While the rested stone has no hope of change, the stone in motion can change and is changing. The soul trapped between the crevices of stationary stones is brought to the brink of despair, but the soul in search of liberation hope moves with dancing stones, creating new spaces and sets of relationships that can transform the topography of the city.

It is time to transform places of despair into what David Harvey calls "spaces of hope."[17] Liturgy, the work of the people, plays a critical role in creating spaces of hope. It offers a spiritual cartography for our work of building just and sustainable urban spaces. The liturgy calibrates

16. Ibid.
17. Harvey, *Spaces of Hope*.

us to festival time and gives us an alternative experience of space in the sanctuary, where each Sabbath we can collectively experience the transformation of places of despair into spaces of hope.

The collective work of liturgy enacts communion among those who are participants. Communion is the context for engendering love, justice, and truth among the gathered people of God, especially the poor and oppressed. Boal's Theatre of the Oppressed offers forums for exploring different configurations of space. When the oppressed lead the drama, the dark structures of injustice are brought into the light. With the injustice and inequity in our urban political economies exposed, the church needs to work toward alternative configurations of space that are just, equitable and sustainable.

The development of the revolutionary subjectivity of the activist finds its fruition in the struggle for structural justice. Theatrical theology today must self-consciously analyze the social location from which it theologizes, including the ever-changing city. In New York City, Youth Ministries for Peace and Justice embodies the spirit of the early church's collective spirit (Acts 2), deploys the theatre of the oppressed, and stands in critique of the capitalist-driven city. It provides an important model of what a theatrical theology can look like when it is politically engaged in the struggle for a more just and sustainable city.

Youth Ministries for Peace and Justice

Youth Ministries for Peace and Justice (YMPJ) in the South Bronx is a youth social justice ministry that is an example of the church as a theatre of the oppressed. Founded by Alexie Torres-Fleming, a Roman Catholic Latina, Youth Ministries for Peace and Justice represents a prophetic, feminist-intercultural movement for justice. Led by a woman of color, Youth Ministries for Peace and Justice has done the demanding work of seeking to challenge the "powers and principalities" (Eph 6:12) in the South Bronx, the poorest congressional district in the country. Youth Ministries for Peace and Justice is effectively using different forms of Boal's Theatre of the Oppressed to dramatize the environmental injustices of the South Bronx for the broader public, building a youth-led people's movement to work for a more just and sustainable South Bronx.

Torres-Fleming was initiated into the movement for justice through her involvement with anti-drug activism in the Bronx. Father Mike

Tyson mentored Torres-Flemming as she became a leader in her youth group at Holy Cross Catholic Church. Father Mike mentored her into a mystical-prophetic theology that flows through the Roman Catholic tradition, especially within the streams of Franciscan monasticism and liberation theology. Youth Ministries for Peace and Justice is an important expression of post-Vatican II Catholic social thought in action through the life of the community. Embracing the power of the sacraments, Youth Ministries for Peace and Justice takes the liturgy of the church outside of the gates of the church in order to unveil the injustices experienced by the people in the community. Through the use of drama, Youth Ministiries for Peace *performed* (rather than perpetrated) injustices for the community to see, so that they could not longer be ignored.

During the 1980s, there was a growing crack epidemic in the South Bronx. Father Mike responded by organizing prayer marches with his parish on the public sidewalks in front of the notorious neighborhood crack houses. In retaliation for his public confrontations, the drug dealers burned down Holy Cross Church in November 1992.

Instead of retreating in the face of this violence, Holy Cross Church had to reimagine itself theologically. Instead of seeing itself as a hierarchical, priest-led, isolated body, it saw itself as a democratic, youth-led community of resurrection. As the youth led creative protest marches on the roads and performed forum theatres in the parks of the Bronx, they were acknowledging that God's true sanctuary was the human body, especially the body of those being destroyed by drugs within the Holy Cross parish and its community. Boldly going into places of despair (unto death), they demonstrated the patience, perseverance, and tenacious resolve needed to break the spiritual stronghold of the gangs and drug lords.

When discerning a way to move ahead, Torres-Fleming said, "Let's march!" She worked with Father Mike and helped to organize local youth to mobilize 1,200 people to march against the drug trade in the neighborhood. The march was successful because it dramatized the oppression and injustice through a youth-led procession for justice in the streets of the neighborhood. Many of the dilapidated crack houses were shut down, often resurrected as homes for families. Because of this witness of transformative theatre and its power, many of the youth at Holy Cross realized that faith could move beyond the walls of the church, that they had subversive moral agency and that, rooted in faith, they could affect positive social change in their neighborhood. With this taste of resurrection, the youth of South Bronx were ready for a new challenge.

Growing up in the Bronx, Torres-Fleming acutely felt the places of death in her community, but also perceived a space of hope where young people could be formed into prophetic leaders. Driven by this vision, Alexie spent the next year discerning what a ministry to youth would look like, and she launched Youth Ministries for Peace and Justice in 1994. They obtained space at St. Joan of Arc Church, and began to respond to many issues of injustice in the community, always focusing on the leadership formation of young people. She sought to raise up a generation of revolutionary disciples, willing to follow the call of Jesus the Jewish prophet through courageously confronting the powers and principalities (Eph 6:12).

When Alexie's son Patrick was diagnosed with asthma, the struggle for justice became personal. Alexie began talking to other mothers and discovered that many of their children had asthma too. These mothers wanted to get to the bottom of their children's sickness. Seeking answers to the problems of this growing health crisis, discovering the sources of particle pollution in the Bronx became a pursuit of utmost urgency for mothers affected by asthma. Their children's lives were on the line. In order to diagnose this health problem, they had to do some cartography to understand the urban ecology of the Bronx.

The South Bronx is crisscrossed by four highways. Post-war urban planning in New York City, under the leadership of Robert Moses, focused on the efficiency of automobile movement throughout the city. Cars and capital, rather than poor people and inhabitable green space, were the primary focus of Moses's urban planning agenda. Through efficient channels of transportation, Moses sought to ensure the efficient flow of labor and capital throughout the New York metropolitan area. Poor neighborhoods like the South Bronx became the target for highway construction. Moses's urban-aesthetic ideal was order and efficiency; however, it was ultimately a white supremacist urban planning model that effectively segregated people into "their place," especially the black and brown bodies of the South Bronx. Eventually, the people of the South Bronx became wise to what was happening to them and started organizing to end poverty and oppression in their borough.

Youth Ministries for Peace and Justice played a vital role in the process. In order to begin to take the land back in the South Bronx, Youth Ministries for Peace and Justice deployed strategies from the Theatre of the Oppressed. Their theatrical campaigns for justice had two foci: the Sheridan Expressway and Concrete Plant Park. While the Sheridan

Expressway had purportedly been built as a necessity because of massive traffic, there was not as much actual traffic as predicted. To dramatize the situation, some Youth Ministries for Peace and Justice staff and volunteers walked out onto Sheridan Expressway during rush hour and laid down in the middle of the road. A photograph was taken and then circulated through the media to show New York City that the Sheridan Expressway was a highly underutilized transportation route. On another occasion, the community coalition organized a picnic on the highway, putting out blankets to dramatize what it would be like to be able to have a park along the Bronx River. Both of these dramatic interventions unveiled an alternative vision for using the land. The highway, which is a place of despair and pollution, could be transformed into a space of health and hope. Theatre of the Oppressed unveils what is wrong in the current system and visualizes what we are moving toward.

Another example is Concrete Plant Park, an old, abandoned concrete plant that was owned by the city and which sat dormant for over a decade in the South Bronx. It was one of two pieces of public land with access to the Bronx River. Youth Ministries for Peace and Justice attended Community Board meetings to reclaim the land. They filed petitions for the land to be turned over officially to the Parks Department, to become waterfront park land and a clean, open green space for the community.

In the process, they discovered that New York State had $11 million in federal money to build a route to move trucks from the Cross Bronx Expressway into Hunts Point Market. They needed to dramatize the injustice, so several young people climbed to the top of the Concrete Plant and hung a sign that said, "Replant the Concrete Plant." However, it was Theatre of the Oppressed that would reach the community's collective psyche most deeply.

In a community where not everyone reads and writes, and many do not speak English, theatre is an effective way to communicate to the people. Individuals from Youth Ministries for Peace and Justice went to the corner with a group of young people and enacted a drama about the death of the river. Taking a portable radio and drums, they made music to draw folks in and conducted a funeral procession about the death of the Bronx River, which was neglected, isolated, and polluted. This performance tapped into the people's hearts and their collective emotional memory of the river. They made a casket and conducted a mock funeral for the concrete plant. They placed a canoe full of flowers into the river, symbolizing how the river was full of death, but could be redeemed by beauty.[18]

Via Dolorosa: Jesús, Recuérdame Cuando Entres en Tu Reino

Given the power of festival time in the life of the church, staging a dramatic intervention during the high holy days is one effective way to wake up the community to the injustices in their midst. During Holy Week, at the end of the forty days of Lent, Torres-Fleming would lead a procession called the "Way of the Cross" through the neighborhood. Often called the *Via Dolorosa* (meaning, the Way of Sorrows), the Way of the Cross is a series of artistic representations of Jesus Christ carrying the cross to his crucifixion during the final hours of his life. The Way of the Cross is often celebrated liturgically within the church building through a series of stations with icons or sculptures that parishioners visit in a spirit of reverent prayer.

Seeking to break the "fourth wall" between the Word and the world, Youth Ministries for Peace and Justice took this holy procession to the streets of the Bronx, seeking to engage the powers and principalities there. During this Way of the Cross procession, they "crucified" various injustices in the community, visiting different "stations" throughout the Bronx. At each station they would focus on a different social sin in the Bronx, nailing it to a big cross that was carried by a young Mexican-American priest, Father Juan Carlos Ruiz. For example, when they walked down to the Bronx river, they engaged the problem of pollution. The Bronx River, which should be a source of life and happiness for the community, had been neglected, polluted, and used as a dump for far too long. Alexie Torres-Fleming says, "When you walk into a Catholic church you dip your hand in holy water as well as when you depart to remember the blessing of baptism. So for us the river represented coming and going into a sacred place. As people of faith, we saw the Bronx river as holy water."[19]

18 There is a good YouTube video about Concrete Plant Park, which can be found at https://www.youtube.com/watch?v=bRvDMSqXYxc.

19. Alexie Torrres-Fleming, interview with the author at New York Theological Seminary, November 21, 2012.

Full of old cars, tires, and oil, the ritual by the riverside was a prayer for the purification of a dying river. Engaging the problem of river pollution was cathartic for the community that longed to swim in the river and drink its water. Tapping into people's hearts and hope, this theatre of the oppressed transformed bad emotional memories into new and positive ones.

St. Paul poetically describes the longing of creation in his epistle to the Romans, writing, "For the creation waits in eager expectation for the children of God to be revealed. For the creation was subjected to frustration, not by its own choice, but by the will of the one who subjected it, in hope that the creation itself will be liberated from its bondage to decay and brought into the freedom and glory of the children of God" (Rom 8:19–21). The whole creation is "groaning as in the pains of childbirth" to be redeemed (Rom 8:22). The cry of creation for healing is connected to humanity's cry for justice. There is a deep interconnectedness between the human community and the community of creation. The destiny of humanity and the earth are intricately and intimately bound together. Visiting the river on the Way of the Cross was an opportunity for the people to worship the Creator and to ask for their own deliverance and the deliverance of the community. The procession continued to the Sheridan Expressway, The Concrete Plant, the sewer system, James Monroe High School, and Bronx River Public Housing Project, bringing to public light other injustices in the community.

After visiting each station and physically nailing the particular sin of that station onto the cross, the young people joined together in singing a praise chorus in English and Spanish: "Jesus, remember me, when you come into your kingdom . . . Jesús, recuérdame cuando entres en tu reino." These crucifixions of the sins of the communities made Jesus' journey to the cross real to the people of the Bronx. Given all of the injustices of the South Bronx, Jesus became a living, incarnate reality of a sacrificial love stronger than death.

Just as the season of Lent ends with resurrection Sunday, so the Way of the Cross procession ended with the resurrection. The spiritual force of the communal ritual bore witness to a world that Scripture describes as a new world, a new covenant, a new birth: the kingdom of God. Inspired by the exodus and resurrection, the Way of the Cross became an event of deliverance, opening up the possibilities of the people's own prophetic moral agency to fight for freedom in the current age. The same "powers and principalities" that sought to crucify Jesus were seeking to crucify the people of the Bronx (Eph 6:12). Youth Ministries for Peace and Justice gives us one concrete example of how the church can become a theatre of the oppressed—a missional movement for social justice and cultural renewal.

Theatre of the Oppressed makes a difference in local communities. As a result of the creative activism of Youth Ministries for Peace and Justice, Congressman Jose Serrano reallocated the $11 million for a greenway to be established in the footprint of the demolished concrete plant. Instead of a route for trucks, there was now a route for pedestrians. The outcry performed by Youth Ministries for Peace and Justice with theatrical flair affected lasting social change. Ultimately, the community received a $30 million dollar grant to build a park. It was a beautifully landscaped green space, including domino tables, seats organized in a circle for reading, and a serpentine pathway to walk and bike along the river. The struggle for green space for the whole community was successful. Today, that beautiful space in the Bronx is called Concrete Plant Park. Some would say the greatest achievement is a restored river and access to a new waterfront, but their use of the Theatre of the Oppressed was more powerful than that; it was a process of transformation that happened among the people who were able to move and speak, emboldened to create the conditions in which they could claim their own voice and power. A new generation of revolutionary disciples was formed, and they continue to lead today. Among them is David Shuffler, who was one of the young adults leading the protests, and who now serves as the organization's second Executive Director.

Conclusion

In summary, Brazilian playwright Augusto Boal's call to break the fourth wall through the cultivation of "*spect-actors*" can unleash the creative power of the church today. Thinking about how to take the disconnected liturgies of the church into the open-air markets of the city is one of the most pressing tasks for the contemporary church. The church, in the power of the Spirit of Justice, can transform urban places of despair into spaces of hope, especially when reimagined as a theatre of the oppressed that moves to the cadence of festival time. Youth Ministries for Justice—a youth-led, faith-rooted, environmental justice ministry in South Bronx, New York—is one example of how the church can be mystically rooted and prophetically engaged, improvising a way forward that leads to a just, equitable, and sustainable urban future.

By being creative, faith-rooted activists and taking liturgy to the streets, the prophetic church today can reimagine space and time through the liturgy, baptizing the community into festival time, and gathering the community to create spaces of hope in the city. Our faith traditions provide vehicles for communicating our message that speaks to the whole brain (left and right) in its wondrous capacity to be shaped and shape the world, as well as to the heart and soul. From the ancient, ringing words of Scripture to our symbols, ceremonies, music, and rituals, we have creative instruments for the transformation of perspectives and the conversion of the heart that go far beyond social analysis and policy recommendations.

Theatre of the Oppressed is often the most powerful, swift, and poignant way to persuade both the ruling powers and the people of the importance of justice. When we seek to spread new ideas among humanity, we should turn to story, poetry, theatre, music, and movement to inspire the heart and imagination. We must utilize these methods in the context of private conversations with the powerful, in formal hearings before official bodies, but especially in the streets as the religious component of nonviolent, direct actions for a more just and loving world.

Theatre of the Oppressed provokes the church to think more deeply about liturgical reform and renewal that makes physical connections and interrupts the actual economics of the marketplace. Churches today need to learn how to translate the liturgical performance of Sunday worship into street theatre freely performed throughout the week. When the church has the courage to open its doors to all God's children in the community of creation, the Spirit of Justice will flow through our city like a mighty stream of salvation, the streets burning bright with shalom as if made of gold.

Bibliography

Boal, Augusto. *Theatre of the Oppressed.* Translated by Charles A. and Maria-Odilia Leal McBride. New York: Theatre Communications Group, 1985.

Certeau, Michele de. *The Practice of Everyday Life.* Translated by Steven Rendall. Berkeley: University of California Press, 1984.

Freire, Paulo. *Pedagogy of the Oppressed.* Translated by Myra Bergman Ramos. New York: Continuum, 1985.

Gadamer, Hans-Georg. *Truth and Method.* 2nd rev. ed. Translated by Joel Weinsheimer and Donald G. Marshall. New York: Continuum, 1989.

Halpern, Manfred. *Transforming the Personal, Political, Historical and Sacred in Theory and Practice*. Edited by David Abalos. Scranton, PA: University of Scranton Press, 2009.

Harvey, David. *Spaces of Hope*. Berkeley: University of California Press, 2000.

Heltzel, Peter Goodwin. *Resurrection City: A Theology of Improvisation*. Grand Rapids: Eerdmans, 2012.

Marx, Karl. *The Marx-Engels Reader*. Edited by Robert C. Tucker. New York: Norton, 1978.

West, Cornel. "Justice Is What Love Looks Like in Public." Sermon delivered at Howard University, Washington, DC, April 17, 2011.

13

Theatre as a Source
of Religious Insight and Revelation

David Brown

THE PURPOSE OF THIS chapter is to consider some ways in which theatre might prove to be a source of religious insight or revelation. I concede at once that this is not a way in which most contemporary theatergoers, even those religiously inclined, are accustomed to think. For them, the expectation is that they will be entertained or moved but not significantly transformed. Not that there is anything wrong as such with these more limited aspirations. To give two recent examples from my own Scottish context, the inclusion of several top hits from the Proclaimers within the play *Sunshine over Leith* offered an excellent evening of enjoyment. Again, few in the audience remained unmoved by Dundee Rep's provocative transfer of Lorca's *Blood Wedding* from Spain to a Glasgow gangland context.[1] Nonetheless, through most of the twentieth century, major playwrights and directors have frequently expressed the wish for something more. It is that "something more" that I want to explore here, not least because it has—somewhat surprisingly, given the secular age in which we live—commonly been expressed in religious terms. So I will begin by outlining some reasons for modern aspirations in this direc-

1. *Blood Wedding* of 1933 was one of the peasant tragedies that Federico García Lorca presented with his university theatre group La Barraca while touring rural Spain. Transferring similar passions to working class Glasgow worked remarkably well.

tion, then briefly sketch what I mean by religious experience and offer my answer to four common objections to giving it such a status. Finally, I will provide several specific examples for readers' consideration from actual stage performance.

Twentieth-Century Background

Let's first go back a little in time. There is no doubt that when L. J. M. Daguerre invented the camera in 1839 he set in motion a process that transformed painting, for although realism initially continued to hold sway, soon artists began to search for alternative means of out-performing the new invention. Thus, one way of interpreting Impressionism and subsequent artistic movements is to see them as offering alternative accounts of what the artist is trying to achieve: not simply a reflection of how we customarily see things, as the camera might propose, but real insight into the way things are.[2] So, for instance, in his famous series of paintings of the facade of Rouen Cathedral (1892–94), Claude Monet encouraged viewers to observe how that facade changed over the course of the day and in different conditions of light. In doing so, he focused on the perception obtained through close attention to immediate experience rather than its customary resolution into dull uniformity created by the mind's antecedent expectations or the picture given by the long-exposure camera shots common in his day.

One might make similar observations about the impact of cinema on theatre, for the spectacle and/or realism that nineteenth-century theatre offered was now produced more convincingly by cinema.[3] For example, cinema could achieve changes of context within a continuing narrative without resorting to artificial props on stage or the reduced impact of waiting while cumbersome stage machinery made the requisite changes. The parallel, however, runs deeper than this. Some visual artists chose new ways of doing things not for the sake of novelty but in

---

2. This is only to indicate how the contrast was felt at the time and for a considerable period afterwards. We now know that issues of realism and truth are no less complicated in photography, not least since Susan Sontag's seminal essay, first published in 1977 and continuously in print since then.

3. I am referring here to realism in stage props and not to the more technical sense of "realism" as a movement towards portraying ordinary life, as seen in Strindberg and Ibsen.

order to recover earlier forms of art prior to the use of perspective,[4] or to refer to earlier styles from other cultures such as Japanese, Oceanic, or African, in what is commonly labeled "the cult of the primitive."[5] Drama in the twentieth century adopted a similar strategy. Both playwrights and directors incorporated elements from earlier forms of drama, ancient Greek drama in particular. So it is important to remember that the type of drama presented in England by T. S. Eliot, Christopher Fry, and John Masefield, with the use of choruses and so forth, was part of a much wider international movement with obvious parallels in the work of W. B. Yeats in Ireland, Paul Claudel in France, Ugo Betti in Italy, and Alfonso Sastre in Spain.

But more relevant to the theme of this chapter is the extent to which a number of leading theatre directors couched their new aims in religious terms. This can, of course, be partly explained by their reliance on Greek drama, given its performance in the context of an annual festival dedicated to the god Dionysus. But there were also deeper motives, and I will highlight two in particular. First, the transformative element in religion—its capacity for holistic change—continues to be seen as a worthy aim even for modern drama (at the very least perspectives should be changed). Secondly, the most effective context for change, it is argued, is not the private, isolated world of cinema, with viewers related simply as individuals to what is happening on the screen. Rather, there is more potential for transformation in a corporate setting, something that is at least potentially feasible in theatre, especially where tactics are employed that directly involve the audience, such as expanding the performance space beyond the stage. In this way, theatre more nearly approaches liturgy, where similar corporate aims are in view. While it is true that Berthold Brecht (d. 1956), perhaps the most significant director of the twentieth century, made no direct appeal to religion in his key notions of the distancing effect or *Verfremdungseffekt* and the breaking down of the so-called "fourth wall," several other influential directors did seek to strengthen their case by religious parallels, and so may be noted here.[6]

4. While Cubism is best known for substituting multiple perspectives for ordinary perspective, other artists did return the canvas to a flat surface. Jean-Édouard Vuillard's treatment of room interiors would be a case in point.

5. Known in France as Japonisme (the term was coined in 1872), Degas, Renoir, Monet, and Whistler were among those influenced by the re-opening of Japan after two hundred years of seclusion. Artists as varied as Picasso and Moore owed debts to Oceanic and African art.

6. The fourth wall, advocated by naturalist approaches to theatre, is the idea that

For instance, the French director Antonin Artaud (1896–1948) argued that theatre is a kind of "soul therapy" concerned to purge the audience of its own wrong emotions, hence the term "theatre of cruelty."[7] While in this aspect he was most influenced by Freud, he also appealed to Jewish Kabbalah for the appropriate breathing exercises that would ensure that actors were in touch with their full emotional and physical resources, while in the use of gesture he appealed to Balinese Hindu dance forms. Again, the Polish director Jerzy Grotowski (1933–99) spoke of how one must remove all elements extraneous to the actor-audience relationship, such as lighting and even sound, and that actors should see themselves not as acquiring extra skills but rather as engaging in a *via negativa*. In other words, they must eliminate anything from their presentation that might inhibit such a relationship, becoming what he called "holy actors," those who are seen to transcend their purely earthly appearance and thus give themselves spiritually to their audience. Finally, we might take note of the British director Peter Brook (b. 1925), whose account of "holy theatre" in *The Empty Space* dates from 1968 and his influential production of *A Midsummer Night's Dream* from two years later.[8] Performed in a white box and using circus acrobatics instead of wings, Brook combined playfulness and seriousness to hint at the possibility of transcendence, with the fairies seen as the very heart of the drama. Contrast the 1997 version by Jonathan Miller who, though influenced by Brook, insisted that a purely human story should be the real focus. Although for Brook "holy theatre" is as capable of emerging through secular themes as religious, he has also sought to revive in the modern West explicitly religious drama through adaption of, for example, the Sufi *Conference of Birds* (1979) or the famous Hindu epic, the *Mahabharata* (1985).[9]

In sum, the possibility of religious experience in drama has surfaced again and again in the twentieth century. But what does it mean to claim

---

the auditorium is the fourth wall of an otherwise realist set which provides the remaining three sides of a room. For Brecht, the auditorium was also part of the stage.

7. I discuss Artaud and other modern approaches at greater length in my *God and Mystery in Words*, 173–85.

8. The endlessly experimental character of his approach is perhaps best indicated in another later work of his, *There Are No Secrets*, in which his repeated changes of mind in approaching *The Tempest* are clearly revealed.

9. Yet, surprisingly, there is less explicit religious content in Peter Brook's adaptation (there is a British Film Institute DVD), for example in use of the *Bhagavad-Gita* section of the *Mahabharata*, than in a more traditional production like the Indian fifteen-hour version (Arrow/Freemantle DVD of 2003).

that religious experience through drama is possible? Before offering some specific examples for consideration, I want first to look at the issue of religious experience more generally.

Religious Experience

Considering some common objections to the very idea of religious experience will help clarify the possibility for theatre to mediate such experience. I will focus on and respond to two common objections from philosophers and two from theologians.

First, philosophers sometimes raise the objection that to talk of religious experience at all is meaningless since God is an infinite being, and so there is nothing in human experience that could count as having an infinite God as its object. In short, we could never know that we had encountered an infinite God with the corresponding range of attributes.[10] This is true, but, as in any encounter with another human being, only some aspects of a person are ever perceived on any particular occasion, and it is from such aspectival perception that a more rounded picture can then be developed. In other words, the experience should not be seen as an isolated phenomenon, and some attempt should be made to integrate it with other aspects of the person's experience and conceptual understanding. For example, a sense of being graced by something larger than one's self can be combined with a more explicit sense of divine transcendence mediated in a different context, as in the presence of an awesome landscape. Indeed, such an experience of transcendence could in itself help suggest the notion of infinity, as with a sea horizon apparently receding infinitely into the distance. That is, the apparent infinity of the horizon conjures up a sense of its divine Creator as similarly infinite.

A rather different sort of objection from philosophers is that such cases are actually only either aesthetic or moral experiences, the more mysterious aspects of both being illegitimately ascribed some sort of religious aura.[11] To demonstrate that they are really the same, the objector points out how the same criteria in fact need to be applied in both cases, with the religious "graced" experience reducible to a sense of gratitude

10. For a version of this objection, see Davies, *An Introduction to the Philosophy of Religion*, 64–76.

11. Similar objections can also be found among architectural historians writing about religious buildings. See, for example, the chapter on "The Absentee Landlord" in Meades, *Museum without Walls.*

without any determinable object, or the "transcendent" experience merely identical to the aesthetic sublime. But although the two types of experience (moral and aesthetic vs. religious) are sometimes confused, even in the percipient's own mind, I would suggest that, in general, different sorts of criteria do indeed operate. Thus, it is not necessarily aesthetically good art that generates religious experience. For example, Bernadette's vision of the Virgin Mary at Lourdes was in part occasioned by a rather indifferent statue of Mary in Bernadette's local parish church. Likewise, experiences of grace are not quite the same thing as a sense of thankfulness. The birth of a child, for instance, if experienced in religious terms, involves rather more than just feeling that one ought to be grateful; there is also a sense of wonder at what has come into the world that goes beyond simply understanding the mechanics of what has occurred. Of course, sometimes the two types do indeed run parallel, as in an aesthetic experience of some great Gothic cathedral that also generates a sense of divine transcendence. To my mind, however, the fact that differences can be detected in other cases justifies us in noting a distinction here as well, even if the differences are less marked. The aesthetic experience will be one of awe in virtue of the nature of the building itself (its lightness despite its weight and it soaring heavenwards), but the religious experience pulls beyond this, in virtue of the symbolism involved, into a sense of that to which such soaring points, God as transcendent and infinite.

No less frequent and insistent are theological objections to religious experience. The first is the worry that God is somehow made subordinate to human experience, when the world is seen as a trigger for experiencing his grace. Should it not be the case that God is entirely free to act wherever and whenever he chooses? Personally, I find this argument somewhat odd. Of course, God could have decided to keep his freedom of action entirely within his own control, but even biblical revelation suggests that this is not so. In the Hebrew Scriptures, the people of Israel are offered repeated assertions and promises of divine presence, while in the New Testament there is not only the promise of Christ's continued presence within the community of faith (Matt 18:20), but also, according to the Catholic tradition, specific powers for its ministers (John 20:23). So there is clearly a biblical pattern of divine accessibility under certain conditions. To such an observation, however, it might well be objected that to speak of similar triggers in the natural world is to go altogether too far, since such availability would exist in the absence of explicit Christian faith, apparently thus suggesting the ability of humanity to tap at will, as it were, into the divine presence. But it is important to note what is and what is not being asserted by any such claim. Certainly, it is to claim that God is universally available to all humanity, through a ubiquitous presence in the created order. But this is in no way to suggest that any further act is required on God's part to make such experience possible; rather, it is human beings that need to open themselves to the already existing divine address. Equally, such a way of viewing matters in no way entails that humanity can manipulate God by, for example, seeking to secure thereby their own salvation. Instead, all that is being asserted is that in virtue of creation taking a particular and divinely ordained form, God is constantly available to human experience, provided the right conditions are met and acted upon. In other words, at the foundation of all reality lies the generosity of God, a standing invitation that, like the cross, admits dismissal and misuse, but which yet, also like the cross, can never expose God to human manipulation.

But perhaps for most theologians the greater worry about such a picture is not so much the kind of exposure it gives to God but the way in which it appears to grant some sort of independent validity to revelatory experiences not derived ultimately from the Scriptures. Such experiences could be interpreted in this way, but it is important to note that their recognition does not of itself carry such an implication. It is still possible to hold that interpretation of these religious experiences remains ultimately subordinate to, and conditional upon, what has been revealed through the Scriptures. Nor is this necessarily to deprive them of their power. It could be argued, for example, that new things are in fact discovered through such forms of general revelation but that these discoveries can lead us to look at the Bible anew and thereby discover what we have previously misunderstood in some way.

Religious experience derived through the arts would fit this general pattern, insofar as the various arts succeed in reflecting aspects of the divine attributes and purposes, which are also available in the created order or through biblical revelation. Yet, even if one accepts such a general account, it might still seem that theatre is one of the less profitable areas to examine in order to substantiate such a possibility. The constant changes of mood throughout a drama might well seem to militate against the possibility of any sustained experience of the divine. So, for example, there are no ready parallels to the constantly repeated refrain of transcendence in Gothic architecture. Even with music, where temporal progression and mood changes are involved, typically it is a particular movement of a symphony, concerto, or sonata that is conceived of carrying divine import. One might think of the sense of transcendence in the final movement of Mozart's Jupiter Symphony and the third movement of Bruckner's Eighth, or again, of thankfulness in the penultimate movement of Beethoven's Pastoral Symphony and in the third movement of his Opus 132 String Quartet. Although there is some change of emphasis within a movement, on the whole the mood remains relatively constant, as indeed is indicated by the general instruction for a particular movement's performance, such as *andante, allegretto,* or *con brio.*

Nonetheless, to deny the possibility of religious experience within dramatic performance simply because of such changes of mood and tempo would surely be a serious mistake, since it would rob much of the Bible of similar possibilities. While there are certainly great moments of biblical experience that comprise a unified mood, such as Isaiah's vision in the Temple, or Job's encounter in the whirlwind, much of the Bible is narrative that fluctuates considerably in mood.[12] Not only that, but much of Jesus' teaching functions similarly, with the story element in his parables exhibiting the same sort of pattern. So it would seem odd if the power of conversion is claimed for parable, but any similar potential denied for the imaginative use of storytelling elsewhere. What I want to do in the last section of this chapter, therefore, is consider a few putative theatrical cases, and explore what it might mean to link them to an actual experience of God.

Theatrical Examples

The examples that follow include some from great Christian drama, although this is in general not the case. My intention in stretching the selection more widely is in no way to decry the virtues of explicitly Christian drama, but rather to indicate how I believe we might perceive God acting more widely. My examples, therefore, come from Ibsen, Wagner, and classical drama as well as the explicitly Christian context with which I begin.

Take, then, the medieval mystery plays. These are commonly presented in terms of Pope Gregory the Great's familiar account of art more

---

12. Isa 6:1–8; Job 38:1—42:6; for a helpful, more detailed discussion of such variety of moods in Scripture, see Ford, *The Future of Christian Theology,* 68–83.

generally as a means for teaching the illiterate.[13] In my perspective, however, something rather different is also going on, perhaps best indicated by the difference between theoretical beliefs and those beliefs that have become part of one's lived experience. That is, it is one thing for a Christian to hold certain beliefs, and even for these beliefs to be expressed through theatre; it is quite another for an individual to gain some sense of God's reality in the here and now. I suggest that this explains what to contemporary Christians often seems a surprising element in such drama, the prominence of humor. One of its main functions was to create a sense of God's presence. No doubt the great majority of those watching them in the later middle ages did not doubt God's existence and the general claims of the church. But the earthiness of some of the humor made it possible to appropriate the reality of God's incarnation into a world not vaguely like their own, but exactly so. This may seem an astonishing claim to make, but despite all the realism of medieval art one must remember how much of it insisted on the holy family as part of the more affluent sections of society. In the art of the time, kings might visit the child but they often did so in contexts in which Mary was no less lavishly dressed and with a solemnity apparently far removed from ordinary life.

Consequently, it must have come as quite a shock to audiences of the time to see the nativity presented as it is in the Second Shepherds' Pageant from the Wakefield cycle, to take what is perhaps the most extreme case in point.[14] The address of the angels to the shepherds is set in the wider context of sheep-stealing, in which the scoundrel, Mak, is aided and abetted by his wife attempting to disguise the stolen sheep as her new-born child. This is, in effect, an alternative nativity set against the incarnation, but even the birth of Jesus is not without its humor, as the shepherds search for suitable presents for the new-born child: one offering cherries, another a bird, and the third a ball for Jesus "to go to the tennis." The Christ Child born into the world of a petty thief like Mak and fumbling, henpecked shepherds must have brought with it a powerful sense of divine reality existing in solidarity with the audience.

More controversially, however, I would like to suggest that such transformative experience of the divine can also be mediated through non-Christian drama. Modern Western drama, as I have already noted,

13. Letter to Serenus, found most easily in Thiessen, *Theological Aesthetics*, 47–48.

14. The text is available in Cawley, ed., *Everyman and Medieval Miracle Plays*, 75–104. Perhaps still the best modern production was the National Theatre's Cottesloe production of 1985.

had its origins in classical drama and in particular Greek tragedy, all of which were performed in the context of a religious festival, the Dionysia. For most of the history of modern interpretation, that religious context has been made firmly subordinate to what has been presented as universal human dilemmas and values. However, as classical scholars are increasingly acknowledging, the presence of the gods in these narratives is by no means just of marginal significance and not merely symbolic of purely human concerns.[15] Rather, they are usually integral to the story. And, if taking this fact seriously may make some of those dramas appear quite remote to our own concerns, nonetheless we ought to hesitate before we resist this new emphasis. Sadly, a reductionism that ignores the divine is now even common in the treatment of Christian mystery plays where the stories are retold, allegedly, to have more universal appeal. I recall, for instance, attending one such presentation in Newcastle, where God had entirely disappeared from the script!

In short, my suspicion is that ancient audiences expected the plays to do something not only for their religious understanding but also for how they experienced the reality of the gods in the context of the performance and in their own lives. Consider, for example, the story of Oedipus. At one level, the grim tale could be read as illustrative of the terrible inevitability of causative forces well beyond any individual's control. As Sophocles's play *Oedipus Tyrannus* makes abundantly clear, there was no way for Oedipus to escape the curse on his family for wrong deeds done by his ancestors, which now visited the next generation. Yet that was not to be the last word, as another of Sophocles's plays, *Oedipus at Colonus*, makes evident. Although from a different cycle, the play suggests a pattern of resolution that Sophocles may well also have adopted for the now lost conclusion to the earlier trilogy to which *Oedipus Tyrannus* belongs: at his life's end, Oedipus is envisaged as being taken up into the life of the gods.[16] It is also, incidentally, Sophocles's own last will and testament, as it were, since the play was only finally produced by his grandson five years after Sophocles's death, in 401 BC. Although finding the play "full of extremes of hatred and devotion, of passion and patience, of misery and power," even someone without religious sympathies like Maurice Bowra admits that its final message is a religious one, with "the justice of

15. See Hugh Lloyd-Jones, *The Justice of Zeus*; and Mary Lefkowitz, *Greek Gods, Human Lives*.

16. Both plays date from the latter part of Sophocles's long life (496–406 BC), *Oedipus Tyrannus* from around 430 and *Oedipus at Colonus* from 406.

the gods . . . vindicated in their treatment of Oedipus," and the "vision of a heroic being who sustains Attica by his presence."[17]

To propose, however, that the concluding scene could have been experienced by some of the ancient audience as an encounter with the divine is not to suggest that the compassionate concern of the Christian God is already fully present in this pagan drama. As Lefkowitz repeatedly emphasizes, more often than not, the Greek gods show callousness even towards those to whom they are especially well disposed. It does suggest, though, that a different picture from such callousness was sometimes offered, with possibilities for relating to the divine that would eventually find fulfillment not only within Christianity but also in some new forms of pagan religion, as in the relation of the third-century Apuleius with the god Isis, in his semi-autobiographical novel *The Ass*.[18]

So it seems not improbable to claim that ancient audiences experienced some sense of divine benevolence and care, providing at least some anticipation of the Christian God. This is to endorse in large part Balthasar's reading of Greek tragedy, though with the hope that its own independent voice might be heard more distinctively and not just as an anticipation of a Christian perspective, for in my view Balthasar goes too far in asserting of Sophocles that "not for one moment, amid the night he is depicting, does he doubt that it is God's night, and therefore God's 'lightless light.'"[19] There is rather more conflict going on, which is well captured in one modern Christian adaptation of *Oedipus at Colonus*, arguably Sophocles's most Christian play. In Lee Breuer's *The Gospel at Colonus*, where most of the text has been retained but given a setting in a modern black Pentecostal church,[20] the interactional character of such worship allows the conflicting thoughts and aspirations of the original to be taken up, even as we are swept beyond longing simply for death to the promise of new life with which the drama ends. In other words, it is not just by offering anticipations of Christianity that Greek drama can allow us to experience God. It is precisely through entering its own conflicts

17. Bowra, *Sophoclean Tragedy*, 355.

18. Modern commentators are now more inclined to treat seriously the claims made to religious experience in the concluding section of the novel. See, for example, Walsh's Introduction to his translation.

19. Balthasar, *The Glory of the Lord*, 4:129. For his discussion of Greek tragedy generally, 101–54.

20. An American text and DVD are available. It was featured at the Edinburgh Festival in 2010, with the Blind Boys of Alabama in the leading role.

and lack of resolution that we can experience God more deeply in the ambiguities of our own lives.

Nor is this by any means the only example from the ancient world of potentially life-changing experiences of the divine within theatrical performance. For most of its history in the modern West, Euripides's *Bacchae* has been read as a warning against unrestrained religious enthusiasm, but from the 1960s onwards it was employed in the opposite direction as an argument that too much sexual restraint might eventually do no less harm.[21] But what if neither human lesson is the point but rather something about how the audience might experience the divine? The focus of the drama is after all the god Dionysus, in whose honor all the plays were being performed. Could not Euripides be suggesting that neither rationalism nor exuberance on their own is the best avenue for experiencing the divine, but that the best approach might include both? If so, the action of the play might have helped some audience members to find the reality of the divine in cultic rituals of the gods that they had previously despised, while other audience members might have at last seen the point of reasoned argument not only in religion more generally but also in the re-structuring of the myths that were sometimes observable within the dramas. As for modern secular audiences, it is intriguing to find Edith Hall, the leading expert on modern reception of Greek tragedy, speculating that one major reason for its huge increase in popularity in recent years has been "the drastic recent secularization of western society." As such, "Greek tragedy can offer an important site . . . for reflecting on metaphysical and (in the broadest sense) theological issues . . . in the fragmented, multicultural (and in north-western Europe at least) post-Christian world of the late twentieth and twenty-first centuries."[22]

The examples I have given so far suggest that theatrical performance has the potential to change our understanding of the divine nature. I began with this observation partly because it seems to me the most neglected aspect of such possibilities, especially in a context where theatre focusing on divine action, in classical or medieval drama, is often presented as merely conveying lessons about humanity. Even, however, where the latter is so, it seems a mistake to suppose that religious experience as such is thereby excluded. Of course, one could take a relatively easy example for my case, such as T. S. Eliot's *Murder in the Cathedral*, deliberately written

21. This was evident most recently in the Scottish National Theatre production of 2008.

22. Hall, "Introduction," 44, in Hall et al., *Dionysus Since*, 69.

in the ancient style of which I have so far spoken. Certainly it is no simple retelling of Becket's murder.[23] Instead, Eliot offers a careful analysis of all the wrong reasons why Becket might have acted before he is seen abandoning even the quest for sanctity and seeking only to do the right thing, leaving all else in the hands of God. Three temptations roughly parallel those of Christ, the first offering personal safety, the second the chance of riches and honor from the king, and the third a way of successfully uniting with the barons against the king. The fourth temptation is the most insidious, acceptance of the call to martyrdom but with the possibility of self-glorification. As Becket himself declares, the worst possible temptation is to do the right thing for the wrong reason. It is perfectly possible for someone watching this play to realize that their own practice of religion has, like Becket's, been essentially self-centered rather than a real attempt to commit all to the providence of God.

But I emphatically do not want to suggest that such experience can only come through the work of Christian writers. God works much more widely than simply through his followers. Consider a play like Ibsen's *The Doll's House* (1879). The plot concerns a wife (Nora), infantilized by her husband (Helmer), who in the end breaks free and leaves not only him but also their children behind to start a new life on her own. On the surface, this hardly sounds like a Christian theme, but Ibsen not only uses religious language but also tries to persuade us, in part precisely through the use of such language, how a proper valuing of this particular woman can only be achieved through these decisions. The play as a whole can in fact be seen to be building up to its final dialogue between husband and wife.[24] So when Nora accuses Helmer of treating her like a mere doll and a puppet reflection of himself, just as her father had done, the audience easily appreciates the rightness of her claim. When Helmer then accuses her of violating her "sacred duty" to her husband and children, it is not difficult to side with her appeal to "another duty equally sacred," that of developing her own distinct identity. But for me the most revealing line is when Nora speaks of her hope that there might have been a miraculous change of perception when Helmer was presented with the opportunity of sacrificing himself on his wife's behalf. Helmer defends himself by

23. The original context and Eliot's subsequent changes to the text are explored in Pickering, *Drama in the Cathedral*, 178–95.

24. For the key scene, see Ibsen, *Four Major Plays,* 78–86.

saying, "But nobody sacrifices his honor for the one he loves," to which Nora gives the devastating reply: "Hundreds and thousands of women have."[25]

So shocked were early German directors of the play, that Ibsen was forced to write an alternative ending for performances in Hamburg and Vienna, in which Nora, when confronted with her children, reluctantly agrees to stay.[26] The latter might seem the more Christian ending, but what interests me here is how an audience seeing the full force of the unadulterated tragedy might be thus enabled for the first time to see the destructive potential of certain forms of marital relationships. Consequently, if they are Christians, they might at the very least seek to read biblical injunctions on marriage in a new way. Of course, the whole process might just be one of inference: hearing the story and then applying it to how they now understand the divine purpose for such personal relationships. But my point is that this need not be so. Instead, the viewing of the play could itself be experienced as a divine summons to change.

There are of course many who for theological or philosophical reasons want to confine experience of God to the rare and the exceptional, and our modern world may seem to support such scarcity in divine availability. But, as scholars such as Charles Taylor have argued, it is precisely such pessimism that has conditioned our contemporaries not to expect such experience and therefore to read the world in this way.[27] In short, human beings no longer have such experiences precisely because they are no longer encouraged to look for them. Yet, even as late as the nineteenth century, even non-believers were continuing to contribute to the possibility of reading the world in a fundamentally Christian way, and thus to the possibility of experiencing God through that world, and indeed through their own work.

Take a fundamental Christian theme like redemption through sacrifice. Neither Verdi nor Wagner was a Christian believer, yet believers attending some of their greatest operas would nonetheless have had their confidence in that fundamental theme hugely strengthened. It is after all basic to the plot of Verdi's La Traviata, as indeed to Wagner's Tristan und Isolde. However, it is the conclusion of Wagner's great Ring Cycle that I want to offer as my final example. I recently saw the accomplished Canadian director Robert Lepage's version, and at the end of the final opera

25. Ibid., 84.

26. For the alternative ending, see Ibid., 87–88.

27. See Taylor, A Secular Age.

Gotterdämmerung I was in tears.[28] So I had to ask myself why. The plot is after all quite absurd: the theft of a ring that results in the destruction of the old divine order. So were those tears just relief that twenty hours or so of theatre were now over, or, more plausibly, was it simply the power of the music that dragged me along? Or was there something deeper at stake in this application of Wagner's concept of total theatre? I venture to suggest that there was: it was a confirmatory experience of how God has in fact shaped our world, with the notion of sacrifice at the heart of a basic pattern built by God into the nature of all reality, which culminates in the crucifixion of Christ.

In my view, therefore, it is not just the liturgy that each Sunday helps to deepen our sense of incorporation into the fundamental narrative of our faith. If we are only alive to hear it, this also happens in the most apparently secular of surroundings: the prostitute at the end of *La Traviata* dying to release her love, and the goddess Brunhilde sacrificing her life to put an end to the jealous quest for power that the ring had come to represent, thus allowing innocence and love to come in its place. But expressed in this way, the point is perhaps still not put as forcefully as it might be. In its desire to appear loyal to divine revelation, much current theological writing on the arts seems to me unnecessarily grudging, as though artists merely perceive what those attentive to biblical revelation already know. As my examples were intended to indicate, the relation is in fact much more complex. Sometimes God is already drawing close in situations far removed from Scripture (*Oedipus at Colonus*). Sometimes a general pattern is established that helps make better sense of a central biblical idea (*The Ring*). Sometimes a secular play might be the very means by which biblical insights are recovered (*The Doll's House*). And sometimes the contribution of theatre can even help us appropriate a reality to which we had previously only given intellectual assent, as with the role of comedy in the medieval mystery plays. This is by no means an inclusive list, but I hope it provides some indication of the potential theological contribution that theatre can continue to make, both as an opportunity for religious experience and as a form of mediated divine revelation.

---

28. In light of what I go on to say, it is intriguing to find Lepage stressing the greater potential of theatre over cinema, and in particular for the possibilities of transformation. See Eyre, *Talking Theatre*, 306–10.

Bibliography

Apuleius. *The Golden Ass*. Translated and edited by P. G. Walsh. Oxford: Oxford University Press, 1994.

Balthasar, Hans Urs von. *The Glory of the Lord*. Vol. 4, *The Realm of Metaphysics in Antiquity*. Edinburgh: T. & T. Clark, 1989.

Breuer, Lee. *The Gospel at Colonus*. New York: Theatre Communications Group, 1989.

Bowra, Maurice. *Sophoclean Tragedy*. Oxford: Clarendon, 1944.

Brook, Peter. *The Empty Space*. Harmondsworth, UK: Penguin, 1968.

———. *There Are No Secrets*. London: Methuen, 1993.

Brown, David. *God and Mystery in Words*. Oxford: Oxford University Press, 2008.

Cawley, A. C., ed. *Everyman and Medieval Miracle Plays*. London: Dent, 1993.

Davies, Brian. *An Introduction to the Philosophy of Religion*. Oxford: Oxford University Press, 1982.

Eyre, Richard. *Talking Theatre: Interviews with Theatre People*. London: Hern, 2009.

Ford, David. *The Future of Christian Theology*. Oxford: Wiley-Blackwell, 2011.

Hall, Edith et al., eds. *Dionysus Since 69: Greek Tragedy at the Dawn of the Third Millennium*. Oxford: Oxford University Press, 2005.

Ibsen, Henrik. *Four Major Plays*. Translated by James McFarlane and Jens Arup. Oxford: Oxford University Press, 1981.

Lefkowitz, Mary. *Greek Gods, Human Lives*. New Haven: Yale University Press, 2003.

Lloyd-Jones, Hugh. *The Justice of Zeus*. Berkeley: University of California Press, 1983.

Meades, Jonathan. *Museum without Walls*. London: Unbound, 2013.

Pickering, Kenneth. *Drama in the Cathedral: The Canterbury Festival Plays, 1928–1948*. Worthing, UK: Churchman, 1985.

Sontag, Susan. *On Photography*. London: Penguin, 1977.

Taylor, Charles. *A Secular Age*. Cambridge, MA: Belknap, 2007.

Thiessen, G. E., ed. *Theological Aesthetics: A Reader*. London: SCM, 2004.

CPSIA information can be obtained
at www.ICGtesting.com
Printed in the USA
FSHW012151050621
81996FS